AMERICA

AND THE

New

ECONOMY

ANTHONY PATRICK CARNEVALE

AMERICA

AND THE

ECONOMY

**How New Competitive Standards
Are Radically Changing
American Workplaces**

 Jossey-Bass Publishers

San Francisco • Oxford • 1991

AMERICA AND THE NEW ECONOMY
How New Competitive Standards Are Radically Changing American Workplaces
by Anthony Patrick Carnevale

Copyright © 1991 by: Jossey-Bass Inc., Publishers
350 Sansome Street
San Francisco, California 94104

&

Jossey-Bass Limited
Headington Hill Hall
Oxford OX3 0BW

Library of Congress Cataloging-in-Publication Data

Carnevale, Anthony Patrick.
America and the new economy : how new competitive standards are
radically changing American workplaces / Anthony Patrick Carnevale.
— 1st ed.
p. cm. — (The Jossey-Bass management series)
Includes bibliographical references and index.
ISBN 1-55542-371-X
1. Labor productivity—United States. 2. Efficiency, Industrial—
United States. I. Title. II. Series
HC110.L3C37 1991
331.11'8'0973—dc20   91-19307
                                                                          CIP

Manufactured in the United States of America

The paper in this book meets the guidelines for
permanence and durability of the Committee on
Production Guidelines for Book Longevity of the
Council on Library Resources.

JACKET DESIGN BY BETH A. LOUDENBERG

FIRST EDITION

Code 9170

THE JOSSEY-BASS
MANAGEMENT SERIES

CONTENTS

TABLES

xi

xii

PREFACE

This book synthesizes several years of firsthand exploration in the world of work. It is the written record of a journey. The journey began in the early eighties, when it became apparent to the nation's leaders in business, government, labor, and the intellectual community that something profoundly different was happening in the world economy. Everyone seemed to have his or her own version of what that difference was. A bewildering array of strategies, each at odds with the next, emerged. As perspectives on the nation's economic prospects diverged and multiplied, it became impossible for American leaders to find enough common ground to form a cohesive response to what were clearly unprecedented events.

One of those leaders was Secretary of Labor William Brock. Before becoming the secretary of labor, Brock had been a chief executive officer, a U.S. senator, chairperson of the Republican party, and the American special trade representative. Secretary Brock was frustrated along with many others at the inability of America's business, governmental, labor, and intellectual leaders to agree on what was actually happening and to form a cohesive response. As a result, he decided to launch a major research effort to forge a common understanding as a guide to action in coping with the overwhelming economic change.

Secretary Brock approached the new reality from two directions. He charged the Hudson Institute with examining work from the outside in. In a project known as "workforce 2000," the institute examined demographic changes in the workforce in terms of how they were likely to affect American competitiveness. I, my research team, and a coalition of American employers were charged with assessing the emerging economic reality from the inside out, by going directly to the nation's workplaces to inventory and analyze changing competitive conditions. Many of our findings have been reported in four other books and an equal number of monographs and articles coauthored by myself and other members of the research team. The task of extracting general conclusions, integrating findings into the current knowledge base, and summing up fell to me.

America and the New Economy summarizes my own sense of what we found in our exploration of the American workplace. It is my belief that we discovered a whole new economy. As the journey progressed, it became apparent that we were in uncharted waters. At first, we encountered small islands of change, a scattered set of institutions that had been transformed by competitive conditions. Eventually, we sighted whole new domains, sufficiently large to constitute a new economy distinct from the economic reality familiar to us at the beginning of our journey.

What follows is both an intellectual map and a guide to action in the new environment. It describes a new economy founded on a new set of competitive standards and strategies that have transformed organizations, technical and product cycles, jobs, skill requirements, and the basic dynamic of economic progress. The emphasis in this book is on the real economy of organizations, people, and technology, not the statistical economy so often reported in secondhand data. *America and the*

New Economy looks at the emerging reality from ground level; its coverage is global, not national.

America and the New Economy integrates the various aspects of the new economy into a cohesive frame. Each aspect of the new order is discussed separately but with careful attention to the relationships between the parts and the whole. Our discoveries are not presented in their natural state. Instead, our findings have been inventoried, sorted, analyzed, and developed into models of best practice. The map that follows includes careful reference to familiar routes and destinations that have led up to the new frontier of economic progress. Once beyond the familiar frontier, this guide charts the new economy both by providing a general sense of direction and by using specific examples as reference points.

Audience

America and the New Economy should be useful to decision makers in employer and labor organizations; leaders in the political, educational, and scientific establishments; and individuals who need to make career choices. As employers in their respective sectors of American society, organizational decision makers are coping with profound change. As stakeholders in the American economy, we are all struggling to find better ways to work together to improve the nation's overall economic performance. As individuals in a society where the price of admission to polity and culture is the ability to get and keep a job, each of us is concerned with job security and career progress. Everyone knows we are in a new economic ball game; this practitioners' guide to the new economy is intended to help us understand and act on what we know.

Overview of the Contents

The introduction to *America and the New Economy* provides a general overview of the new environment and places America in it. The remainder of the book details the new terrain in four parts. Part One offers a basic description of competitive standards and technical change processes in the new economy. Part Two presents details on the impact of the new economic reality on organizations and industries. Part Three discusses the impact of the new economy on job and skill demands and how to teach and measure needed skills. Part Four suggests new strategic thinking, crucial to success in the new economy. The conclusion discusses the challenges facing America in the new economy.

Included in Part One are three chapters that explain the new competitive reality. Chapter One traces the evolution of economic competition from the single-minded focus on productivity characteristic of mass production to today's more complex economic environment in which productivity is no longer sufficient by itself to capture and retain market share. Included is a discussion of the principal factors that led to this fundamental restructuring: increasing wealth of nations, globalization of economic activity, diversification of tastes, increasing value of time, commercialization of previously free labor, consumers' increasing participation in production and delivery, and advances in technology.

Chapter Two describes the new, expanded set of competitive standards, beginning with productivity, which continues to have great importance, and continuing with quality, variety, customization, convenience, and timeliness. This chapter explains these standards in concept and by example and discusses America's past performance and prospects in meeting them. The chapter concludes by explaining how these standards overlap to form a flexible, mutually reinforcing framework and how this framework evolved.

Chapter Three presents the three dominant philosophical viewpoints concerning the role of technology in social and economic change and then discusses the dynamics of technical change in more detail. This chapter demonstrates that although technical revolutions can create major economic and social disruptions, most technical change is evolutionary, moving in small steps and conforming to social and economic conditions as well as shaping them. Junctures of choice, barriers to change, and available technologies all affect the path of technical progress. It is the availability of technical flexibility—in the form of the computer—that is bringing us into the new economy. Chapter Three concludes by explaining how the classic, five-phase economic life cycle has changed in the new economy, becoming less sequential, less orderly, and faster moving. Institutions can successfully leapfrog the initial phases in the cycle, borrowing innovations and exploiting their economic potential. Success in such circumstances requires flexibility, broadly skilled employees, and continuous learning at all levels of the organization—not heroic invention.

Part Two, consisting of Chapters Four and Five, considers the impact of the new economic reality on organizations and industries. Chapter Four explains that top-down mass production structures and the fragmented structures characteristic of service, craft, and professional work are converging on a common format—interdependent, nested networks of people, work teams, and organizations. As we move into the new economy, distinctive types of networks are emerging in different industries. Each type represents a solution to the fundamental paradox that networks must offer integration, so as to achieve the benefits of scale, and yet allow the autonomy necessary for flexibility. By balancing these two virtues, along with scale, scope, and focus, networks foster an organization's ability to meet the new competitive standards. Also, given the importance of incremental improvements in the new competitive environment, capturing, communicating, and applying knowledge at all levels of an organization has become a critical process, and networks are conducive to such pervasive institutional learning.

Chapter Five assesses the competitive prospects of thirteen critical U.S. industries, showing how they are changing and what competition they are facing from abroad. Some industries, such as the automobile industry, have the potential to adapt to the new economic reality, but face daunting challenges. Others, such as the computer industry, have excellent prospects. In all cases, however, future success will depend on the ability to make the transition to the new economic standards by developing effective networks and exploiting institutional learning.

The three chapters in Part Three consider how jobs and

skill demands are changing in the new economy. Chapter Six focuses on jobs. Although the number of jobs in the U.S. economy is likely to grow over the current decade, the distribution of this growth will be uneven because of the effects of new technologies, the globalization of economic activity, and organizational changes. Specifically, the increasing importance of service functions in every industry is causing the proportion of service jobs to increase while the proportion of manufacturing and extractive jobs is decreasing. In addition, job growth is increasingly being concentrated in population centers, particularly the East and West Coasts. The distribution of wage increases is also uneven, with education and on-the-job learning becoming the key to higher income. Women's earnings are growing, but African Americans, Hispanics, and other minorities are not making similar economic progress. Demands for organizational flexibility are resulting in decreased employment security, so workers need to take more responsibility for their own career development. Chapter Six concludes with some observations on patterns of career development in the new economy: Bosses are becoming brokers, technical specialists are becoming increasingly important, craft work is disappearing, and professional jobs are being partitioned into jobs for teams of specialists and paraprofessionals. In general, career ladders are becoming shorter as lateral ports of entry multiply, and jobs are becoming more generalized and similar to one another.

Chapter Seven explores how skill requirements are changing. The extension of technical and machine capabilities creates a complementary extension of the complexity and scope of the human role in exploiting these new capabilities, so workers in the new economy need both great depth of skills and great breadth of skills. Flexible organizations and job structures require equally flexible employees. Work increasingly involves hands-off tasks and personal interaction with co-workers and customers. In sum, employers in the new economy need workers with general skills, abstract skills, and the ability to handle exceptions. These trends are evident in a growing proportion of jobs, resulting in a convergence of skill requirements throughout the economy.

Chapter Eight takes a closer look at the sixteen job skills crucial to success in the new economic environment. These skills fall under the categories of learning to learn, academic basics, communication skills, adaptability, developmental skills, group effectiveness skills, and influencing skills. The chapter explains the need for each skill, summarizes what an effective curriculum should include, and briefly discusses standards of competency.

In two chapters, Part Four suggests strategies for competitive success in the new economy. Chapter Nine begins by considering strategies for meeting each of the new competitive standards. A successful productivity strategy requires a long-term perspective centering on the importance of innovation. To meet the quality standard, people must develop commitment and a sense of responsibility for the overall work effort. Flexibility is the key to variety and customization, and convenience, the quality standard most focused on the interface with the customer, relies on meeting all the other standards as well as on good customer service. Organizations must be careful not to pursue timeliness to the point of diminishing returns, becoming so speedy that they cannot meet the other competitive standards or investing more in an innovation than can be recouped over its life cycle. The final section of Chapter Nine looks more closely at organizational structures suited to the new economy, describing work teams, the need to emphasize process over function, and the crucial role of networks that link organizations upstream and down.

Chapter Ten analyzes the interactions between learning and economic enterprise by discussing a set of eight loosely connected processes: scientific inquiry, invention, innovation, dissemination, networking, investment, commercialization, and cumulative learning. These processes result in economic progress by encouraging the continuing accumulation of knowledge, creating new knowledge, and embedding it in economic systems. The book concludes by noting that we cannot take economic progress for granted. The new economy presents us with formidable challenges, and we will succeed only if we value economic progress sufficiently to meet them.

Acknowledgments

Special thanks to Michele Nathan for her invaluable editorial assistance, Marge Weathers and Grenda Townsend for their administrative assistance, and Alice Grindstaff for her assistance in the final production of this book.

Washington, D.C.   Anthony Patrick Carnevale
July 1991

THE AUTHOR

Anthony Patrick Carnevale is executive director of the Institute for Workplace Learning of the American Society for Training and Development (ASTD), an association of more than 55,000 human resource professionals in major business organizations. He received his B.A. degree (1968) from Colby College in intellectual and cultural history. Between 1969 and 1972, Carnevale received an M.A. degree in social science, another M.A. degree in public administration, and a Ph.D. degree with a concentration in public finance economics from the Maxwell School of Public Affairs at Syracuse University.

Prior to joining ASTD, Carnevale was government affairs director for the American Federation of State, County, and Municipal Employees (AFSCME). He also served as co-moderator for the White House Conference on Productivity and as chairman of the Fiscal Policy Task Force for the U.S. Council on Competitiveness. Carnevale has held positions as senior policy analyst for the U.S. Department of Health, Education, and Welfare; senior staff economist for the U.S. House of Representatives Government Operations Committee; and senior staff member for education, employment, training, and social services for the U.S. Senate Committee on the Budget.

He has authored numerous research reports, books, and articles on macro- and microeconomic issues associated with national employment, training, and competitiveness issues. Carnevale is also coauthor of the principal affidavit in *Rodriquez* v. *San Antonio*, a U.S. Supreme Court action to remedy unequal tax burdens and unequal educational opportunities.

AMERICA

AND THE

New

ECONOMY

AMERICA'S PLACE IN
THE NEW ECONOMY

There is a widely-shared sense that we are entering a new economic order. Indeed, the new economy is already upon us. It is pulling threads from the weave of our economic past, creating a whole new cloth. At this writing, the future economic order is perceived only dimly. We know the traits of its lineage but have little knowledge as to how these traits will recombine. Prior attempts to name our economic future have not worn well. Terms like *postindustrial economy* and *service economy* oversimplify and point us toward an economy that will not work. We will not survive by deindustrializing and "taking in each other's wash" or becoming a nation of hamburger flippers. Nor will our manufacturing industries prosper without the support of complementary service and natural resource capabilities. In short, it is premature to name our economic future. We do know that the future economy will be new, however, so the analysis that follows refers to it simply as the "new economy."

The most obvious change in the texture of the economic

1

fabric is the growing complexity in the pattern of standards that we must meet in order to win in economic competition. In the old economy, nations competed principally on the basis of productivity and prices. Our success as a nation was measured by our ability to produce higher volumes of goods and services with the same or fewer resources. In the new economy, our national competitiveness is based not only on productivity but also on quality, variety, customization, convenience, and timeliness. People are demanding high-quality goods and services that are competitively priced, available in a variety of forms, customized to specific needs, and conveniently accessible. In addition, people do not want to wait patiently for state-of-the-art goods and services.

These new market standards are the result of profound economic and social changes in America and around the world. In the new economy, consumers are richer than they were in the old economy. They devote more time to making money than to spending it. Today's consumers can afford something better than they used to. They demand, and new technologies allow, quality, variety, customization, convenience, timeliness, and mass production prices. And in the global economy, if American industry does not meet these standards, somebody else will.

Central to the new economy are flexible and information-based technologies. In fact, today's most important technology is our friend the computer. In its various disguises, this information-based technology raises our potential for higher productivity and quality. It provides sufficient flexibility to tailor goods and services to smaller markets and even to individual customers. In addition, by integrating producers and consumers into economic networks, it helps create an environment in which goods and services can be delivered globally or locally in a convenient and timely manner.

As new economic and technical forces change the standards for economic competition, they also affect organizational structures, skill requirements, and jobs. Organizational formats are shifting toward flexible networks that use information to integrate organizations, expedite strategic changes, and improve customer service. The physical energy necessary to extract resources, manufacture goods, and deliver services is becoming less important than the information required to respond to markets quickly. Increasingly, information is becoming the basic raw material of economic processes and the end product of economic activity. This shift to information networks is evident in the large hierarchies of big business and the structures of the service and small-business sectors. Today's employers in large hierarchies are driving authority, skill, and resources toward production and service delivery, flattening the middle tiers of the hierarchies. In industries with typically small, autonomous, and isolated organizations, new market demands and the capacity of new information technologies are reducing fragmentation and integrating small structures into effective networks.

This book explains the new economy from the point of view of people at work. Specifically, it examines the impact of changing competitive standards, new technologies, and emerging organizational structures on jobs and skill requirements in the American workplace.

As the new economy emerges, the role of people at work is also changing. Capital-to-labor ratios are continuing to grow, and direct labor participation in the processes of resource extraction, manufacturing, and service provision is declining. As a result, human responsibilities and skill requirements are increasing and becoming less job specific, job assignments are becoming more flexible and overlapping, and employees are spending more time interacting with one another and with customers.

Overall, we are experiencing an increase in service functions and service jobs in all industries. The new market standards and the declining hands-on participation of labor at work are creating a new competitive reality that emphasizes service. At the same time, unpaid household labor is being absorbed into the service economy as the value of human capital and time increases.

In the new economy, flexible work teams and information networks within and among economic institutions are the basic units of production. The demand for state-of-the-art goods and services requires flexible, integrated work organizations that get innovations off the drawing board and into the hands of consumers quickly. The need to customize a wide and everchanging assortment of products requires closely integrated working groups that can shift fluidly. Similarly, market demands for quality and convenience are difficult to meet without teamwork, and the new information-based and flexible technologies result in organizations and work processes that rely on shared information. The trend toward more general and overlapping work assignments and skills forces employees to interact to meet shared responsibilities. Economic activity becomes more of a collective activity conducted by groups of people.

The New Economy in Historical Perspective

Every economic era has its characteristic signature — a dominant mode of providing services and of extracting natural resources to produce goods. Two major economic eras, those of craft production and industrial mass production, preceded and influenced the new economy. The age of craft production was characterized by the autonomy of skilled farmers, miners, and artisans. Organizations employed only a few individuals. Artisans, who occupied the upper tiers of a relatively flat occupational hierarchy, were broadly skilled and used general-purpose tools to turn out a wide variety of customized goods. Each artisan usually worked in a single medium, such as cloth, wood, metal, glass, or leather. Both the medium and the tools were subservient to the skill. The conception, execution, and control of work were unified in the individual. Remuneration was based on skill and output.

The characteristic signature of the mass production era was the rationalization of economic activity: simplifying and increasing the scale of activity in order to provide large quantities at lowest costs. In the mass production economy, the autonomous artisan gave way to the dependent employee who worked in the context of a workforce and an organization. The artisan's unity of conception, execution, and control at work was fragmented in the mass production workplace: Jobs were organized into segmented hierarchies. The machine substituted for the artisan's tool. The human scale of cottage and shop was replaced by the industrial leviathan. The natural rhythms characteristic of the craft and farm economy bowed to bureaucratic procedure and the machine cadences of the factory. The tool was an extension of the artisan's skill and purpose; the worker was an extension of the machine. The artisan was paid for skill embodied in the final product; in the mass production economy, wages were attached to jobs rather than skill or final products.

The craft economy did not disappear with the advent of mass production but survived in an uneasy existence in its shadow. Markets for short-run production and specialized services have persisted. Someone has to invent and make the mass production machinery. Moreover, the mass production system requires employees with the ability to tailor machine-made products to specific uses. The pipe fitter, the machinist, and the tool and die maker are cases in point. Some industries, such as construction, have been difficult to rationalize with the available technologies and have continued in the craft tradition. Moreover, professional and administrative services have grown as a result of mass production, urbanization, and increased disposable income, and this growth has provided new opportunities to expand the craft model. The urge to rationalize craft and professional work through mechanization and Taylorist work practices persists, however, in the interest of greater efficiencies and cost savings.

The similarities and differences between the new economy and the craft and mass production economies are instructive. The new market standards of customization, variety, convenience, timeliness, and quality are similar to those in the craft economy. At the same time, the new economy utilizes a powerful capital base to produce craftlike products on a scale and at prices more akin to those of mass production than the low-productivity craft economy. The urge to rationalize economic activity and thereby extract resources, manufacture, and provide services at least cost is far from spent. The new economy retains the productivity standard and adds to it.

Unity of conception, execution, and control over work, characteristic of the craft economy but fragmented in the mass production system, reemerges in the new economy (Baran and Parsons, 1986). Employees do not work as independently as artisans did, but there are also differences from the mass production economy: Employees are more autonomous and do not work in the rationalized hierarchies typical of the mass production system. The new context for work is loosely knit teams and networks flexibly organized around information. As in the craft economy, control is exerted through common values and goals arrived at by consensus-building processes and cooperation rather than through authority-based control systems.

Although the new economy represents a return to craft standards for remuneration, wages are increasingly dependent on the overall skill and performance of the group rather than the individual. "Gain sharing" and other forms of group incentives are on the rise, automatic cost-of-living increases have declined dramatically, and employees are generally more attuned to the effect of organizational performance on their earnings.

In sum, the emerging new economy retains the volume and productivity standards of mass production and weds them to the craft standards of quality, variety, customization, convenience, and timeliness. A notable difference is that autonomous artisans and anonymous mass production workers are replaced by interdependent work teams.

At present, our general understanding of the new economy far exceeds its acceptance in the American workplace. In short, we know where we need to go, but we don't know how to get there. The reasons are plain enough. The path of economic progress is rarely smooth. Our path toward the new economy narrows as we encounter economic, social, technical, and political bottlenecks. Our ability to move beyond these bottlenecks, to embrace the future, will require hard choices. In our previous economic transitions, we have encountered other barriers, and there is much to be learned from them. They provide the context for our current economic dilemmas. They reflect our values as a nation and our common sense of the appropriate balance between the competing claims of public and private institutions, employers and employees, and present and future generations.

Transport proved the first hurdle in the path of American economic and technical development. The interior regions of the New World were rich in natural resources, livestock, and produce. Meat, poultry, coal, and crops produced in western Ohio or Pennsylvania tripled in value by the time they reached New York, Philadelphia, or Baltimore (Liebergott, 1984). Yet in 1800, it still took days of hard riding to get from Detroit to Pittsburgh. By 1820, the race between the canals and the railroads was on. The canals won the early rounds. In 1825, the Erie Canal provided the first gateway to the East, connecting Ohio, Indiana, and Illinois to New York Harbor. No longer did shipments have to be moved through Montreal, where the harbor was frozen for almost four months every year (Liebergott, 1984). The railroads finally overtook the canals as the principal means of moving goods from west to east because the railroads were faster and could carry heavier loads.

American manufacturing was born in New England at the turn of the nineteenth century and grew over the next fifty years as a result of borrowed technology and protection from foreign competition by the artificial oceans of embargo and tariff. Yet as late as 1860, only 14 percent of Americans worked in manufacturing, whereas 53 percent still worked in agriculture. Because the preponderance of economic activity was still in agriculture, the rationalization of economic activity, usually associated with manufacturing, had its first and most powerful impact on the farm. By the time the first shots were fired on Fort Sumter in 1861, agricultural productivity had increased enormously compared with productivity rates at the turn of the century. Careful breeding had increased the livestock yield dramatically, and between 1810 and 1860, this same process of unnatural selection had doubled the fleece per sheep (Liebergott, 1984). Over the same period, improved seed had increased the yield from a single cotton picker from 50 to almost 200 pounds of cotton per day, and the cotton gin, a machine that separated cotton seed from raw cotton, had increased the number of cleaned bales produced in a single day eightfold. The number of hours required to produce a bushel of wheat or corn had been cut roughly in half over the same fifty years.

Rapid advances in industry arrived after the Civil War in the form of new energy sources and manufacturing processes. The principal technological bottleneck to the advance of American manufacturing was energy, and the shift from water to steam power after the Civil War and the subsequent shift to electricity between 1880 and 1930 made quantum changes in the power and productivity of manufacturing processes. Production systems became both more powerful and more flexible, ultimately moving the locus of production from rural to urban settings. New manufacturing processes that developed after the Civil War also expanded output. For instance, new processes for making cheaper and better steel and aluminum increased output and reduced prices more than tenfold between 1850 and 1880.

As the nation raced toward the twentieth century, the increased productive capacity in agriculture and industry encountered new educational, organizational, and financial barriers to economic progress. As productivity increased, agriculture began shedding unskilled labor. As private industry developed off the farm, the lack of complementary infrastructure became a barrier to further expansion. The nation required an urban, industrial labor force made up of highly skilled white-collar and technical employees and blue-collar laborers. In addition, substantial investments were required to pay for railroads, roads, and the communications infrastructure that would move raw products from west to east. The urban infrastructure, including electrification and sewage treatment, demanded a huge capital outlay. Private employers needed new institutions and financial mechanisms to support the expensive technical and organizational infrastructure of mass production. In the end, the government paid for the urban infrastructure, the industrial labor force, and the roads. Private industry built new financial institutions large and powerful enough to afford private development of factories, railroads, and new communications infrastructure.

The urban industrial economy that emerged in the twentieth century relied on extensive investments in both machine and human capital from both public and private sources. But the new system also required stable production and constantly increasing consumption to justify the costs of the infrastructure and to maintain the increasingly wage-dependent urban work-force. With time, strikes and recessions proved that the new bottleneck in the development of the nation's economic system was an instability in the workplace and in consumer markets.

Eventually, managers were able to promote stability in the workplace without surrendering substantial control by paying higher wages and maintaining a more accommodating rela-tionship with nonsupervisory employees and their unions. The stability of markets was improved by increasing the buying power of individual consumers, extending credit, and control-ling national economic performance by regulating the money supply and government spending. Consumer credit, which had been available since Singer began selling sewing machines in the late nineteenth century, was offered for International Har-vester's farm implements shortly thereafter and for Ford's and General Motors' automobiles in the 1920s. Further extension of credit was interrupted during the Great Depression, but credit became generally available after World War II. The Depression and the war demonstrated the need for new tools to stabilize the national market. After the Depression, a financial safety net was created for the unemployed, the underemployed, and other dependent populations, guaranteeing demand in slack periods. War production demonstrated the ability of the national govern-ment to sustain aggregate demand through the manipulation of taxation, government spending, and control over the money supply.

By the beginning of the postwar era in the United States, all the aspects of the economic system seemed to have been reconciled. Both production and overall demand had stabilized. World War II had unleashed our economic system and gradually created a new optimism based on economic success. The hot-house economy of the postwar boom produced abundance on an unprecedented scale. The pent-up demand for consumer goods continued to stimulate the resources mobilized for war production. The result was effortless growth. Our economic system seemed to have the self-sustaining power of a social gyro. Once set in motion, it spun free at an ever accelerating rate. Public policies braked or nudged the freely spinning wheel at the point of demand—a political convenience for a society concerned with the excesses of planned societies in the East.

The pace and path of economic development ran into new obstacles in the early 1970s. A productivity decline suggested to some observers that something was wrong with the way we were using technology, people, and the organization of work. Others blamed the decline, at least in part, on the infusion of new female and young workers who had less experience and educational preparation than previous workers. Shortages of energy and other raw commodities proved another barrier to effortless growth in the 1970s. Bottlenecks arose in markets as well. By the 1980s, postwar productivity resulted in a saturation of mass markets at home, encouraging the globalization of competition. Eventually, global demand became saturated as well, with a glut of production in an increasing number of industries. Growth has become stagnant since the early 1970s, and the economic and technical arrangement rooted in the industrial revolution seems to have exhausted the possibilities for stabilizing either production or markets.

In this the last decade of the twentieth century, the nation is blazing a path toward the new economy. But numerous new obstacles impede our progress and have become the focus of enormous social, economic, and scientific energy as pressure for growth continues to build.

Inside the workplace, flexible technology needs to be matched with more skilled and autonomous workers and work teams. New, more flexible work organizations that drive authority and resources toward the point of production, service delivery, and the customer are also required if we are to take advantage of the inherent potential of new human-machine combinations.

Barriers that impede progress toward the new economy are apparent outside the workplace as well. Environmental limitations to growth await a technical solution. The new economy is emerging in the midst of a financial dilemma—one that is fraught with savings-and-loan bailouts, junk bonds, and foreign debt. Furthermore, although the new economy will require massive public and private investments in the nation's human, organizational, and technical infrastructure, the financial capital necessary for this overhaul is being absorbed in an orgy of public and private consumption. In addition, it is increasingly clear that our ability to stabilize domestic markets is no longer enough; the new economy has gone global, and global economic events tend to affect and impinge on our domestic economy. The unpredictability of global economic events requires new mechanisms for stability. Finally, the demographic surpluses of the 1970s are giving way to longer-term demographic scarcity. The number of available workers is declining rapidly. Moreover, more employees will come from populations in which our human capital investments prior to work have been insufficient (Johnston and Packer, 1987).

Nevertheless, we can be cautiously optimistic about America's prospects in the new economy. Much will depend on our ability to break through the barriers. While other nations face many of the same obstacles, the United States moves into the new economic era with the additional burden of its past successes. Old and formerly successful habits die hard.

The pages that follow attempt to provide a more complete description of America and the new economy. The discussion will weave the threads of past and present into a new cloth. Because the past, present, and future are so inextricably bound, the past and present economies serve throughout as reference points for describing the emerging economic reality.

There is no logical spot at which to break into the seamless weave of forces that is creating the new economy. There are many strands to choose from, and the forces of change are hopelessly tangled. It is impossible to separate changes in markets, technology, strategies, organizational structure, job design, and workforce quality. Therefore, the examination that follows begins with a discussion of the increased breadth and depth of standards for competitive success in the new economy. Arguably, markets are a good place to start because they represent the separate strands of the economic system made whole.

Part One

THE NEW
COMPETITIVE REALITY

Chapter One

DISCOVERING THE NEW
MARKET STANDARDS

Markets are the nexus where producers and consumers come together. A market represents the distillation of human wants and needs into material goods or services. Moreover, markets are a relatively uniform motif in the disjointed pattern of economic change. The basic human wants and needs expressed in markets do not vary much over time: food and drink, housing, health care, education and training, communication, transportation, entertainment, community, physical and emotional security, and safe and pleasant surroundings. Ultimately, the new economy will be measured by its ability to satisfy these timeless wants and needs efficiently and fairly.

Market Standards: A Thumbnail History

In 8000 B.C., humans settled down to farm (Grayson and O'Dell, 1988). Early agricultural production was used mostly for subsistence or to pay tribute or rents and was rarely sold competitively.

Competition and competitive standards were primitive. Subsequently, in 4500 B.C., small communities and tool-based manufacturing appeared along with early crafts (Grayson and O'Dell, 1988). The labor-intensive craft and agricultural economy developed gradually over the next several hundred years. Competition in agricultural markets accelerated slowly with urbanization, as townspeople created a growing demand for farm surpluses.

Output per person remained relatively flat until the eighteenth century— 10,000 years after the first farms (Grayson and O'Dell, 1988). Thereafter, the economic history of the world became the story of ever expanding consumption of goods and services as the frontiers of human wants and needs receded before the onslaught of increasing productivity.

Productivity—the ability to get more with the same or fewer resources—has been a self-starter ever since. Supply and demand have been like the proverbial chicken and egg. Selling goods and services has generated spendable earnings to fuel further expansion. With the aid of productivity increases and invention, expansion continues to elude the limits to growth. The spiral of relatively effortless growth has dumbfounded naysayers from Malthus to the Club of Rome, as one doomsday after another has been posted, come, and gone; and the world still has not run out of land or gas.

The Mass Production Economy: Meeting the Productivity Standard. The astonishing productivity growth that began in the eighteenth century and continues today stems from the genius of mass production. In the mass production system, goods and services were reduced to their smallest and most reproducible parts. Machines were then designed to make each individual component. In the stereotypical mass production institution, white-collar and technical elites invented standardized products, designed production jobs and machinery, and orchestrated the piecemeal output of specialized workers and narrow-purpose machines within carefully organized top-down hierarchies.

A mass production economy feeds upon itself. The degree of specialization is limited only by the volume of output. Higher volumes justify the cost of ever more specialized machinery and workers. Higher volumes also justify lower prices, which in turn expand market sizes, allowing more mass production.

The mass production model is usually associated with manufacturing, but as the dominant and most successful economic paradigm, it has been tried in all sectors of the economy since its inception. The model invaded agriculture, mining, and other natural resource industries early and continues to have its greatest successes there.

Craft work and service work were less amenable to mass production techniques. The crafts did not disappear with the evolution of mass production but continued in areas of economic activity where mass production techniques had yet to penetrate, such as in the apprenticeable trades. Yet the apprenticeable trades coexisted uneasily with mass production, especially in manufacturing—working cheek by jowl with the mass production system that would deskill them if it could find a way. The mass production model was most difficult to implement in services because it is so difficult to standardize service delivery en masse. To the extent possible, however, industries such as finance, insurance, transportation, public services, and health care organized large hierarchical structures to take advantage of service delivery on a large scale.

Productivity is the competitive standard of the mass production economy, and goods and services are ever more available and cheaper. The Dutch were the world's first productivity leaders, setting the pace beginning in 1700, and the British surpassed the Dutch in 1785. The United States took the productivity lead from the British in the 1890s (Grayson and O'Dell, 1988), and has set the world standard for mass production techniques and productivity since then.

The American Postwar Economy. United States productivity performance peaked in the American boom that followed World War II. The pent-up demand for consumer goods in the postwar era, in combination with the manufacturing infrastructure built for war production and nurtured out of harm's way, pushed America's productivity performance to unprecedented levels beginning in 1946. The hothouse economy made it seem as though Americans could produce goods and services on such a grand scale that material want would eventually be drowned in a sea of resources. Our abundant society was both an economic and political miracle. It short-circuited the two toughest questions facing any society: Who gets what? What do we do first? There was enough for everybody; all that was required was "an equal opportunity" to share in the largesse of productivity. Abundance also solved the priority problem because there was sufficient wealth to afford a cornucopia of both public and private goods. New needs could be funded without reducing existing shares in the growing economic pie.

Our successes set the tone for relationships between government and industry as well as labor and management. Cooperation was unnecessary. Rather, success created an environment of peaceful coexistence punctuated by episodes of hostile bargaining, with each party minding its own interest.

The government played a positive but aloof role in the management of the economy while preserving private ownership. Government policies manipulated macroeconomic aggregates, leaving the day-to-day management of businesses to private employers. The government's macroeconomic policies emphasized the manipulation of aggregate spending and the availability of an expanding supply of money. The government stimulated economic growth from a distance by moderating the amount of income available for spending. Spending translated into demand for goods and services and stimulated production, and production generated employment and more income for spending.

Our public economic policies encouraged stable growth, stable prices, and employment by controlling the general supply of money and regulating government spending and taxation in order to moderate the overall balance between savings and investment. Income growth also resulted in public revenues that eventually had to be spent before they became a fiscal drag on the economy. These revenues could be used to paper over the social failures of the economy and pay for its negative external effects, such as environmental pollution and unemployment.

Similarly, after the "Red scare" in the early fifties, American unions separated themselves from strategic concerns in the workplace. Managers ran the businesses, while unions focused on getting better working conditions and a fair share of the growing profits. Not everyone agreed; for example, the auto workers' Walter Reuther continued to argue for more worker involvement in business decisions. Labor leaders of Reuther's stripe were called "red-headed"—a reference to Reuther's red hair and radical ideas.

Our productivity performance and the abundance it produced became the centerpiece for our claim to global leadership. American political and economic institutions, as much as goods and services, became a principal export. Our economic success demonstrated the superiority of democratic individualism as opposed to the collectivist systems to the east. Global relationships were intended to leverage our way of life more than our exports. Trade policies were politically and ideologically driven rather than developed with the national economic interest in mind.

The postwar boom was supposed to launch the "American Century" and the "end of ideology." Our principal problem, as we ran pell-mell toward the "postindustrial society" in which productivity made work unnecessary, was to provide for meaningful leisure (Bell, 1983). Many facts demonstrated our postwar success, among them the following:

- In 1945, Europeans were living on 1,500 calories per day and Asians on 1,000. The average American consumed approximately 3,500 calories per day.
- In 1947, the United States produced half the world's manufactured goods, 57 percent of its steel, 43 percent of its electricity, and 63 percent of its oil.
- Also in 1947, U.S. citizens owned 75 percent of the world's cars, and U.S. companies manufactured 80 percent of the cars built.

- By the 1950s, most of the world's gold supply was safely stored in Fort Knox (Carnevale, 1985).

Meanwhile, in Europe and Japan. In the 1950s, as the Europeans and Japanese dug out from under the rubble of World War II, their first instinct was to follow the American example. But copying our mass production system proved more difficult than they first imagined. The war had taken a fearful toll, and the Europeans and Japanese had profound competitive liabilities. Primary among these liabilities was the relatively small size of their consumer markets. The American market was eight times the size of the next largest domestic market. The scale economies of mass production could be realized fully in the United States without going offshore and competing abroad. In Europe and Japan, however, domestic markets were too small to permit an emphasis on high-volume production of standardized goods for domestic sales alone. As a result, European and Japanese companies were forced to sell abroad.

The complexity of international markets compelled the Europeans and Japanese to pay more attention to their diverse customers. German car manufacturers, for instance, had to produce cars not only for Germans but for Swedes and Italians as well. The Swedish market demanded cars for harsh winters and rural driving. Fuel efficiency was not a prime concern because gas taxes were low. In Italy, on the other hand, the climate was more forgiving and driving more urban, gas taxes were high, and registration fees were based on engine sizes (Womack, 1989). The German carmakers learned to produce weather-resistant cars for Swedish consumers and lighter, more fuel efficient cars for the Italian market.

Fragmented markets forced the Europeans and Japanese to focus on flexibility—toward human resources and machine technologies—to provide a variety of goods and services tailored to market segments. Moreover, because the Europeans and Japanese could not realize economies from the sheer scale of production, they were forced to adopt more complex competitive strategies and to look for market niches. Rather than confront the United States head-on in the large-scale mass production markets, they took the path of least resistance. The Europeans offered the Volkswagen Beetle instead of big gas-guzzlers. Similarly, mimicking MacArthur's strategy by leapfrog-ging across the Pacific by avoiding major Japanese strongholds, the Japanese decided, as MacArthur did, to "hit 'em where they ain't." The Japanese entered American markets by gaining a toehold in niches neglected by the domestic American pro-ducers, often after taking on the Europeans first.

To compensate for their inability to match American productivity and scale economies, the Europeans and Japanese focused on quality. If they could not reduce costs per unit of output simply by increasing volume, they achieved alternative savings. For example, they reduced the costs of reworking prod-ucts by increasing quality in production; they focused on effec-tive work processes, flexible organizational designs, and supe-rior integration of human and machine capital.

Our competitors also had to compensate for the Ameri-can advantages on the human side of production. The Euro-peans and Japanese had fewer, less-qualified workers as they entered the postwar competition. The glut of American workers, especially as the baby boomers entered the workforce in the 1960s, allowed American employers to substitute unskilled la-bor for more expensive human capital. The relative paucity of labor, especially skilled labor, in Europe and Japan encouraged a more careful utilization of human capital and a more ag-gressive focus on learning at school and on the job (Dertouzos, Lester, and Solow, 1989). In addition, American technical per-sonnel, homegrown and imported, were of a superior quality, and the sheer size of the U.S. population guaranteed a greater quantity of white-collar and technical employees. As a result, the Europeans and Japanese could not compete in the development of major innovations. Instead, they competed on the basis of their ability to develop new applications quickly.

The Europeans and Japanese also had to compete against the flexibility of American labor markets. In Europe, a strong craft tradition and a powerful left-wing political movement con-siderably reduced employers' authority to hire, fire, and re-design work. In Japan, employers were forced to provide "lifetime employment" to blunt the more radical policies of a powerful Marxist labor movement, especially in industries manufacturing internationally traded products. American employers were able to reduce costs by shedding skilled labor and substituting mass production machinery in combination with unskilled labor. In sharp contrast, the Europeans and Japanese were forced to treat labor as a fixed cost of production and could not easily eliminate expensive skilled labor by substituting machinery and unskilled labor. As a result, the Europeans and Japanese had powerful incentives to develop and use human capital, whereas American employers were encouraged to rely on special-purpose machines and unskilled labor to drive productivity.

The Europeans and Japanese also found it difficult to match the sheer quantity of American intellectual and financial capital. In relative terms, the United States has never been a leading saver or investor, yet the nation is so large and wealthy that setting aside even a modest proportion of its gross national product (GNP) for investment results in more capital available per worker than is possible in many other nations. In the 1950s, for instance, Japanese families saved three times as much of their income as did American families but earned only one-eighth as much. As a result, total investment was twice as high in the United States as in Japan. Similarly, the United States made relatively low investments in intellectual capital, but because of sheer size it fielded the world's largest group of white-collar and technical workers and largest cache of basic research resources.

To compensate for America's advantages in the scale of intellectual and financial resources, the Europeans and Japanese tried to make better use of their smaller quantities of resources. They turned to networks both within and outside employer institutions. While government, business, and labor in the United States bargained over slices of the growing economic pie, government, business, and labor in Japan and Europe joined together to make the pie grow, forging more tightly integrated relationships among development, design, production, and delivery than did the United States. Japan and Europe encouraged cooperation between managers and labor, strengthened linkages between employers upstream and downstream in the production process, and fostered relationships between institutions that provided critical intellectual and financial capital. Governments played a critical role in these networks by promoting research, disseminating best practices, and acting as arbiter among competitors.

The Europeans and Japanese also compensated for a lesser quantity and quality of human resources by devising ways to make more effective economic use of these resources. The United States was good at educating and utilizing white-collar and technical elites, but students who were not college bound received second-rate educations and were given relatively little responsibility or opportunity to develop on the job. This system was consistent with the mass production economy that employed white-collar and technical workers in responsible positions at the top of institutional hierarchies and relegated nonsupervisory workers to narrow tasks at the bottom.

The Europeans and Japanese organized their educational systems and workplaces to make more effective use of students not bound for college and nonsupervisory workers. The Europeans built elaborate apprenticeship structures that mixed work and learning. The Japanese provided high-quality elementary and secondary education to all students. In the workplace, employees and their representatives shared responsibility and authority in an evenhanded exchange among team members up and down the line.

Our competitors also sharpened a more applied point on their intellectual pencil, focusing scarce financial and intellectual resources on real-world questions. Product development and process innovations were emphasized over basic research, and applied learning was emphasized at school and at work. The European use of apprenticeship, the Japanese use of group processes in school, and the emphasis on problem-solving teams on the job in both Europe and Japan are obvious examples of this applied focus. In contrast, American schooling sequestered students from the real world, broke down knowledge artificially into theoretical disciplines, broke disciplines into component pieces, and demanded that students commit fragments of knowledge to memory. Applications were reserved for pen-and-paper exercises at the back of the chapter. Interdisciplinary applications were rare, and applications in the context of working groups were even rarer. At work, new products, technologies, and work processes were installed from above and implemented below. There was little emphasis on capturing knowledge while the product was made, the service was delivered, or the customer was served.

The Emergence and Effect of New Market Forces

Something happened as we entered the final decades of the American Century. We still held the lead in the productivity race, but many of our competitors were running faster and threatening to overtake us by the turn of the century. More disturbing was the fact that we were losing market share in many industries and product lines despite our superior productivity. Apparently, productivity was still a necessary condition for competitive success but no longer sufficient by itself to capture and retain market share.

By most reports, the Europeans and Japanese seemed to have turned their weaknesses into strengths. By pursuing quality, variety, customization, convenience, and speed in getting to market, they not only expanded the terms of competition beyond productivity but found new routes to productivity as well. For instance, by designing quality into products as they were made, the Europeans and Japanese reduced the need to rework products and curbed waste, ultimately increasing productivity as well as quality. By the mid 1970s, mounting evidence began to suggest that productivity, on the one hand, and quality, variety, customization, convenience, and rapid change, on the other, were not only compatible but also mutually reinforcing competitive standards. Mass production was not the only route to competitive success.

Somewhere along the road to the second American Century, the rules of the economic game changed. The fundamental restructuring of the standards of economic competition in the postwar era had many roots, but principal among them were the following:

- Increasing wealth of nations
- Globalization of economic activity
- Diversification of tastes
- Increasing value of human time
- Commercialization of free labor
- Increasing participation of consumers in production and goods and service delivery
- Technical advances

Wealth of Nations. One reason people are demanding more than mass-produced goods and services is that they can afford more. The buying power of the average American has grown enormously since the end of World War II. The average car, for instance, was five times as expensive in the 1980s as it was in the 1950s. To afford such a car, however, the average family had to work twenty-six weeks in the 1950s but only twenty-three weeks in the 1980s. Moreover, the average car in the 1980s was of much higher quality and usually included a number of additional features: a digital radio, air-conditioning, and generally superior performance in the power train and assembly. In general, American workers had to work only half as many hours in 1988 as they did in 1950 to buy the same basket of goods (see Table 1). Of course, not everything we buy has become a better deal. For instance, we have to work more hours to buy used cars, public transportation, health care, and medical insurance.

The increase in the wealth of Americans is not all good news. Most of the increase in earnings occurred prior to 1973: The earnings of the average fifty-year-old American male rose from $15,529 in 1946 to $32,701 in 1973 but increased only to $36,228 in 1986 (Levy, 1987). Average family income doubled from roughly $14,000 to $28,000 between 1950 and 1973, growing at an average annual rate of 3.1 percent, but then it stagnated at a growth rate of 0.9 percent between 1973 and 1979 and 0.3 percent between 1979 and 1987 (Litan, Lawrence, and Schultze, 1988).

Table 1. Percentage Change in Hours of Work Required
to Buy Goods and Services.

	1950 to 1960	1950 to 1970	1950 to 1980	1950 to 1988
Durable Goods				
New autos	−79	−51	−41	−36
Used autos	+118	−105	−116	+144
Furniture and household equipment	−62	−38	−28	−21
Nondurable Goods				
Food	−76	−62	−63	−57
Clothing and shoes	−70	−56	−39	−31
Gasoline and oil	−78	−56	+96	−52
Tobacco products	−83	−75	−61	−81
Services				
Housing	−81	−61	−57	−60
Electricity	−69	−46	−54	−52
Gas	−84	−58	+96	+91
Water	+110	−98	−104	+124
Mass transit	+111	+121	−96	+116
Bus ticket	−88	−72	+89	+104
Airline ticket	−74	−57	−67	−64
Hospital care	−90	−88	+93	+107
Physicians' care	−93	−91	+98	+118
Dental care	−85	−77	−76	−81
Health insurance	−71	−70	−57	+87
Private education	−86	−76	−84	−82

Note: This table shows that it took 36 percent less work time in 1988 to purchase a new auto than it did in 1950; it required 144 percent more work time in 1988 to purchase a used auto than it did in 1950; and so on.

Source: Adapted by H. C. Kelly from U.S. Department of Commerce, Bureau of Economic Analysis, 1989.

The sources of income growth are equally disturbing. Until 1973, productivity drove income growth, but since then other factors have been responsible. Americans are not earning more now because they are working smarter. They are working harder. Although the average number of hours spent at work per week has declined for most European and Canadian workers, Americans have consistently worked about forty hours per week throughout the postwar period (U.S. Congress, 1988). Only the

Germans, Dutch, British, and Japanese work more hours. Americans are also increasing family incomes by putting more family members to work. Over the postwar period, participation in the labor force has declined from roughly 85 percent to 75 percent of men, but among women, participation in the labor force has increased from about 30 percent to almost 60 percent. We have learned to spread our money farther by marrying later and having fewer children. We are marrying two years later on average than we did in the 1950s, and there is roughly one less person in the average household (Levy, 1987).

Americans have increased their buying power, especially since 1980, by spending more, saving less, and borrowing. Average net savings stayed at approximately 7 percent from the beginning of the postwar era until 1980; then it plummeted toward 1 percent, where it has stagnated ever since (Litan, Lawrence, and Schultze, 1988). Until the 1980s, Americans produced sufficient savings to pay all their debts and still hold a savings surplus of between 3 percent and 7 percent of the GNP. Since 1980, we have lost our savings cushion altogether, and we are now forced to borrow an amount roughly equivalent to 3 percent of our GNP from foreigners to make ends meet (Litan, Lawrence, and Schultze, 1988). Since 1980, the federal debt has tripled, not counting the $250 billion we have to borrow to bail out failed savings and loan institutions. Household debt grew from $1.6 trillion in 1980 to $2.6 trillion in 1990. Over the same period, corporate debt increased from $1.0 trillion to $1.6 trillion. In 1980, the United States was a net lender to the rest of the world—the world owed us $106 billion. In 1990, we owed the rest of the world more than $500 billion.

Americans' increased buying power has been more than matched by improved buying power around the globe. In 1950, the average West German family earned only 40 percent as much as the average American family. By 1986, this figure had increased to 84 percent. The average Japanese family earned only 17 percent of the earnings of the average American family in 1950 but 77 percent in 1986 (Smith, 1987). The Japanese domestic market, which was one-eighth the size of the U.S. market in the 1950s, grew to almost half the size of the U.S.

market in the late 1980s (Dertouzos, Lester, and Solow, 1989). By the mid 1980s, the earnings of the average French family were 79 percent of the earnings of the average American family; corresponding figures elsewhere were 66 percent for the British, 54 percent for the Italians, and 47 percent for the Soviets.

Globalization. As everyone knows by now, the genie of international trade has long been out of the bottle. The combined value of imports and exports is equivalent to roughly a quarter of our GNP. The trend toward globalization is rooted in a variety of factors:

- Tastes have been homogenized as earnings have equalized worldwide; media, marketing, and travel have integrated demand.
- Higher incomes have given rise to international markets for national specialty products and services, such as Italian textiles, Swiss watches, and Japanese consumer electronics.
- A worldwide reduction in trade barriers began in the 1950s and continued through the 1980s despite painful trade-related dislocations (Doz, 1987).
- Advances in communication and transportation technology allowed multinational companies to serve large, homogeneous international markets from the home country, permitted decentralized worldwide production and sales, and reduced the costs for the newly industrialized nations to enter markets (Vernon, 1987).
- Organizational experience in American, European, and Japanese multinational corporations allowed rapid expansion when global markets became robust after the mid 1960s.

By the mid 1960s, these changes in global tastes, wealth, trade, and organizational capabilities resulted in the potential for rapid globalization. The spark that ultimately ignited global competition was the need to find new markets for mass-produced goods when existing markets became saturated. Increased productivity in combination with the natural cycles of boom and bust in domestic markets began to create persistent oversupply in the mid 1960s. As domestic markets became saturated, more and more nations began to compete for international customers. Because of increased mass production around the world, the list of basic commodities, goods, and services that were oversupplied grew constantly. By the late 1980s, production exceeded demand by at least 20 percent in steel, petrochemicals, semiconductors, and cars (Stokes, 1986). In a perfectly functioning free market, a glut would drive down prices and the least efficient producers would go out of business. But in the modern global economy, a variety of forces inhibit natural demise. Institutions are reluctant to shut down and accept the loss of huge start-up costs. Government support for basic industries can guarantee survival beyond the natural life cycle of economic viability.

The impact of the globalization of economic competition has been profound and in some ways unexpected. At its simplest level, globalization has increased the intensity and nature of competition. In a world where supply exceeds demand, the competitive importance of productivity and prices is reduced; quality, variety, customization, convenience, and timely delivery of state-of-the-art goods and services become the competitive edge. In global markets, demand fragments, requiring competitors to tailor goods and services to local tastes and needs. In addition, the complexity of and distances involved in global markets require increased service functions in order to deliver goods and services. The rule of thumb in global competition is, to borrow a phrase from the environmentalists, to "think globally and act locally."

Globalization also seems to have shattered the "product cycle," a self-perpetuating hand-me-down process of international economic development that has been in place for time in memory. Until recently, the logic of the product cycle was historically proven and difficult to challenge. According to this logic, global economic development began in the developed world, principally in the United States, where the markets were the wealthiest and largest, the labor force was the highest paid and most skilled, and the financial capital was the most readily

available. The American market was the logical seedbed for the
development of new technologies and products and, as a result,
the place where products were first developed and sold. Eventually, in every product line, the genius of mass production
reduced production systems to simple tricks requiring a small
cadre of elite white-collar and technical workers who managed
relatively unskilled labor and standardized technology. Once
simplified, mature production systems were passed on to less
developed nations that could use simple technologies in combination with cheaper and less skilled labor. In the meantime,
the United States moved on to the next wave of new technologies
and products. In this hand-me-down system, the developed and
developing nations of the world moved in lockstep up the development ladder. Advancement in the developed world eventually
raised all nations worldwide and did so without disrupting
American superiority.

    This comfortable cycle has broken down under the weight
of the new economic reality. Development has made human and
financial capital more available outside the United States, and
markets outside the United States have accrued sufficient wealth
to drive new product demand. Further, new global wealth, in
combination with new communications, transport, and information technologies, has reduced the scale advantages of the
American domestic market. The Japanese market is now almost
half the size of the American and growing. As economic integration proceeds in Europe, market size, buying power, and per
capita income there and in the United States are becoming
roughly equivalent (Dertouzos, Lester, and Solow, 1989). In addition, new technologies and the dismantling of trade barriers
have made the size of domestic markets less important. The
Japanese, for instance, sell six times as many videocassette recorders (VCRs) around the world as they sell at home.

    The most profound assault on the international product
cycle has come from a general breakdown in its sequential
nature. Today the nation that develops a new idea may not profit
from it before handing it to a lesser economic power. Technology is footloose. The quality of the indigenous human capital
is increasingly equal worldwide. As a result, nations can step

into the product cycle at any given point. Indeed, it is often best to let others bear the cost of development and to focus resources on subsequent phases of the product cycle. There is pride in invention, but there is money in developing products, making small improvements in efficiency and quality, and developing new applications for existing technologies, goods, and services (Teece, 1987; Ergas, 1987).

Globalization has been a mixed blessing for Americans. In a robust global market, the possibilities for economic expansion are impressive. The potential demand for goods and services in the world economy is vastly greater than current production levels. For instance, we now have one car for every 1.5 Americans, but in China, there is one car for every 2,122 citizens (U.S. Department of Commerce, 1989b). At the same time, globalization has helped change competitive standards in ways that do not play exclusively to our strengths. Productivity and the price reductions it brings are necessary, but not sufficient, for successful competition in global markets. Our scale advantages are eroding as Europe and Asia become more cohesive market spheres. In addition, the Europeans and Japanese have more experience than we do with the flexible production systems necessary to succeed in the highly fragmented global marketplace.

In the final analysis, however, we have no choice but to embrace the complex competitive standards of the global market and to devise a new set of rules and procedures to stabilize world trade. Our domestic markets are no longer large enough to satisfy our productive capabilities, and the extension of economic activity into the global market is necessary if we are to continue to increase our own standard of living. Moreover, if we are allowed access to foreign markets, we cannot deny others access to ours.

Diversification of Tastes. Plain vanilla is not good enough anymore. Variety and customization of goods and services have become key competitive principles. Consumers' tastes have diversified because of a mix of economics and demography at home and abroad. Increasing economic wealth contributes to diversity in demand in two ways. First, it changes what people want. As people get richer, a smaller share of their income goes for the basics of food, clothing, and shelter, and they begin demanding variety, quality, tailoring, convenience, and state-of-the-art goods and services. They also want more intangibles. For example, they can afford to let environmental, health, and nutritional concerns influence their purchasing decisions.

Second, growing wealth gives economic voice to underlying ethnic, geographic, cultural, religious, and gender differences that were there all along. No nation, with the possible exception of the Soviet Union, is more diverse than the United States. Moreover, our tastes become increasingly diversified. Demographic changes at home have resulted in a more complex domestic market. The aging baby boomers continue to create waves of new demands and to leave deflated markets in their wake. The American family has decreased in size and increased in variety. Enormous increases in wealth and life expectancy have resulted in new markets to serve older Americans (Kochan, Mitchell, and Dyer, 1982). The globalization of economic activity has also been a major external force in the diversification of tastes. There are many neighborhoods in the global village.

Importance of Time. In general, although Americans have more money than they used to, they have less time to spend it. Americans, especially American women, are busier than ever (see Table 2). Although men are working a little less, women are working a good deal more, and both men and women are spending more time commuting. Indeed, Americans and Australians have the longest commutes in the world. Sixty-four percent of Americans spend more than fifteen minutes commuting to work (U.S. Congress, 1988). Americans also enjoy fewer national holidays and have less access to paid leave than do the citizens of most other modern nations (U.S. Congress, 1988). Men are doing about an hour's more housework per week now than they did in the mid 1970s, but women are doing almost four hours' less housework per week. Both men and women are spending a little less time with their children and less time eating at home. Men have lost slightly more than two hours of

Table 2. Change in Weekly Time Budgets of Men and Women
Between 1975 and 1985.

Activity	Men	Women	Average
Contracted Time	+18 mins.	+6 hrs. 48 mins.	+3 hrs. 30 mins.
Work	–24 mins.	+5 hrs. 54 mins.	+2 hrs. 42 mins.
Travel to work	+42 mins.	+54 mins.	+48 mins.
Committed Time	+1 hr.	–4 hrs. 30 mins.	–1 hr. 42 mins.
Housework	+1 hr. 18 mins.	–3 hrs. 54 mins.	–1 hr. 18 mins.
Child care	–12 mins.	–36 mins.	–24 mins.
Shopping	+6 mins.	No change	+6 mins.
Family travel	–12 mins.	No change	–6 mins.
Personal Time	+36 mins.	+1 hr.	+48 mins.
Eating at home	–18 mins.	–48 mins.	–30 mins.
Eating out	–42 mins.	+6 mins.	–18 mins.
Personal care	+1 hr. 36 mins.	+1 hr. 42 mins.	+1 hr. 36 mins.
Free Time	–2 hrs. 6 mins.	–3 hrs. 18 mins.	–2 hrs. 42 mins.
Education	–24 mins.	–6 mins.	–18 mins.
Volunteer organizations	No change	–42 mins.	–24 mins.
Social activities	–1 hr. 24 mins.	–2 hrs. 18 mins.	–1 hr. 48 mins.
Recreation	+18 mins.	–24 mins.	–6 mins.
Electronic media	–1 hr. 12 mins.	–18 mins.	–42 mins.
Other media	No change	+18 mins.	+6 mins.
Leisure travel	+36 mins.	+12 mins.	+24 mins.

Note: This table shows that in 1985, men were working 24 minutes less and women were working 5 hours and 54 minutes more than they did in 1975. Both men and women spent more time traveling to work in 1985 than they did in 1975. In general, Americans, especially women, were spending more time in work-related activities.

Source: U.S. Congress Office of Technology Assessment, 1988, p. 69.

free time per week and women more than three. Women are working two shifts: the first on the job and the second at home (Hochschild and Machung, 1989).

The increasing scarcity of consumer time has had an enormous impact on competition for consumers' dollars and loyalty. Busy people have neither time nor patience for shoddy goods or second-rate services. They want goods and services tailored to their needs. They want readily available information on the range of offerings, and they will be loyal to institutions that consistently provide high quality or information on where high-quality products are available. Above all, busy people want goods and services that can be consumed conveniently.

Commercialization of Homemaking and Personal Care. Scarcity of time has encouraged the development of markets for time-sensitive goods and services. Americans are interested in buying products that help them work at home more efficiently, and they are willing to pay for goods and labor to do the chores they would otherwise do themselves. More and more of the work traditionally done off the job is being commercialized. The commercialization of homemaking, recreation, and personal care stems in part from the new work roles of women and changes in the structure of the American family. Child care, cleaning, care for the elderly, and other domestic activities were once largely foisted on women in the context of the traditional family. Increased opportunities for women, growing financial pressures, and the increasing number of families with nontraditional structures suggest that the commercialization of homemaking and personal care will continue to be an important engine driving market changes for decades to come.

This kind of commercialization inevitably expands market standards beyond price competition. For example, price is not the only criterion for choosing how to care for our loved ones, young or old. We want quality, choice, and services tailored to our individual needs. We may not have the time or expertise for home cooking, but we still want varied, high-quality, convenient meals. We may be too busy to teach our children, but we demand high-quality, customized education for them.

Expanding Consumer Participation in Production and Delivery of Goods and Services. A distinctive feature of the new goods and service markets is the extent of consumer participation. Consumer participation has always been the hallmark of service delivery: The patient needs to interact with the doctor to formulate a diagnosis; the diner needs to work with the waiter to order the food; the potential claimant has to work with the insurance salesperson to choose the right policy; and the novice needs to work with the dance instructor to learn the right steps.

Customer participation is nothing new in manufacturing either. Traditionally, makers of household gadgets, products used for home-based entertainment, and recreational equipment have expanded consumption by creating hardware that requires unpaid consumer labor to produce the final service or goods. The number of commercial laundries, for instance, was dramatically reduced with the introduction of mechanical washers and dryers that combined user friendly technology with consumer labor.

Although consumer participation in production and delivery is not new, now there is more of it. Both technical and organizational changes have facilitated this expansion. New user friendly machinery can harness technology for the user's purposes through flexible software. Customer-focused organizational structures increase the ability of producers to tailor products by involving customers in production or delivery.

Consumer participation helps institutions meet new market standards. For example, computer-based technologies can allow customers to participate in designing goods and services tailored to their individual needs and preferences. Examples range from the growing proportion of shorter and more tailored production runs in manufacturing to the design of houses and insurance packages. The increased involvement of customers in the use of goods and services can have the same effect. For example, the automated teller machine provides convenience and allows the consumer to customize services; the VCR is more convenient than the movie theater and allows more variety than television; self-service at the gas pump is convenient; and the salad bar varies and customizes a restaurant's menu.

Advances in Technology. The new market standards would not have been possible without an equally new role for technology. In traditional manufacturing, for instance, machinery was hard wired for narrow purposes. Each machine made a piece of the good, and a new good or a new piece required a new machine. The fragmented markets the Japanese and Europeans faced, however, required a more flexible use of existing technologies. In the 1950s, the Europeans and Japanese developed work processes for using narrow-purpose and relatively inflexible equipment more fluidly. For instance, they learned to use team-based production to reset machines or roll different machines in and out of the assembly line quickly to reduce downtime when changing from one version of a good to the next (Womack, 1989; Piore and Sabel, 1984).

Eventually, information-based technologies allowed employers to locate flexibility in the technology itself, as well as in the work processes for using the technology. With flexible software, a few keystrokes at a control board can reprogram whole production systems and work processes. The computer has brought a new level of built-in flexibility and precision in production and service delivery. Employers who have fully exploited the flexible new technology, by using it in conjunction with equally flexible workforces and organizational formats, have raised the level of competition and increased the range of competitive standards. The new technology also provides convenience. User friendly software makes technical complexity as invisible to most customers and workers as the carburetor is to most drivers of cars.

Chapter Two

SIX STANDARDS OF SUCCESS: HOW AMERICA MEASURES UP

Productivity and Beyond

It takes more than productivity and low prices to win the competitive race. American productivity in computer chips, for instance, has been as good as or better than that of our competitors, yet in the late 1970s, we lost our market share because our chips were not as reliable as those produced in Japan (Clausing, 1989). Similarly, our productivity in textiles is world class, and our German and Italian competitors have higher wage costs, more aggressive unions, and less government protection. Nevertheless, we continue to lose market share to both the Germans and the Italians (Berger, 1989). In short, although productivity is still primary in the mix of competitive standards in the new economy, it has been joined by a new set of standards. None of the forces that have given rise to the new competitive standards shows any sign of relenting. The inevitable conclusion

37

Table 3. The Productivity of Other Nations as a Percentage of
American Productivity, 1950–1989.

Country	1950	1960	1970	1980	1989
United States	100.0	100.0	100.0	100.0	100.0
Canada	69.5	72.0	78.1	92.1	94.2
Norway	49.9	56.7	61.6	79.0	81.4
Sweden	59.1	66.6	76.3	76.7	75.1
Japan	16.1	28.8	55.8	66.1	74.9
West Germany	36.0	61.1	67.9	74.3	72.8
France	44.4	54.4	65.8	73.1	70.1
Denmark	51.5	62.1	69.1	70.6	69.2
United Kingdom	60.4	66.5	64.9	66.2	68.6
Belgium	46.4	50.8	60.9	69.9	68.0
Italy	31.7	44.9	57.3	67.1	67.3
Netherlands	53.4	61.4	69.4	72.4	66.6
Austria	31.4	47.0	55.0	66.2	65.0
Korea	N/A	9.5	12.9	20.9	34.4

Note: American productivity is shown as 100.0 percent in each year, and each nation's productivity is expressed as a percentage of American productivity rate. In general, the table shows that although the United States is still the world's overall productivity leader, other nations are closing the gap. For instance, in 1950, the Canadian productivity rate was 69.5 percent as high as the U.S. productivity rate. By 1989, Canadian productivity had risen to 94.2 percent of American productivity. Japan's productivity rate was only 16.1 percent of the American productivity rate in 1950 but had risen to 74.9 percent of U.S. productivity by 1989.

Source: U.S. Department of Labor, 1990a.

is that our economic status among the community of nations will depend on our ability to meet these new standards.

Productivity. The American productivity rate is still the world standard (see Tables 3 and 4). Yet the rate of increase in productivity is much greater among our competitors than it is in the United States, and other nations will catch up and pass us if present trends continue (see Tables 3, 4, and 5). Evidence suggests that the United States is already losing the productivity race to Japan in some industries, including chemicals, steel and other primary metals, electrical machinery, and transportation equipment (Sadler, 1977).

**Table 4. Value of Output per Person in the United States
and Other Nations, 1950–1989.**

Country	1950	1960	1970	1980	1989
United States	$9,972	$11,559	$14,777	$17,369	$20,891
Canada	$6,926	$ 8,322	$11,545	$15,999	$19,679
Japan	$1,605	$ 3,325	$ 8,238	$11,483	$15,655
West Germany	$3,593	$ 7,066	$10,037	$12,908	$15,211
France	$4,428	$ 6,290	$ 9,729	$12,689	$14,646
Korea	N/A	$ 1,101	$ 1,912	$ 3,631	$ 7,184

Note: The dollar value of economic output per person is shown for each country. For instance, if we had divided our total output evenly among all Americans in 1950, each of us would have received $9,972 worth of goods and services. By 1989, our total output was sufficient to afford each American $20,891 worth of goods and services. In general, although the table demonstrates that we are still the world's wealthiest people, other nations are catching up.
Source: U.S. Department of Labor, 1990b.

America's recent productivity problems are well known. Our rate of productivity boomed between 1948 and 1965, averaging 3.5 percent per year. The rate slowed to 2.0 percent per year between 1965 and 1973, however, before collapsing and turning negative in 1974 (– 2.1 percent). After 1974, the rate barely held its own, registering a disappointing average increase of 1.1 percent per year until 1977, when it fell below 1.0 percent. Productivity improvement in the 1980s remained well below the long-term average of 2.0 percent per year.

The American productivity story is not completely gloomy, however. We need to increase our productivity by only 1.2 percent a year in order to improve our standard of living by about 1.5 percent per year, a rate sufficient to afford us our accustomed life-style. A 1.2 percent increase in productivity would be a difficult but not an unattainable target (Freedman, 1989).

The best productivity news has come in manufacturing, where we need productivity most to maintain our competitive position in the global economy. Manufacturing productivity improvement collapsed in the early 1970s but made a remark-

Table 5. Percentage Increase in Productivity per Year, 1950–1989.

Country	Percentage Productivity Increased
Japan	6.0
Korea	5.7
Italy	3.9
Austria	3.8
West Germany	3.8
Norway	3.2
France	3.1
Belgium	2.9
Canada	2.7
Denmark	2.7
Netherlands	2.5
Sweden	2.5
United Kingdom	2.2
United States	1.9

Note: The rate of increase in overall economic output per year is shown for each nation. For instance, between 1950 and 1989, overall U.S. productivity increased by 1.9 percent a year on average. Over the same period, Japanese productivity increased by 6.0 percent a year on average. As a result, although the United States is still the productivity leader, Japan and other nations are catching up.
Source: U.S. Department of Labor, 1989, 1990.

able comeback in the 1980s, growing at an annual rate of more than 3 percent beginning in 1982 (Morris, 1989). This rate is roughly equivalent to our best productivity performance in manufacturing and almost twice the overall productivity trend in the postwar era. Although the Japanese, Germans, Swedes, French, British, and Italians are still running faster than we are, we appear to have finally reacted to the chase (Fullerton, 1989). Moreover, although most industrialized nations have experienced a productivity slowdown since 1973, the United States and the United Kingdom are the only two nations that have had a productivity turnaround and matched their pre-1973 performance (Fullerton, 1989).

With even a small acceleration in our rate of increase in productivity, our competitors will be hard pressed to catch up given our current lead. If we are to hold the lead, we will have to continue to improve our performance in manufacturing, but even more will depend on our ability to jump-start the stalled productivity engine elsewhere.

The principal drag on the nation's overall productivity comes from the service sector. For instance, if white-collar workers in the service sector had been as productive as white-collar workers in manufacturing, the overall productivity rate would have risen by more than an additional 0.5 percent per year in the 1980s, bringing the overall productivity rate above 2.0 percent— a rate consistent with our pace prior to 1973 (Roach, 1989).

Demographic and technological trends already in place could help sustain the boom in manufacturing productivity and extend it to other industries. The size of the workforce will decline over the foreseeable future, especially at the entry level. This trend represents a dramatic turnaround from conditions in the 1960s and 1970s, when the baby boom encouraged employers to substitute relatively cheap labor for skill and technology. This practice made the United States the world's best job creation machine in the post-World War II era but probably led to some significant share of the nation's mysterious productivity decline after 1973 (Morris, 1989). As we look to the future, the continuing decline in the overall size of the workforce will boost investments in human and machine capital. A smaller workforce will have to be more skilled and utilize more technology to maintain output. The result will be an increase in output per worker, which means increased productivity. The demographic news at the entry level is not all good, however, because a growing share of our entry-level workers will come from populations in which our human capital investments have been woefully inadequate. As a result, the cost of developing workers with necessary skills will increase.

The best demographic news comes at midcareer. After decades of expensive preparation, the baby boomers are finally on the job. We have already paid the productivity price of integrating these workers into the workplace and can now look forward to more than thirty years of continuous productivity improvement as they learn formally and informally at work. Available evidence suggests that individual performance does not peak until workers reach their late fifties. The average age of the American workforce will not reach the fifties until 2050. As a result, we can expect productivity improvements until the middle of the next century, when the workforce will start getting younger again.

In addition, as the baby boomers age and the demographic center of gravity in the United States shifts toward middle age, more financial capital will become available for investment in both human and machine capital. The baby boomers are entering their prime saving years. Moreover, because virtually all baby boomers who can afford houses have already bought them, less capital will be absorbed in the mammoth housing sector and more capital will be available for investments in machines and people. Demographically driven housing demand is likely to fall off by as much as 30 percent. Already the inventory of homes available for sale has risen by a third since 1972 (Morris, 1989).

Trends in technology are also favorable for the nation's future productivity performance. The application of profound technical changes usually takes a long time. Electricity, for instance, was generally available by 1860 but was not commonly used in American homes and businesses until the 1920s. And although electricity declined in price by more than 400 percent over the same period, the sale of steam engines did not peak until the early decades of the twentieth century (Liebergott, 1984). The flexible technologies of the new economy, especially information technologies, are in their infancy. We are still in the most primitive phases of applying these technologies at home and at work.

Quality. Quality appears to be primary among the new competitive standards. Remarkably, in 1989, when the nation established its first major award for economic excellence, it was an award for quality, not productivity. By act of Congress and with the enthusiastic support of American industry, the award was called the Malcolm Baldrige National Quality Award (named for the former secretary of commerce) (Segalla, 1989).

Quality is measurable from two points of view. One set of

quality measures looks at a good or service from the inside out, a point of view usually adopted by the maker of the good or the deliverer of the service. Another way to look at quality is from the outside in, a point of view that emphasizes the consumer's perspective.

Inside-out measures are usually concerned with built-in quality, which is achieved in the design and production of a good or the design and delivery of a service. Built-in quality in manufacturing, for example, is usually measurable by an engineering standard such as the number of defects or mistakes per quantity of a good. In services, built-in quality is usually measured by the extent to which state-of-the-art processes, personnel, or machines are used. A medical examination, for instance, meets quality standards if it is delivered by certified personnel who follow recommended procedures.

The complementary outside-in view of quality presumes the proof of the pudding is in the tasting and relies on the consumer's estimation of quality. Measures of this more external standard tend to assess the performance of the final good or the effects of the service. Automobile performance standards and the effects of heart transplants on longevity are cases in point. Performance standards, especially measures of customer satisfaction, are often more subjective than measures of built-in, or internal, quality.

American performance in terms of quality is mixed. In automotive manufacturing, for instance, the number of defects per American-made vehicle is decreasing dramatically. The built-in quality of our cars is currently on a par with that of European cars, but we still manufacture twice as many defects per vehicle as the Japanese (Womack, 1989). Independent auto watchers J. D. Power and Associates reported, in a 1986 survey of customer satisfaction, that the United States scored 94 points; the Europeans, 106; and the Japanese, 119. In 1989, the United States scored 112; the Europeans, 111; and the Japanese scored highest at 130 (*The Power Report*, 1989). In the consumer's estimation, we have overtaken the European auto manufacturers by a hair's breadth, but the Japanese still hold the market standard for quality.

Data on the quality of textiles, computer chips, steel, and many other American products are mixed, and data on consumer electronics, chemicals, and machine tools are downright disappointing (Dertouzos, Lester, and Solow, 1989).

Yet the United States sets the world's quality standard for other industries, such as aerospace, aircraft, large computers, appliances, and health care. Indeed, General Electric, Whirlpool, Maytag, and other American appliance manufacturers initiated quality improvements before being challenged by overseas competitors. Since 1980, these manufacturers have cut defect rates by more than three-quarters and customer service and warranty claims by half (Dumaine, 1989).

There have also been individual turnarounds in quality in every industry. NUMMI, the GM-Toyota plant in Fremont, California, averages only 0.55 defect per car, a level equal to Japanese production quality and almost twice as good as the American average (Womack, 1989). Motorola, one of the first three recipients of the Malcolm Baldrige National Quality Award, lowered its defect rate from no more than 5,000 defects per 1,000,000 chips to 500 defects and then to 3.4 defects per 1,000,000 chips (Galvin, 1988). Xerox, one of two Baldrige award winners in 1989, installed a companywide quality standard and overtook the Japanese lead in the photocopier market. And Harley-Davidson, which reached a manufacturing defect rate of 50 percent in 1972, has since cut defects to 1 percent of production (Reid, 1990). Additionally, GM's Cadillac division whose earlier reputation for quality had suffered in the 1980s, rebounded in 1990 as the first automotive winner of the Baldrige award (Paton, 1991).

Variety. The once standardized offerings of mass production have given way to an explosion of choices.

- Americans now choose among 572 different models of cars, vans, and trucks compared with just 408 in 1980. In the mid-1980s, vehicle manufacturers counted a combined total of seven distinct market segments for cars and trucks. As we entered the 1990s, manufacturers identified nineteen distinct market segments for cars and eleven for trucks (Ingrassia and Patterson, 1989).

- Consumer banking has expanded from six basic services in the mid-1970s to more than a hundred today (Noyelle, 1989).
- Retail specialty chains like Toys "Я" Us, the Gap, the Limited, Circuit City, and Esprit have cut into the market shares of major department stores by offering more specialty items. New specialty stores are emerging daily for everything from telephones to Christmas decorations.
- Between 1979 and 1989, the number of items carried on supermarket shelves rose from 12,000 to 24,000 (Noyelle, 1989). The number of breakfast cereal brand names jumped from 152 to 271. The number of soup brand names increased from 55 to 83.

The explosion in variety comes from the same forces that have set the new quality standard. People can afford variety. The fragmented global market demands it. New flexible technologies allow it at mass production prices. The saturation of domestic and global markets also encourages variety. Once large-scale markets for standardized products mature, variety can be an effective way to gain market share. This pattern is evident in the recent histories of the retail banking, communications, chemical, and steel industries.

In retail banking, institutions competed throughout the 1950s and 1960s on the basis of their ability to sell checking and savings accounts through a growing network of branch offices. In the 1950s, only 20 percent to 30 percent of American, German, and French families had checking or savings accounts. As the 1980s approached, almost 90 percent of these families had such accounts. Competitive pressures eventually expanded banking services, revitalizing the competition and ultimately transforming the banking business into the financial services industry (Noyelle, 1988b).

In the 1950s and 1960s, the communications industry was the telephone business. Saturated by the mid 1970s, this business escaped the declining prospects of maturity by expanding goods and services to include data transmission and new communication services.

By the late 1960s, the chemical industry had matured. At the same time, the available technology had diffused throughout the world, greatly increasing world capacity for chemical production. The net result was chronic overcapacity. Generally, from 20 percent to 30 percent more commodity chemicals were available than anyone wanted to buy. Moreover, as new capacity came on line, prices dropped faster than costs, a common phenomenon in mature markets for basic commodities. In response, the industry has gone through a worldwide restructuring, deemphasizing commodity chemicals and diversifying into a greater variety of more complex goods produced in smaller quantities (Wei, 1989).

The same process has occurred in the steel industry. Growing capacity in world steel production has long since resulted in a glut of steel on the market. Foreign producers have been able to produce steel more cheaply than we have, and in the past twenty-five years, the American steelmakers' share of domestic steel markets has fallen from 95 percent to 60 percent (Kendrick, 1988). American steelmakers, no longer the low-cost producers of the basic commodity, have had to shift to a strategy emphasizing the new competitive standards, including variety. The most obvious evidence of this shift has been the growing importance of specialty steel and minimills and the relative decline in markets for large-scale producers. By 1988, specialty steel represented only 5 percent of U.S. production but a much higher proportion of total revenues; since 1980, the number of minimills has doubled from thirty to sixty (Kendrick, 1988). The minimills had captured 13 percent of the market for carbon steel by 1980 and 21 percent by 1985; they are projected to hold a market share of 40 percent by the year 2000 (Flemings, 1989).

Customization. In the family of competitive standards, customization is first cousin to variety. Busy people with more buying power want more choices in goods and services to meet their individual needs. At a minimum, this demand results in increased variety designed to satisfy market segments; in a growing number of industries, the urge to move from a one-size-fits-all approach to a more tailored market strategy is resulting in customization. As human capital and machine capital become more flexible, the relationship between scale and production costs weakens, and fewer units of output are necessary to realize scale economies. The ability to customize represents the victory of flexibility over scale. Ultimate flexibility is achieved when the cost-effective scale of production reduces to one.

At present, many employers are trying to combine variety and customization. A bank, for instance, provides a variety of financial services and with the assistance of information technology can develop a customized package of such services for the individual.

The textile and apparel industries provides another case in point. The textile market, especially in doubleknit fabric, was saturated in the early 1970s. The apparel market was saturated at about the same time, and many garments were left on the rack as demand declined further with the oil price increases after 1972. Many manufacturers turned to shorter production runs of fiber, garments of higher quality and more variety, and customization. At Milliken, textile lot sizes were reduced from an average of 20,000 yards of cloth to 4,000. Dan River reduced lot sizes from 12,000 yards to special runs of as few as 1,800 yards while offering more than 2,000 varieties of fabric (Berger, 1989). At Melbo Apparel in Japan, lot sizes for suits were reduced to one. A similar trend in Germany and northern Italy suggests that the apparel industry may have come full circle from tailoring prior to the industrial revolution in the 1700s to mass production after 1800 and back to tailoring in the new economy, which is emerging in the closing decade of the 1900s. Both the Japanese and the Italians are heading toward a system in which an individual order specifying fabric, style, and size will be filled in a few weeks by means of highly responsive, electronically driven networks of retailers and apparel, textile, and fiber manufacturers (U.S. Congress, 1988; Piore and Sabel, 1984; Berger, 1989).

Convenience. Busy people crave convenience. More and more consumers can afford it. And flexible technologies can provide it. In the complex global economy, delivering a good or service conveniently can provide the competitive edge that differentiates one company from another.

There are three kinds of convenience: built-in convenience, convenient delivery, and high-quality customer relations. Built-in convenience comes with effective product designs and the exploitation of user friendly technologies and software. Remote controls, automated teller and other self-service machines, home entertainment centers, car phones, and computer dating networks are examples.

Convenient delivery becomes more important as domestic markets fragment and competition goes global. The growth in the number of "convenience stores" is one bit of evidence. There are almost 8,000 7-Elevens in the United States and another 4,000 overseas, with an average of 1,000 customers per store daily. One-stop shopping is on the rise. Drive-in islands that offer gas, fast foods, and myriad banking services are appearing everywhere. Supermarkets are currently devoting 25 percent of their space to specialty departments such as self-service delis, pharmacies, and bakeries. "Hypermarkets" — which are essentially malls without walls — are the latest in convenient delivery. They range in size from 200,000 to 250,000 square feet and carry upward of 70,000 items.

The third type of convenience, that of successful customer relations, can also be a powerful selling tool. Dissatisfied customers will not buy again, and each will relate his or her unhappiness to roughly ten other people (Desatnick, 1987). Moreover, according to one survey, for every customer complaint, another twenty-six customers have the same problem, and anywhere from 65 percent to 95 percent of those noncomplainers will eventually stop doing business with the offending company.

Losing customers is serious. It costs five times more to get a new customer than it does to keep an old one. In *Service America!*, Albrecht and Zemke (1985) cite some generally accepted statistics on the value of customer loyalty. For instance, in the auto industry, a loyal customer is worth $140,000 over a lifetime of car buying. In terms of appliances, a loyal customer is worth $2,800 over a twenty-year period. At the local super-market, a loyal customer is worth $4,400 a year (Desatnick, 1987). A survey of "why customers quit" provided the following information: 3 percent move away, 5 percent develop personal loyalties to other businesses, 9 percent choose other suppliers' more competitive products, 14 percent are dissatisfied with the good or service, and 68 percent perceive that they were treated badly or with indifference (LeBoeuf, 1987).

By all reports, the expectations for service are increasing, and Americans are expressing a growing dissatisfaction with the customer service they are receiving. A Conference Board survey of 6,000 households suggested that Americans are reasonably satisfied with the quality of goods but pervasively dissatisfied with service quality. The *Yankelovitch Monitor* surveyed 2,500 Americans about their satisfaction with customer service and found that respondents believed that only airline service had improved over time (Denton, 1989). But a closer look at airline customer service does not bear out the *Yankelovitch Monitor's* good news. Zemke and Schaaf (1989) report that in 1987 the U.S. Department of Transportation received more than 44,000 complaints from airline passengers, an increase of 25 percent over 1986. Also in 1987, only 66 percent of airline flights arrived on time and airlines lost 11 out of every 1,000 pieces of luggage.

Timeliness. The early bird will win market share in the new economy because time is money. According to one study of high-tech markets, products that come to market on budget but six months late will earn 33 percent less profit over five years than products that come out on time but are 50 percent over budget (Nasar, 1987).

Institutions compete in several successive races against the clock:

> First event: Develop a major innovation, whether a technology, a product, or a new work process.
> Second event: Move the innovation off the drawing board and into the hands of consumers.
> Third event: Race up the learning curve to improve the

innovation by increasing efficiency, improving quality, or developing new applications.

Final event: Use the knowledge accumulated in the race up the learning curve to make a breakthrough to an-other major innovation. This event occurs after institu-tions have wrung all possible incremental improve-ments and new applications out of the original innovation.

A single employer or nation rarely wins all these events. In the nineteenth century and the first half of the twentieth century, the United States became a leading economic power by borrow-ing ideas from abroad. We were not the best at invention, but we were first in the race to get these borrowed ideas off the drawing board and into the hands of customers. After World War II, however, Americans became the wellspring of invention. The United States ended up with the lion's share of the world's intellectual, financial, and physical capital. These resources in combination with our postwar leadership in defense and space-related research ensured that we would be the first to develop most large-scale innovations.

Since the end of World War II, the United States has been the global leader at invention, but our relatively rigid mass production techniques and organizational structures are hold-ing us back in the race to commercialize, improve, and multiply the products of invention. Additional disadvantages are our overly specialized human and machine capital and inattention to the development of human capital and organizational learn-ing at the point of goods production and service delivery and at the interface with the customer, where inventions are turned into commercial successes.

Evidence of our inability to beat the clock has been ac-cumulating for some time, as the following four examples make clear. Japanese auto manufacturers renew their designs every four years, whereas American companies attempt to make a basic design last as long as ten years. Because the Japanese automakers develop and design faster, they introduce a new line of products every seven years, but Americans wait as long as fifteen years to turn over a basic product line (Womack 1989). In another example, dies, the metal molds used to stamp or cut metal to specific shapes, play a key role in changing automobile models. The ability to set new dies and to change dies in production quickly is critical to variety and customization. It takes the automaker in Japan twelve months to set new dies compared with twenty-three months in the United States. On the factory floor, die changes that can take as long as eight to twenty-four hours in U.S. auto plants can take as little as five minutes in Japanese plants (Dertouzos, Lester, and Solow, 1989). In the steel industry, it takes four to five years to design and build a new blast furnace in the United States but only three years in Japan and two years in Korea (Dertouzos, Lester, and Solow, 1989). In the apparel industry, it takes most American institutions up to sixty-six weeks to get from fiber to finished garment. Many European and Asian companies reach the customer in twenty-three weeks, and at least one Japanese manufacturer hopes to reduce the time to a few weeks (U.S. Congress, 1988; Berger, 1989).

On the other hand, some American industries, such as aircraft, computers, and appliances, have led in all four of the competitive events throughout the postwar era. In addition, the United States boasts examples of speedy institutions in almost every industry: Milliken in textiles; WalMart in retail; Motorola, Xerox, and Hewlett Packard in high-tech manufacturing; and Harley-Davidson in low-tech manufacturing. Even in industries where whole companies are not model performers, there are always individual plants, like NUMMI in auto manufacturing, that lead the pack.

The New Competitive Framework

The new competitive standards are mutually reinforcing and develop simultaneously. They are understood best as a flexible framework in which each standard makes sense only in the context of the others. Individual employers who begin by emphasizing one standard usually end up embracing them all because each overlaps and leads to the next.

Productivity. Productivity is pursued differently in the new economy than it was in the old. In the organizations of the old economy, white-collar and technical elites increased productivity principally by rationalizing organizations, mechanizing work processes, and reducing personnel costs by using fewer or cheaper employees. The essential goal of the productivity strategy was greater efficiency — more output for less cost. The main target for cost cutting was personnel costs because they represented the largest share of costs in every organization. By automating work processes and instituting rigorous organizational designs, employers in the old economy reduced skill requirements and could therefore use cheaper labor, realizing even more substantial savings by reducing the size of the workforce.

The old-time religion of productivity with a single-minded focus on cost reduction does not work in the new economy. Highly rationalized bureaucracies are too rigid to respond to the fast pace of change that characterizes the new competitive environment. The organizations of the old economy hoarded authority and resources at the top. The presumption was that general access to authority and resources would result in profligacy and waste. Yet in the new economy, access to authority and resources is required at the point of production and service delivery and at the interface with the customer if the organization is to provide quality, variety, customization, convenience, and timely innovations. Moreover, authority and access to resources are required down the line to encourage full utilization of the new flexible information and communications technologies at the core of the new economy.

Increasing productivity by reducing costs results in lean organizations, narrow-purpose technologies, and unskilled workforces that are cheap but too inflexible and anemic to respond to the new, broader set of competitive requirements. The new economy requires organizations, technologies, and workforces that are flexible and robust. In the old economy, organizations, technologies, and workforces were targets for cost reduction; in the new economy, they are resources to be developed in order to add value.

Productivity–Variety–Customization. A basic tenet of the mass production economy was that increased standardization and higher volumes drive prices down, whereas greater variety and lower volumes drive prices up. One rule of thumb said that cutting variety by half raises productivity by 30 percent and cuts costs by roughly 15 percent; doubling the volume of a standardized good or service decreases cost per unit of output from 15 percent to 25 percent (Stalk, 1988).

In point of fact, as competition heated up in the postwar era, high-volume production became a competitive box with no easy exit. Global production capabilities increased, volumes went up, and prices kept going down, reducing profit margins. American employers continued to retreat into high-margin markets, surrendering low-margin niches to newcomers. Narrow product lines and rigid production systems dedicated to fewer and fewer products also limited options for growth in product lines.

The Japanese and Europeans had different problems. As noted earlier, their domestic markets were small, leaving little room for high-volume production at home and forcing them to provide variety for diverse markets abroad. Only narrow, low-margin niches were left for high-volume products; the United States and other industrial leaders had left these niches behind.

To resolve their competitive dilemma, the Japanese and Europeans eventually broke the link between scale and variety by making more flexible use of their human, machine, and organizational capital. For example, one U.S. producer of automobile components produces ten million parts per year and offers only eleven varieties of components, whereas its Japanese competitor produces only three and a half million units per year but offers thirty-eight different varieties. More important, with one-third the scale and three times the variety, the Japanese producer has a labor productivity one and one-half times that of the U.S. company and produces at half the unit cost (Stalk, 1988).

Ultimately, the pursuit of variety begets customization. The distinction between these standards is a matter of degree.

Variety becomes customization as a production or service institution becomes more flexible and the goods or services sold come close to being one of a kind.

Productivity–Variety–Customization–Timeliness. Variety and customization eventually encourage speed. The need to shift from product to product or to vary products without losing productivity forces an emphasis on speed. By way of contrast, rigid mass production systems require long lead times to refit human resources and machine technology to new goods or services. The problem is that long lead times cost money, reduce responsiveness to markets, and force an excessive reliance on forecasts of demand, which are often wrong. Poor forecasts result in either excess inventory costs due to overproduction or losses due to underproduction. Bad forecasts lead to more planning, less risk taking, and even longer lead times and less accurate forecasts.

A focus on time increases productivity and saves money. In traditional manufacturing, products are being worked on only 0.05 percent to 2.5 percent of the time. Tighter production systems can result in enormous savings, as shown in the examples that follow.

- A just-in-time production system installed at Hewlett-Packard resulted in inventory reductions of more than 60 percent, reduced space requirements more than 30 percent, and lowered labor costs more than 20 percent (Clausing, 1989).
- Harley-Davidson reduced the time it took to make a motorcycle from thirty days to three and cut production costs by more than 50 percent (Smith, 1987).
- In 1982, Toyota could manufacture a car in two days but required another fifteen to twenty-five days to close a sale. The sales and distribution function was consuming 20 to 30 percent of the cost to the customer, an amount greater than the cost of manufacturing the car. By 1987, Toyota had reduced the distribution time to nine days, with a commensurate reduction in cost.

- In the U.S. apparel industry, on average, it takes more than sixty-five weeks to move from fiber to a finished good available to customers (Berger, 1989; U.S. Congress, 1988). The material is actually being worked on for only fifteen of those weeks. One industry study found that the snail's pace of production and delivery resulted in a 25 percent increase in costs and losses:
  - — 6.4 percent in extra carrying costs to maintain inventory,
  - — 4.0 percent in losses because retailers did not have the product on hand, and
  - — 14.6 percent in losses because of forced markdowns due to late arrivals (Berger, 1989).

  Some companies have been able to shorten response time to twenty-one weeks, reducing the price of apparel by almost 13 percent (Berger, 1989; U.S. Congress, 1988). Industry experts tend to agree that there is no technical reason why response times cannot be reduced to a few weeks.

Productivity–Variety–Customization–Timeliness–Quality. The quality standard has become the emblem of the new competitive framework. Experience teaches that pursuing quality invariably improves performance on a host of competitive standards. For instance, the customer's view of quality certainly includes the convenient and timely availability of a variety of state-of-the-art goods and services tailored to the customer's needs. A high-quality car that runs well is a convenience to the customer. A tailored suit provides both quality and customization. Quality tends to improve as the state of the art advances in any line of goods or services. As a result, quality and timely delivery of state-of-the-art products are inseparable.

Most experts agree that the typical factory invests 20 percent to 25 percent of its operating budget in finding and correcting mistakes and another 5 percent in doing recall work after mistakes have left the factory gates (Port, 1987; Allaire and Rickard, 1989). The experience of particular companies tends to verify the relationship between quality and productivity. For example, the Xerox quality program reduced production costs by 20 percent (Allaire and Richard, 1989). At Harley-Davidson, focusing on quality manufacturing techniques reduced the cost of reworking defects by 60 percent (Port, 1987). General Motors' Lansing assembly plant drove costs down by 21 percent with embedded quality procedures (Hampton and Schiller, 1987).

Thus, quality is often the best antidote for a productivity problem. Because 80 percent of quality problems stem from design rather than production defects (Port, 1987), improved design can mean big productivity gains. For example, more "robust" designs that allow high performance despite production errors have slashed performance defects at ITT by more than half and saved more than $60 million (Port, 1987). In another case, Ford redesigned an instrument console for the 1987 Escort, using only six parts rather than the twenty-two parts used in the original 1984 model. The change reduced material costs by 39 percent, drove down labor costs by 83 percent, and improved the defect rate by 10 percent.

Productivity– Variety– Customization– Timeliness– Quality– Convenience. In the final analysis, the pursuit of any of the new competitive standards ultimately translates into convenience for the customer. Variety and customization beget convenience because they offer choices that meet the specific needs of certain groups or individual customers. The pursuit of timeliness leads to convenience as well. Employers who try to build speed into their goods and services inevitably end up closer to their customers, and these close ties are a fresh source of information on customers' needs and desires. Attention to speed also increases convenience because, for a busy consumer, convenience is largely a matter of time saved. Higher-quality goods and services are convenient because they work better.

Every competitive victory in the new economy results in more convenience for the customer. For example, in the traditional mass production mode, component parts of shirts are manufactured and then brought together for final assembly. If a shirt factory requires a week to fill the average order and ten orders come in the same day, it will be ten weeks before the last order is filled. More advanced companies, however, are organized into small units, each capable of making entire shirts. If there are ten such units in a factory, ten orders can be filled in one week. Indeed, part of each order can be shipped each day. In one company that used this strategy, productivity increased by 5 percent, individual shirts were available to customers in half a day, the share of defective shirts dropped from 2 percent to 0.2 percent, and space requirements for inventory and production were cut in half (Bailey, 1988c). The big winner in this kind of reorganization is the customer, who gets shirts cheaper, faster, and with fewer defects. In another example, the Aid Association for Lutherans replaced specialized functional departments in its insurance services with teams responsible for providing full service to individual regions. As a result, personnel costs were cut by 10 percent, and the overall number of cases handled increased by 10 percent. Overall productivity increased by 20 percent, and the time it took to process a case was reduced by 75 percent (Hoerr, 1988). The association's insurance customers got their insurance cheaper, faster, and in packages customized for their individual needs.

Chapter Three

DYNAMICS OF TECHNICAL CHANGE AND THE NEW ECONOMIC CYCLE

The Role of Technology in Social and Economic Change

Human beings have a long-standing love-hate relationship with technology. Technology improves and extends our lives but at the same time manages to disrupt and even threaten our existence. Some of our discomfort with technology results from the fact that it has never been entirely clear whether people or machines are in the driver's seat.

Because technology plays many roles in the human drama, the alternative portrayals of technology as monstrous villain, hero, and agent of the ruling classes are all convincing. Technology is always there when we round up the usual suspects after some social or economic calamity; but it is just as often the hero that arrives in the nick of time to extricate us from some social or economic impasse. On balance, the optimistic depictions of technology have prevailed in the Western Hemisphere. Armed with the characteristic European and American faith in technical progress, the champions of technical change have persuaded us to rejoice in our technical victories over the natural world and the human condition and to accept our losses grudgingly.

Historically, there have been three dominant perspectives on the role of technology in social and economic change. One dark perspective often espoused in the arts, theology, and philosophy pits humanity against the machine in a constant struggle for dominance and survival. This view portrays technology, the natural world, and the human condition (death) as a triumvirate of forces that must be overcome to allow human ascent to some higher state.

The notion of a titanic struggle between humanity and the machine is a persistent theme in modern intellectual and cultural history. In the early days of industrialization, Ned Ludd and his roving bands asserted dominance over machines by smashing them (Garraty, 1979). Since then, the Luddites among us have tended to characterize the advance of technology as a Faustian pact with the devil: We receive material progress in exchange for a reduction in the quality of our private and working lives.

Those who subscribe to this view write the history of work as a tragedy in which work is dehumanized by mass production technology that constantly encroaches on human skill. As they see it, the mass production system breaks final goods and services into their smallest components and then dissects the talents of whole persons into narrowly elementary skills that are combined with specialized technologies to produce those components. "Tools" that allow the artisan to embody human talent in final goods or services become "machines" that subordinate the worker to the technology. To make matters worse, institutional structures utilize top-down hierarchical authority to recombine the fragmented skills and components into final goods and services. The net effect is the sublimation of the whole person at work, a loss of human autonomy as technology advances, and a shift in the pace of work from the natural and human rhythms of farm and craft to the artificial cadence of the machine (Arendt, 1970; Piore and Sable, 1984).

This titanic struggle with technology is most often and best expressed in the arts. Science fiction provides an excellent listening post for eavesdropping on humanity's hopes and fears for the role of technology in our future. In the classic science fantasy *2001: A Space Odyssey*, for example, a monolith sent by beneficent aliens discovers promise in a prehistoric humanity. The device instructs Moonwatcher, an apelike human, in the uses of violence. The story flashes forward to the modern day, when humans have subdued nature and built powerful technologies. Because of the flammable mix of aggression and technology, the world is on the verge of nuclear annihilation. At this point, human evolution requires mastery of the machine and natural aggression. The alien device reappears, the *deus ex machina*, and lures humanity into space in hot pursuit. During the journey, a confrontation develops between the human protagonist, Dave, and the supercomputer, Hal. Dave pulls the plug on Hal, narrowly winning the right to lead the evolution of earthly intelligence into space. With the assistance of the extraterrestrials who sent the monolith, Dave is reborn and returns to earth, destroying nuclear satellites along the way, on a mission to end human aggression.

A second perspective, common among historians and political theorists, is equally fatalistic but more analytic and optimistic. This perspective ascribes social and economic change to a combination of technical, social, and economic factors. In highbrow versions of this view, the interaction of these complex forces in a "dialectic" guarantees "progress" and a happy ending.

According to this view, the interaction of technology, culture, economy, and polity ultimately forces a convergence of cultures, political systems, and economies around the utilization of higher human capacities (Kerr, 1983). Economics is the engine of cultural and political change, and technology is the fuel. The sometimes nasty side effects of technical and economic development are to be tolerated as the price of progress. In the usual scenario, technology pushes productive capacity and creates wealth; rising wealth and expanding markets in turn push technology forward. The march of technical invention automates repetitive tasks, ultimately leveraging the importance of human knowledge at work while eliminating some jobs and deskilling others along the way (Bell, 1983).

For proponents of this second view, the industrial economy is a way station along the route to something better. The version of the future most widely accepted in the United States is the notion of a coming postindustrial era, a vaguely perceived economy in which human intellectual and social skills will dominate technical capability. Economic possibilities will be constrained only by human ingenuity, not by the limits of materials, muscular power, dexterity, or memory (U.S. Congress, 1988). In the postindustrial era, information-based technologies and other flexible machinery will supplant rigid mass production technology. The relationship between people and technology will have come full circle from human control to technical domination and back to human control again. Like the artisan's tools, the new flexible technologies will conform to the user, extending his or her productive capacity and reasserting human control over technology (Piore and Sabel, 1984). The technical aspects of making objects and performing services will be minor parlor tricks. Machines will take on the more rigorous and mechanical aspects of skill, leaving personnel with more human labors. For most jobs, the primary task will be interacting with colleagues and customers, and the required skills will be those needed to imagine designs, to tailor products and services to consumers' diverse tastes and needs, and to teach, learn from, nurture (physically and psychologically), amuse, and persuade other people.

A third perspective assigns technology a more passive role and tends to view technical change as the consequence, not the cause, of social, political, and economic circumstances. Technology is neutral and malleable, taking on shapes that mirror the culture and polity in which it is embedded, and thereby extends the reach of broad cultural and political forces into the workplace and into our private lives. Proponents of this view put people in the driver's seat. The issue, as they see it, is not the car, but who gets to be the driver.

The notion of submissive technology has found its great-

est currency among the various sects of leftist politics and economics and among some sociological and anthropological
schools of thought that regard reality itself as a social construct
(Berger and Luckmann, 1966). The view from the left is that the
shape of technology conforms to the inherent conflicts between
classes. Principal among these class struggles is the conflict
between managers and workers over control of the means of
production. According to the Marxist interpretation of history,
managers and technical elites installed at the pinnacle of organizational hierarchies assert their control by designing jobs and
technologies that minimize dependence on workers' skills (Braverman, 1974). Workers resist the employers' attempts to de-
grade labor into a homogeneous class of low-skilled machine
tenders. This conflict results in a complex bargaining process,
which in turn produces a hierarchy of jobs in which technical
control and rewards at work are disproportionately distributed
to white-collar and technical elites, while the mass of workers are
relegated to the blue- and pink-collar proletariat. Moreover,
according to the leftist critique, this distinction between people
who use technology and those who are abused by it reinforces
the racial, gender, and other prejudices characteristic of the
larger society.

The Dynamics of Technical Change

The origins of economic and technical change are shrouded in
myth. Once expelled from the Garden, humanity was forced to
use technology to tame nature in order to survive. Myth tells us
that Prometheus stole the makings for fire from the gods. The
ability to make fire may have been the first major technical
breakthrough. The subsequent development of farming and
husbandry eliminated the nomadic life-style for the majority of
humans, but we still had no notion of economic or technical
progress. The animistic religions made no distinction between
the natural and supernatural worlds. In a world where all things
were gods' handiwork, the impetus for developing human tools
was frustrated. Judaism and then Christianity broke through
this impasse by separating this world from the next and encour-

aging humanity to do work in the world as a form of worship and proof of worthiness. The seventeenth-century "enlightenment" separated science from religion as an end in itself. Subsequent improvements in the productivity of farming and population growth created surplus labor, craft production, and the growth of towns, which intensified and accelerated the industrial revolution.

Technological Revolutions

Where do revolutionary changes in technology come from? Since the beginning of human history, curiosity has been a sufficient reason to tinker aimlessly with technology. How else can we explain Leonardo da Vinci's fascination with helicopters, the early interest in subatomic physics, and nineteenth-century experimentation with waterpower, steam, internal combustion, and electricity? In retrospect, a fair share of our experimental fantasies seem silly — the search for a "philosopher's stone" that would turn all base metals into gold, elixirs that promised eternal life, and "phlogiston," the essence of fire. Occasionally, however, aimless tinkering makes an abrupt entrance into human history in the form of startling inventions that almost always inspire horror in some people and rejoicing in others. Technological change sometimes arrives like a bolt out of the blue, accompanied by "gales of creative destruction" that uproot the current technology and clear the way for some new technical marvel (Schumpeter, 1989).

Cold and hot wars have been the context for unveiling some of our nastiest technical surprises. For example, the metal stirrup gave increased support when fighting from horseback and provided the edge that allowed the Mongol hordes to sweep across Europe and Asia only to be defeated by a hurricane — a "kamikaze" or "divine wind" — that sank their invading flotilla off the coast of a defenseless Japan (Fairbank, Reischauer, and Craig, 1978). Gatling's machine gun, the atomic bomb, the patriot missile, and the stealth bomber are all more modern examples of technical surprises used on unsuspecting enemies in warfare.

Sudden availability of a developed technology where it was previously unknown or resisted can create major discontinuities in social or economic arrangements. Francis Lowell provided the engine of American industrialism when he pirated the design for the Arkwright power loom, smuggled it into the United States, and set up the earliest American textile factories in Lowell, Massachusetts, and Saco, Maine (Gibbs, 1950). In New England, the subsequent shift from trapping, logging, and cottage industries to factory work was a wrenching change that brought the social context of work from the outdoors and the family hearth to the artificial environs of town and factory. The Japanese economy and culture made a sharp turn to the West when Admiral Perry, President Fillmore's emissary, arrived on a modern warship bristling with cannon and carrying gifts of modern revolvers and a small working locomotive (Fairbank, Reischauer, and Craig, 1978).

Technical Evolution

People who tend to view technology as a revolutionary force do not ascribe much economic importance to incremental technical change. They are less interested in the process of building a better buggy whip than in the development of the automobile, which made the buggy whip a museum piece. Yet technical shocks are rare. Most technical change comes in relatively small bites in the process of applying technical breakthroughs. Using and commercializing new technologies triggers a series of evolutionary changes and new applications that represent a large share of technical progress. Indeed, major breakthroughs in technical knowledge usually result from the accumulation of incremental innovations in the real world. Science may owe more to the steam engine than the steam engine owes to science.

A close look almost always reveals that the achievements of geniuses like Darwin, Freud, and Einstein are more synthesis combined with timely and convincing presentation than unprecedented thinking (Stromberg, 1975). What appears to be a fresh assault on the established order is often, in fact, an internal collapse of an intellectual house of cards under the weight of real-world contradictions that have accumulated over long periods of time and can be denied no longer. Even at the installation of the new order, anomalies begin to accumulate as the new axioms are applied outside the ivory bastions of pure thought, and the siege begins anew (Kuhn, 1970).

Technical Push and Social Pull

Ultimately, technology is one factor among many in the complex evolutionary process of economic and social change. Technology is sometimes the catalytic agent that transforms elements in the social and economic systems and sometimes a by-product of change that begins elsewhere. For instance, the dramatic growth in agricultural invention resulted both from technical changes and from the complementary growth of urban populations that needed to be fed. The nomadic hunters and gatherers were pushed off the trail by new agricultural techniques that allowed people to settle down close to crops and livestock. Tools, new methods, and machine technology improved agricultural yields and pushed surplus labor into cities, creating an industrial labor pool. At the same time, new agricultural techniques were pulled along by the creation of urban populations that depended on and could purchase farm output.

Some social and economic systems pull technical changes along faster than others. Culture and religion in the Eastern and Southern hemispheres have favored rigid social structures and the preservation of natural balances. The result, until recently, has been a general technical passivity and even resistance to change in general and technical change in particular. By way of contrast, Western cultures have exhibited biases in favor of change and progress. These biases, in combination with capitalist economic systems that provide enormous rewards for technical successes and substantial penalties for falling behind, have been powerful engines for technical progress in the Western world (Rosenberg and Birdsell, 1986).

The intricate connection between societies and technology is evident in the story of the wheel. The wheel appears to have been invented anonymously in Sumeria in the Middle East.

The Sumerians did not invent the wheel overnight. They began in 1500 B.C. by using draft animals to haul sledges on runners. The runners eventually became rollers in the shape of solid tubes, then rollers with the ends thickened to roll straighter, and finally wheels attached to axles. Other civilizations in Europe and Asia did not reinvent the wheel but borrowed the idea from one another, finding the wheel useful to make money and war. With the help of merchants and conquerors, the wheel arrived in what is now Great Britain in about 500 B.C. In contrast, the Incas reinvented the wheel independently but used it only to make toys and cult objects. Apparently, the long developmental process that began with animals hauling sledges never occurred in the Americas. The Incas used people for hauling. Indeed, almost 3,000 people died hauling one particular stone, according to available chronicles (Adams, 1984).

The evolution of the typewriter keyboard presents another interesting case for studying the interaction of culture and technology. In the early development of the keyboard, technical push dominated social pull, but lately social conventions have proven more important than new technical developments. The original typewriter arranged keys in alphabetical order, but the metal type pieces arranged in a circular basket under the carriage were prone to jamming at high typing speeds. Christopher Sholes solved the problem by moving the typing keys that were most frequently used the farthest apart from one another on the keyboard and in the basket of type pieces. The result was the "qwerty" keyboard, named after the top row of letters on the left-hand side of the keyboard. Sholes sold his typewriter to the Remington gun company and the rest is history. The qwerty keyboard still survives despite the fact that subsequent improvements in word processing technology make it unnecessary. The state-of-the-art keyboard is the Dvorak keyboard, developed by August Dvorak at the University of Washington and patented in 1932. This keyboard is designed to provide easiest access to the most used keys. All vowels are in the home row of keys, and the location of keys favors the right hand slightly. Numerous studies demonstrate this keyboard's superiority, but the weight of convention and expended intellectual and financial costs in the qwerty keyboard impede acceptance.

In Asia, culture puts even greater demands on word processing technology. The Chinese language includes thousands of characters. As a result, the typical Hoang keyboard packs a mind-boggling 5,850 characters on a frame that is two feet by seventeen inches. The better Chinese typists can handle eleven words a minute. The Chinese eagerly await voice-activated word processing.

Junctures of Choice

Viewed retrospectively, the process of economic change and the role of technology in that change always seem obvious. Social scientists armed with historical evidence project past events into the present and tend to encourage the view that past and future are joined along an inevitable trajectory. In reality, however, although there is an element of inevitability in economic and technical change, there is also an element of choice — and sometimes there is more choice than at other times. Periodically, new possibilities or an impasse will create a juncture of choice, which becomes the focus of tremendous social and technical energy. Uncertainty arises and increases risk and potential rewards for risk takers; new trails are blazed. Eventually, one pathway becomes the beaten track while others become overgrown or less traveled. Thereafter, the track narrows as the chosen course is reconciled with other aspects of the social and economic landscape.

Currently, we are at a wide place in the path of technical progress, awaiting choices that will narrow the track of economic and social change. During periods such as this, real and imagined changes can be disruptive and painful. If history is any guide, however, we are unlikely to experience any more disruption than we can handle. There appear to be a variety of forces that counterbalance the possibilities for runaway technical change.

Impediments to Technical Progress

Theory into Practice. The interplay between theory and practice is one factor that sets a deliberate pace for technical change. The state of the technical art is almost always ahead of the technical practice because of an inevitable hiatus between the acceptance of new ideas and their embodiment in new technology. In addition, a considerable amount of tinkering usually occurs before patent office clerks and historians pencil in someone's name alongside a working invention. Our heroic view of history encourages us to forget the tinkering. When a workable invention finally arrives, the bouquets go to the people who happen to be upstage for the curtain calls. Their names become part of the cultural lore to be forever chanted like mantras by American schoolchildren. The Wright brothers are "first in flight" everywhere but in Connecticut, where the legislature has decreed that Gustav Whitehead made the first flight at Bridgeport in 1901, a year before the Wright brothers' flight at Kitty Hawk, North Carolina.

The Weight of History. Once invented, new technologies are not immediately adopted. Fear, superstition, vested interest, and instability give the past and present a powerful hold on the future. Examples abound. At the turn of the twentieth century, more than fifty years after the first automobile was introduced in England, Parliament still decreed that speeds not exceed two miles per hour in the city and that each car be preceded by a man on foot carrying a red flag. Cast-iron plows were available in 1937 but were not used widely for more than forty years thereafter because farmers believed iron plows would poison the soil. In the early days of the railroad, stagecoach companies persuaded local authorities to stop locomotives at the edges of New York, Philadelphia, and Baltimore so that each railway car could be pulled to its final destination by a team of no less than four horses (Liebergott, 1984).

Sunk Costs. Both the economic and the intellectual investment in current technology and its accompanying infrastructure can impede technical change (Hayes and Garvin, 1982). For example, the shift from water to steam energy was accomplished rather easily because changing the source of power had relatively little impact on other production factors. The shift was relatively inexpensive and did not require major changes in technologies or work processes, jobs, and skills. Water and steam energy depended on the same system of drive shafts and gears to transmit power to the same factory machines and workers.

In contrast, when an electrical energy supply became available in 1860, existing factories were heavily invested in water or steam and their machine and human complements. Electrical energy had great advantages. Electricity was cheaper to use than water or steam and kept getting cheaper; costs per kilowatt-hour declined by 400 percent between 1880 and 1930. The new energy source was portable, allowing employers to locate close to customers, raw materials, or suppliers instead of near the fast-moving water necessary for water or steam power. The new power source also allowed a more efficient factory layout. The layout in water- or steam-powered factories was driven by the mechanical transmission systems and the need to locate machines in a straight line, with those that required the most energy closest to the power source. In factories using electricity, each machine could be powered by its own electric motor or be wired to a central energy source with no loss of operating power regardless of placement or distance from the energy source. And perhaps most important, the new electrical energy greatly increased the speed and power of machinery: The steam and water mechanical transmission systems lost power with distance from the energy source and could not approach the peak power levels possible with electrical current. With increased speed and power, machines could take on new tasks and be used more productively.

Despite the fact that electrical power had made water and steam obsolete by 1880, the use of steam did not peak until 1910 (Rosenberg and Birdsell, 1986). In 1890, only 4 percent of American employers and 3 percent of American homes used electricity, and in 1910, the corresponding figures were still only 19 percent and 15 percent. By 1920, 50 percent of employers and 35 percent of homes had joined the electrical energy age. But even as late as 1930, only 78 percent of employers and 68 percent of homes were using electricity (Liebergott, 1984).

Sound but shortsighted business practices were a major stumbling block to the expanded use of electrical energy. Cost accounting told the employers of the last century that the cost of a new power system and its accompanying infrastructure was substantially more than the cost of using the obsolete power source. Standard accounting has changed little since the nineteenth century. The balance sheet rarely reflects the long-term cost of not switching to a new technology, the competitive position of the institution in the distant future should the competition adopt the new technology, or the barely measurable potential benefits that will eventually accrue up and down the line from the technical change.

The inability to swallow the cost sunk in a current technology and its accompanying infrastructure is a persistent cause of the loss of the competitive edge to those who are willing to push technical frontiers in mature industries. Established technology and supporting infrastructure are especially vulnerable to the competitors who are least invested in the status quo. For example, American manufacturing lost its competitive position to foreign companies that moved to leverage small technical niches into major market shares. German companies, invested in a labor force strong in the crafts and mechanical arts, ultimately lost share to others whose workforces were better able to adapt to flexible computer-based automation, which relies more on the technician than the mechanically skilled craft worker (Ergas, 1987).

Failures of Imagination. Often an inability or unwillingness to discern the potential benefits of a new technology is due more to a failure of imagination and nerve than to an overreliance on the arithmetic of cost accounting. Most new technologies are used initially to substitute for the technologies they displace. Subsequent changes in the immediate family of compatible technologies and the accompanying infrastructure of the workplace occur incrementally, following the path of least resistance. Thus, in many cases, electricity was used to power the old belts, pulleys, and gear transmission systems that connected water and steam to machines and workers. In a more modern case, flexible manufacturing machinery is sold as a substitute for skilled labor and used with its flexible controls "locked" (Adler, 1988). Similarly, high-powered personal computers are used as typewriters in the office and to store grocery lists at home.

Lack of Complementary Assets. Once the decision to invest in an invention has been made, a compatible family of technologies is usually required to realize the full potential of the invention. The stereo needs compatible speakers. The automated workstation requires further automation upstream and downstream in the work flow so that the increased productivity will be fed and consumed. In most cases, infrastructure even beyond the immediate family of accompanying technologies is required. For instance, before the Model T could be produced successfully for mass consumption, Henry Ford needed a labor force with the skills and organization to produce the car, a pool of consumers with enough money and credit to buy it, and roads for it to ride on.

Technical Capability

Choices as to how to combine people and technology at work are limited by the capabilities of available technologies and the energy sources that power them. Ancient kings could have afforded jet planes but could not have them. Certainly the preindustrial citizenry would have welcomed high-quality goods at low prices, but mass production was impossible without waterpower, steam energy, or electricity and certain advances in the mechanical and eventually electromechanical arts. Who would not want goods and services that meet the standards of the new economy? But these goods and services were not possible until flexible, information-based technologies came along in the last quarter of the twentieth century.

To some extent, the history of economic systems is the

history of technical capability. Each economic era has been limited by the technical state of the art. In the primitive era of hunting and gathering, energy came in the form of raw muscular power. Eventually, levers, wheels, and primitive implements and weapons multiplied muscular power. In the age of agriculture and craft production, animal power and wind and water energy were harnessed to drive mechanical technologies in farming. Production and service technologies came in the form of general-purpose tools that augmented and extended human skill. The characteristic technologies of the preindustrial eras were incapable of producing high volumes at low prices. As a result, neither natural resources extracted from the earth nor manufactured goods were generally available, severely limiting the material wealth available to the average person.

In the industrial era, people harnessed wind, water, and then steam and electricity to drive increasingly powerful and fast machinery that produced ever higher volumes of extracted resources, manufactured goods, and services at consistently declining prices. When industrial technology is introduced, it tends to spread. Once a workstation is mechanized, productivity increases, forcing mechanization upstream and down in order to provide a sufficient volume of feedstock and handle output. The mechanization process ebbs, however, when it confronts jobs and responsibilities that are difficult to reduce into elementary repetitive tasks for mechanization. Goods and services produced in small quantities and service functions both within and outside manufacturing have stymied mechanization, for example. Moreover, within manufacturing and extractive industries, relatively unskilled machine tenders have had to be complemented by more highly skilled craft, white-collar, and technical elites, who make the machines, manage the production process, and provide specialized staff services such as installation and repair.

Both human and machine capital in the mass production system are relatively inflexible and not easily shifted to alternative uses without incurring prohibitive costs for retraining, capital, and reduced productivity due to downtime. This inflexibility eventually became the system's tragic flaw and ultimate technical limitation when, in the early postwar decades, consumers began to demand quality, variety, customization, convenience, and timeliness at mass production prices. New computer-based technologies are now bringing us into the new economy by increasing flexibility so that the standards of the craft economy and of the mass production economy can be met at the same time.

Indeed, the computer is the seminal technology of the new economy because of its intrinsic malleability. Almost every other technology is significant only for doing something better than some previous technology (Blackburn, Coombs, and Green, 1985; Piore and Sabel, 1984; U.S. Congress, 1988; Bailey and Noyelle, 1988). The new communications technology, for instance, substitutes satellites for cable and can transmit information as well as voice. Biotechnology makes what used to be grown. Laser technology cuts finer and faster than previous tools.

The capabilities of the new information technology take us where we have never gone before. Computers extend the penetration of technology into human endeavor, ultimately expanding both the technical and human domains. In manufacturing, computers give us more control over the transformation and movement of material. In addition, they have the potential to break down barriers between technology and service functions. By automating paper shuffling, a major work responsibility for clerical workers and managers, who make up almost a third of the workforce, computers can effect major productivity improvements that until now seemed impervious to technical penetration (U.S. Congress, 1988). The new information technology also breaks the iron link between rigidity and efficiency. Mass production technology has to be scrapped or reconfigured to do a new job, but with flexible software, a good or service can be modified quickly at little additional cost.

The new information technology also increases the value of its attendant human capital by allowing a fuller utilization of human capacities. Mass production machinery has a rigid structure to which workers must conform, but user friendly software adapts to employees' talents and work styles (U.S. Congress,

1988; Bailey and Noyelle, 1988). Information technology can also improve the contributions of an organization and its work groups by linking individuals and work teams within the organization as well as by linking the organization with external suppliers, customers, and clients. Information links can improve the performance and market sensitivity of entire networks, sometimes with unforeseen consequences, as in the case of the stock market crash of October 1987.

Evidence suggesting the centrality of technical flexibility in our progress toward the new economy is abundant. One important piece of evidence is the rapid penetration of information-based technology: Investments in this technology now absorb more than 40 percent of all investments in new plants and equipment compared with 20 percent in 1980 and 6 percent in 1950. In 1987, factory shipments were valued at $48 billion for computers, $18 billion for semiconductors, and $6 billion for copiers. In the same year, commercial software on the market was worth $320 billion, and software developed by employer institutions for their own use was worth $200 billion (Clausing, 1989).

Two-thirds of the recent investment in information technology has gone to improve service functions, raising capital-to-labor ratios in services to the level of the ratios in manufacturing (U.S. Congress, 1988; Vernon, 1987). The microcomputer is a principal investment. One study showed that there were about nineteen employees for every computer in the American workplace in 1985 (Hirschhorn, 1988). Another study revealed that about 12.5 percent of American workers used computers on the job in 1984 (Goldstein and Fraser, 1985).

The pivotal role of technical flexibility in the emerging economy is also evident in attempts to reconfigure technologies that are not computer based in order to make them more flexible (Bailey, 1988c; Piore and Sabel, 1984). Experimentation with technical layout is an example. In the mass production system, technology and people in manufacturing, extractive, and service industries tend to be grouped on the basis of process or function. For example, there are drilling, stamping, and typing pools. Increasingly, however, machines are being grouped in families and used by broadly skilled employee teams capable of turning out final goods and services. This new arrangement is intended to provide better service, facilitate customizing production runs, and provide fast turnaround (Blackburn, Coombs, and Green, 1985).

The Classic Economic Life Cycle

Economic structures are constantly evolving, following a path not dissimilar to an organic life cycle. As a result, the way to use people optimally at work depends on the stage in the life cycle of the particular organization, technology, product line, service, or work process. Traditionally, economic life cycles tended to have five phases: installation, competition, maturity, and eventual breakthrough to a new life cycle.

Innovation

In the innovation phase of the economic life cycle, theory takes its initial leap into practice. The process of making new ideas workable is generally fluid, open-ended, and experimental, and applications tend to show considerable variety. At this stage, economic institutions struggle to exploit new ideas in meeting and shaping market demands. Work processes and organizational formats are generally flexible and characterized by trial and error. The scale of operations is generally small. Job assignments are flexible and overlapping, and skill requirements are general. General-purpose technologies are utilized to allow flexibility and experimentation. Competitive advantage resides with organizations that are entrepreneurial, flexible, and creative.

Installation

In the installation phase, each institution settles on a version of the innovation suited to the institution's culture and market niche. Consequently, a variety of product designs enter the marketplace at varying costs and quality. Machine capital be-

comes more specialized to fit the particular designs. Job responsibilities, work processes, and organizational formats become
more stable, specialized, and standardized. The scale of operations begins to grow as volume increases, price declines, and
market demand accelerates. Skill requirements become more
specific and technical. Organizations with the capacity to install the innovation quickly and efficiently have the competitive
advantage.

Competition

In the competition phase of the economic life cycle, the impact
of the innovation results in a rippling wave of minor innovations
with economic cycles of their own. Individual institutions begin
perfecting their market entries, incorporating incremental innovations in cost-effective production, delivery, and quality. In
addition, new applications for the basic innovation are discovered and new markets spin off. Work processes, technologies,
job designs, and skills are perfected and become more focused
and specialized to match refinements in the original innovation.
The scale of production or service delivery increases. Competitive advantage lies with organizations that can capture incremental improvements in the original innovation most effectively. The capacity for continuous learning is especially critical
down the line where the good is made, the service delivered, and
the customer served.

Maturity

The maturity phase of the economic cycle is characterized by
the emergence of a dominant design and use for the original
innovation (Utterback, 1987). The product begins to take on the
characteristics of a basic commodity, and the experimental quality of the earlier phases begins to wane. The dominant design
allows increasing scale and lower costs for production and delivery. Lower costs expand markets rapidly. In turn, the emergence
of a dominant design and expanding markets substantially reduces the risks of adopting the innovation and accelerates its

dissemination. Competition shifts from innovation to price and marginal differences in quality, variety, convenience, and service. Advertising and sales become more important than research and development or marketing. Job design, skill requirements, work processes, and machine capital become more stable and predictable. Ultimately, the competitive benefits from the innovation are captured. Institutions compete for smaller and smaller increases in demand, and markets stabilize or become saturated.

Breakthrough

In the mature phase of an organization's life, the flow of incremental innovations slows to a trickle. The original innovation is generally available and highly refined. Breaking through to a new cycle of improvements is difficult for a variety of reasons: Mature innovations do not improve rapidly. The central ideas that founded them are usually spent. As a result, the economic returns to further innovation along the same intellectual lines decline. Incremental innovations do not promise substantial increases in markets, yet they tend to require substantial costs because a change in one part of the production and delivery system usually requires other changes elsewhere. Consequently, sunk costs tend to make incremental changes more costly than they are worth in and of themselves in the short term.

In mature markets, breakthroughs are especially difficult for established institutions because of their sunk costs in the status quo (Lehnerd, 1987). Such organizations can make breakthroughs only if they are willing to (1) risk resources on innovation despite low returns in the short term, (2) incur the high costs of replacing expensive human and machine capital, and (3) maintain organizational formats, work processes, and workers capable of generating innovations after markets have matured. In contrast, new institutions do not have to carry sunk costs or the costs of changes to capture incremental innovations and are therefore often the source of breakthroughs.

Forever Young: The New Economic Life Cycle

The structure of economic life cycles and associated skill requirements are not the same in the new economy as they were in the past. Life cycles used to be predictable. They followed a consistent sequence of phases from birth to growth, maturity, and eventually stability and decline (Flynn, 1989; Guile and Brooks, 1987). In addition, the life cycles of technologies, products, work processes, and organizations tended to be simultaneous, interrelated, and roughly consistent. Young organizations, for instance, sold widely varying goods and services in markets where relative shares were still unstable. Technologies and work processes were varied and experimental. Mature organizations tended to utilize highly evolved and standardized technologies and work processes to produce fairly standardized goods and services in stable markets.

The traditional view of the economic cycle is that it is an inexorable ratchet that progressively deskills work, combining ever more specialized human and machine resources with Taylorist work processes and hierarchical organizations to produce cheaper outputs in greater quantity (Braverman, 1974; Flynn, 1989). Economic cycles in the new economy operate differently. They are more open-ended, less sequential, and generally less orderly. For example, today's global institutions leapfrog the initial developmental phases of the classic economic life cycle. They borrow innovations and compete on the basis of ability to exploit them, focusing efforts on the latter phases of the economic cycle, when most of the money is made (Ergas, 1987). In the mature phase, competitors have been able to challenge established institutions with high sunk investments by entering niche markets and adopting incremental improvements in available technologies. Often, established institutions in mature markets are vulnerable because they have overly rationalized their technologies, workforces, and work processes to the point of losing all flexibility and becoming incapable of recognizing or adopting incremental innovations or making major breakthroughs. It is difficult for such institutions to maintain the flexibility necessary to stay abreast of change (Dertouzos, Lester, and Solow, 1989; Lehnerd, 1987).

In the new economy, the need to make improvements continuously and quickly makes flexibility of workers and organizations essential in all phases of the economic cycle and at all levels of the organization. In the classic economic cycle, there is a tendency to require flexibility only from senior, white-collar, and technical personnel and only in the initial, innovative phase. In successive stages, the ratchet of specialization tightens to reduce costs and increase the scale of identical outputs. In the new economy, however, it is becoming clear that a labor force segmented into broadly skilled elites and narrowly skilled nonsupervisory employees and a top-down organization hierarchy can result in costly delays in installing innovations, improving them incrementally, developing new applications for original ideas, and capturing and using learning to encourage breakthroughs.

Economic cycles also seem to be speeding up. As mass markets have expanded, competition has become more global and intense. As a result, cycle times have shortened, and employees at all levels need deep and broad skills and a reserve skill capacity beyond the requirements of their current jobs to handle the new challenges that come with accelerating economic change (Ford, 1989). The lean, narrowly skilled organization is unlikely to have the flexible resources to manage change.

The growing importance of continuous innovation in the new economy is another novel factor that increases skill requirements and demands flatter, more flexible organizations and broadly skilled employees. In the traditional economic cycle, innovation is a heroic process easily tracked by economic statistics and patent applications. White-collar and technical elites generate innovations and then design and install specialized machinery and narrowly skilled jobs to exploit them. In the intensified competition characteristic of the new economy, however, inventing and installing major innovations is only the tip of the iceberg of change. Incremental improvement, a process of continuous learning invisible to conventional indexes of economic change, has assumed a growing competitive importance.

Moreover, the process of continuous learning involves the whole organization, not just white-collar and technical personnel. In the new economy, learning occurs from the bottom up as well as the top down, often in the process of making the good, delivering the service, or interacting with the customer. The competitive emphasis on incremental innovation has turned on its head the traditional heroic view of innovation in the economic cycle. The later phases of the cycle and innovative contributions down the line in the organizational hierarchy have increased in importance (Ergas, 1987; Gomory and Schmitt, 1988).

The traditional model has been altered further as markets and organizations have become more complex. Thus far, many enterprises have responded to the new complexity by subdividing institutions into a variety of establishments with work processes, workforces, technologies, and products focused at different stages of the product cycle (U.S. Congress, 1988). Ultimately, however, if the intensity of competition continues to grow, the traditional cycle will foreshorten until it telescopes into a single phase. The human, machine, and organizational capacities associated with each stage of the traditional economic cycle will be required simultaneously.

Part Two

PEOPLE AND ORGANIZATIONS
IN THE NEW ECONOMY

Chapter Four

NEW STRUCTURES THAT
LINK ORGANIZATIONS,
INDUSTRIES, AND MARKETS

Two traditional organizational formats have survived to form the context for organizations in the new economy: large, centralized mass production monoliths and small, decentralized structures characteristic of services, small business, and craft work. The mass production model for organizing work has survived and become dominant because of its superior ability to generate higher levels of productivity. The trades, crafts, professions, and services have been resistant to this model and survive in uneasy coexistence with mass production organizations.

Mass Production Structures

The dynamic of price competition in mass production has a bias toward standardization, bigness, and conflict. As price competition intensifies, profits from individual units of goods or services decline. Lower unit profits encourage higher volumes. In order to get higher volumes at lower prices, the production or service delivery process is further rationalized and standardized.

The organizational structures of mass production are continuously seeking greater scale. Large scale begets larger scale as volumes of goods or services increase to cover the fixed costs of more and more specialized and inflexible human and machine capital. In addition, the scale of production encourages even higher volumes in each specialized production unit in order to create buffer stocks of good or service components to ensure uninterrupted production or service delivery. Managers must be sure that the whole enterprise will not be lost for want of a nail. Moreover, mass production organizations are always extending their boundaries in order to squeeze costs and exert more control. When Henry Ford needed power for his factories, he built or bought power plants both to obtain electricity more cheaply and to ensure that it would be there when he needed it.

Mass production is biased toward control and competition more than flexibility and cooperation. As an organization grows in scale, the ratchet of specialization makes it more fragmented internally and more dependent on the actions of external parties—suppliers, customers, and governments. Inside the organization, the combination of increasing size and growing fragmentation requires more authority and carefully designed work rules to integrate and balance the production or service delivery process. In its external relationships, the organization attempts to control customers in order to ensure demand and to control suppliers by establishing legal relationships and encouraging competition. Governments are regarded as potential sources of cost and destabilization through regulation and economic policy, so the organization attempts to blunt governmental influence through political action.

Services, Independent Crafts, and the Professions

Mass production techniques do not translate easily to all kinds of work structures. Even within manufacturing, it is impossible to standardize the work of white-collar and technical workers and to rationalize the work of trade and craft workers down the line. Craft work outside manufacturing, especially in the construction trade, has highly fragmented operations. The entrepreneurial small-business sector also seems impervious to increasing scale and productivity, and the professions, such as law and medicine, operate as isolated small businesses with minimal attachment to larger organizations.

The primary reason for the limited extension of mass production technologies and methods in the crafts and professions is that there is a large element of service in each of these kinds of work. Service work has been resistant to the mass production model because it is difficult to fragment service delivery into standardized components. Almost every crafted good, professional interaction, and service interaction is different.

Generally, work in services, crafts, and the professions is less repetitive than work in mass production. Typically, workers are more broadly assigned and skilled. Pay is based more on skill and certification. The work is not standardized, and it is therefore difficult to produce high volumes at low prices by means of mass production technologies. Because the advantages of scale are more difficult to attain, work outside mass production tends to be organized in smaller institutions that produce smaller volumes of goods and services in local markets rather than national or international ones. Moreover, although there have been technical advances in service functions in the form of job aids, service delivery has been resistant to mechanization. The craft worker, professional, or service worker tends to use tools and job aids to deliver a variable good or service; this work is rarely dominated by technology.

Some progress has been made in improving productivity in the crafts, the professions, and service delivery by utilizing mass production organizational formats, careful job designs, and technical job aids. Large-scale organizations, typing pools, typewriters, copiers, and other innovations have allowed the service sector to squeeze some economies of scale.

Organizing the New Economy: The Shift to Networks

Mass production organizations have their virtues: mobilizing capital, conducting research and development, and realizing economies of scale. Even so, these organizations often provide shoddy quality and are too rigid to offer variety, customization, convenience, and timely innovations. The fragmented organization of professional and service work also has its virtues. It focuses on quality, tailoring, and face-to-face customer service. Yet this fragmented structure operates without the benefit of scale; productivity is low, prices are relatively high, capital is unavailable for state-of-the-art improvements, and individual organizations are too isolated to deliver consistent quality.

In the new economy, the top-down industry behemoths and the fragmented service organizations are giving way to new work structures that meld the strengths of prior economic formats and add some new twists. The new economy's work structures are attempting to meet the standards of both mass production and craft, service, and professional work. Flexibility is becoming the driving force. The volume of products may be high or low, and the geographic reach of the organizations in the new economy contracts and expands to serve local, national, and global markets.

As the new economy emerges, work structures are converging on a common institutional format of interdependent networks of people, work teams, and organizations. Mass production institutions are turning to networks to transform their top-down rigidity into more flexible organizational formats; service and craft institutions find themselves using networks to foster greater integration and the benefits of scale.

Network structures grow from within and eventually extend beyond the boundaries of traditional organizational structures. Inside the organization, individuals become members of work teams. Work teams, the smallest networks, are the basic building blocks of larger networks. The whole organization becomes a network of working teams. In turn, the organization is a member of a network made up of other organizations that are its suppliers, customers, regulators, and financial backers. The rubber, steel, plastics, and electronics industries depend on auto sales. The banker depends on the health of the industries in the bank's portfolio.

The interdependence of economic institutions is not

news. The news in the new economy is the growing importance of effective networks. Organizations no longer compete as single institutions but as members of competitive networks. Global competition and the expansion of competitive standards demand stronger organizational linkages, and new communications and information technologies allow organizations to connect easily with one another and with their customers. As a result, organizational relationships in every industry are becoming more interdependent and complex.

The networks that provide final goods and services in the American economy are displayed in Table 6, which shows that most of what we buy requires a mix of natural resources, manufacturing, and services before it becomes a final good or service. Only fifteen cents of a dollar spent on food goes to the farmer, but twenty-six cents goes to manufacturing institutions that prepare and package the food. About thirteen cents of a dollar spent on housing goes to the construction sector. Only thirty cents of our transportation dollar stays in the transportation industry. A little more than half of our health care dollar actually buys health care services. More than twenty-five cents of our education dollar pays for things other than instruction.

There are important differences among economic networks. In general, the more a network produces a pure service, the less complicated the network, whereas the more a network produces a tangible output, the more complex the network. For example, the networks for delivering food, housing, clothing, personal care, and transportation are complex; the networks for health care and recreation are slightly less complex; and the networks for education, personal business and communication services, and government are relatively simple.

The competitive performance of a network depends more on the ability of the partners to work together than on their separate performances. In the clothing business, for instance, the chemical company manufactures and treats the fiber; the textile firm turns it into cloth; the apparel manufacturer turns the cloth into clothing; the wholesaler distributes the clothing to retail outlets; and the retailers sell the clothing to

Table 6. Economic Networks.

Sector	Food	Housing	Transportation	Health	Clothing and Personal Care	Education	Personal Business and Communication	Recreation and Leisure	Government	Federal Defense	Exports	Total
Natural resources	15.0%	9.7%	14.5%	4.3%	4.9%	4.0%	2.6%	6.0%	5.2%	4.4%	16.4%	9.1%
Construction	3.3	12.9	6.1	3.7	2.4	5.2	2.8	3.7	11.0	3.8	3.4	6.2
Low-wage manufacturing	1.5	3.2	2.7	1.5	17.0	1.2	1.1	3.5	1.9	1.4	3.8	3.2
Medium-wage manufacturing	16.8	6.8	7.8	6.6	5.2	4.8	6.7	12.1	6.1	10.9	19.4	9.7
High-wage manufacturing	8.1	5.7	16.1	5.9	7.6	3.3	2.9	7.1	5.0	17.6	19.5	8.7
Transportation, wholesalers, and retailers	39.1	12.8	30.1	10.3	39.1	4.1	6.0	21.7	8.0	8.1	18.8	19.3
Transactional activities	12.7	44.7	12.3	15.6	12.8	7.0	70.9	15.4	12.4	9.0	16.1	23.5
Personal services	1.6	2.3	8.0	1.4	10.0	0.6	3.2	14.4	1.4	1.2	1.5	3.7
Social services	1.8	2.0	2.3	50.8	1.1	69.9	3.7	16.2	49.1	43.4	1.1	16.4
Total	100.0	100.0	100.0	100.0	100.0	100.0	100.0	100.0	100.0	100.0	100.0	100.0
Percentage of Total National Output	15.0	23.0	9.0	10.0	6.0	6.0	6.0	7.0	4.0	6.0	8.0	

Note: The U.S. economy may be viewed as a series of interconnected networks; the product of one sector works in conjunction with the products of other sectors to satisfy the demand of a consumer for a final good or service. For instance, approximately 15 percent, or fifteen cents, of every dollar spent on food went to the farmer, who works in the natural resource sector of the economy. Almost forty cents of every dollar spent on food went to pay for transportation.

Source: Kelly, 1989.

final consumers. If the retailers do not sell to the final consumers, all the other companies lose business.

Improving the performance of the clothing network is not simply a matter of improving productivity among its component parts. Imagine you are a trucker who delivers fiber to the textile firm, cloth to the apparel manufacturer, and clothes to the wholesaler and retailers. You will maximize your productivity and be able to charge lower prices if you always arrive with a full truck. Yet if you move smaller batches of materials and final products, you could speed up the performance of the network, encourage cost savings from just-in-time performance, reduce "stock outs" at the retail stores, shorten planning horizons, increase the variety of fashion seasons, allow for more tailoring, and generally bring the network closer to customers. At the expense of your own productivity, you could improve the overall performance of the network.

Networks are dynamic, not static. Both the extent of interdependence and the mix of partners change with time. Available evidence suggests that America's economic networks are becoming more interdependent as they respond to more demanding competitive standards and are more easily linked by new information and communications technologies.

One way to measure interdependence is by calculating how much of each dollar earned by an organization is paid out to suppliers. A study by the Office of Technology Assessment shows that of each dollar earned by American industries, the average share that went to suppliers increased by 5 percent between 1970 and 1980 (U.S. Congress, 1988). Some industry networks are becoming more interdependent than others. High-wage manufacturing, for instance, spent 15 percent more of earnings on its suppliers in the late 1980s than it did in the early 1970s—a rate of increase three times the national average. A dollar spent on natural resources in 1972 turned over enough times to eventually increase earnings by another $1.30 outside the industry; by the 1980s, a dollar spent on natural resources eventually multiplied into $1.80 in new income outside the industry. Low-wage manufacturing and some service networks became less interdependent during these years, indicating a growing separation between the organizational formats of the old economy and the networks of the new economy (U.S. Congress, 1988).

The recipe for producing final goods and services has also changed in virtually every network since the 1970s. Institutions that operate in complex and highly integrated networks are now involved in an increasing number of transactions and devote more resources to transactional activities. These activities—including accounting, legal work, business services, and consulting—have increased by an average of 5 percent in the economy as a whole. The overall increase in spending for wholesale and retail trade, advertising, and communication also reflects the increasing volume of transactions among institutions and the growing complexity of networks in the global economy (U.S. Congress, 1988).

In the new economy, each industry network is evolving toward a distinctive organizational mix of large and small institutions. No one size fits all, but some typical patterns of change are discernible.

Oligarchs. In some sectors, a relatively few firms with tightly controlled subsidiaries dominate. The domination of the American automobile industry by General Motors, Ford, and Chrysler is a case in point. The domestic giants control an extensive network of suppliers. Traditionally, suppliers and dealers were loosely connected to auto producers and forced to compete for business. The new trend, however, is a loosening of top-down control inside organizations, with the integration of suppliers and dealers into production networks.

Federations. Federations are large enterprises that traditionally do their business through a network of autonomous organizations, branch offices, or franchises. In the interest of capturing economies of scale and developing a greater variety of state-of-the-art goods and services, federations in the new economy are using new information and communications technology to provide stronger integration. Banking and franchising are good examples. Central operations provide economies of scale in product development, financial services, purchases of machine capital and other resources from suppliers, training and staff services, and information systems maintenance.

Families. Another traditional pattern is a network dominated by a large firm that provides an economic umbrella for a large family of suppliers whose goods and services bear the unmistakable stamp of the dominant company. IBM and parts of the Bell system are typical of this model. IBM has set de facto standards in software and peripheral hardware for some time. As the new economy emerges, these kinds of networks appear to be becoming more integrated. The relationship between the umbrella organization and suppliers of peripheral goods and services is becoming more explicit. The participation of IBM and other high-tech industry leaders in Sematech demonstrates that they realize the mutual dependence between small computer chip makers, independent software developers, peripheral manufacturers, and service firms on the one hand and the industry giants on the other.

Loners. Some sectors of the American economy have been dominated by highly isolated institutions that produce the same or similar products in relatively small-scale organizational settings. Up until now, these sectors have operated almost entirely without the benefit of scale or integration. Classroom education, small-scale farming, health care, and home construction are examples. As the new economy emerges, the institutions in these sectors are likely to become larger and to develop more closely integrated networks. For instance, the market share of builders with volumes greater than 100 houses per year grew from less than 7 percent in 1959 to 67 percent in 1986. And health care agencies, facing cost and regulatory pressures, are sorting out institutional roles according to cost advantages. Outpatient clinics handle a greater share of noncritical care than do hospitals, which are concentrating on critical and intensive care. Nursing homes and hospices are focusing on longer-term residential care that does not require critical services.

Entrepreneurs. Another typical institutional category includes autonomous, relatively small firms and self-employed entrepreneurs. The high-tech firms of Silicon Valley and Boston's Route 128 are typical of the former; artists, craft workers, accountants, consultants, lawyers, and doctors are typical of the self-employed. In the new economy, these entrepreneurial institutions are seeking the benefits of integration and scale by forming information networks and trade and professional associations and by joining larger enterprises through purchase or hire. One result has been a steady decline in self-employment. The self-employed formed almost 20 percent of the workforce in 1950 but only 7 percent in 1986 (U.S. Congress, 1988).

Finding a Balance

There is a paradox in the operation of the networks of the new economy. These networks simultaneously encourage both integration and autonomy of individuals, work teams, and organizations. Networks are an attempt to have it both ways: They are formed for competitive purposes but cannot operate effectively without cooperation. By integrating, subunits enjoy the productivity and resources that come with large-scale delivery. At the same time, maintaining autonomy for network members allows for the variety, customization, and quality that come with decentralized, more focused production and service delivery. In the final analysis, the success of networks inside and outside organizations depends on the ability to find a balance among competing organizational virtues.

Balancing Organizational Integration and Autonomy. There is a long-standing tension in organizations between the need to integrate and focus employees' efforts on strategic goals and the competing desire to allow employees sufficient autonomy to make their full contributions to the work effort. If employees' efforts are not focused on strategic goals, organizational efforts will disintegrate into a cacophony of wasted energy. At the same time, employees need discretionary authority to make efficiency

and quality improvements and flexibility to provide good customer service.

Mass production hierarchies and the organizations typical in crafts, the professions, services, and small businesses face
different challenges as they move to balance organizational
integration and employee autonomy. The mass production hierarchies, which are already tightly integrated, need to emphasize
reforms that promote decentralization and employee discretion
down the line. Moreover, as these hierarchies give way to decentralized authority, mass production organizations need to
find cohesion through integrative forces other than top-down
authority and rigid work rules. In contrast, the decentralized
craft, professional, service, and small-business work structures,
which tend toward autonomy, need to emphasize greater integration in order to improve performance.

In large mass production organizations, the attempt to
balance hierarchy and autonomy has led to a common organizational response: a flatter, more decentralized organizational
structure that drives autonomy down the line. The relative autonomy of subunits in the organizational network encourages
flexibility to help meet competitive standards and exploit new
flexible technologies fully. These subunits are integrated by new
communications and information technologies, mutually
agreed upon values and commitments, new leadership and
communication roles for managers, and outcome standards for
work.

Managers in large organizations of the new economy
relinquish control of work processes to work teams and instead
provide organizational integration through leadership and the
monitoring of outcomes. They also act as listening posts, communicating strategic information down the line and new organizational learning up the line. Managers are responsible for
communicating standards and measuring results; when work
teams do not meet outcome standards, managers intervene to
provide assistance and direction as necessary.

In the networks emerging in professional, service, and
craft work, technology is a prime mover in the attempt to
achieve greater cohesion. Flexible information-based technolo-

gies are capable of automating once impenetrable service and craft functions, and artificial intelligence promises even more possibilities for automation. Performance and pricing standards are emerging in diverse professional and service functions from health care to education.

The isolation of crafts, the professions, services, and small businesses is already giving way. Small retail outlets are being integrated into networks by their suppliers. Franchises and chains are taking the place of mom-and-pop operations. Physicians work in health maintenance organizations and other forms of organized practice. Architects, engineers, and management consultants work as employees in business service firms. Increasingly, housing is manufactured indoors in modules rather than built entirely outside by construction crews, one house at a time.

Balancing Scale, Scope, and Focus. The organizations of the new economy require the ability to produce large-scale runs of standardized goods and services for national and global markets as well as smaller volumes for local markets. In addition, organizations must be able to focus on individual goods or services in order to meet state-of-the-art quality and efficiency standards. Organizations also need to expand the scope of their offerings in order to provide variety and customized goods and services to satisfy increasingly diverse demands.

The ability of organizations to balance scale, scope, and focus depends on their flexibility. With flexible technologies, especially information-based technologies, matched to flexible organizations and workers, small volumes of output, variety, and customization add relatively little to price.

One way an organization can achieve scale, scope, and focus simultaneously is to create a network of highly focused subunits. The parent organization can provide capital and infrastructure. Subunits can be dedicated to individual goods or services at different stages of the economic cycle, and they can also focus on different competitive virtues. For instance, in a manufacturing setting, one subunit can focus on meeting production standards (productivity, quality, and state-of-the-art product development), while another subunit can focus on customer-sensitive virtues (variety, customization, and convenience). Unlike a traditionally integrated structure, a network can support both sets of organizational values.

Available evidence tends to indicate that there is indeed a trend toward using this strategy. Parent enterprises are making more products and emphasizing scope, while individual subunits are focusing on fewer products and delivering scale and focus. The number of products made by individual manufacturing firms increased by 15 percent between 1963 and 1982. Over the same period, each of the subsidiaries and establishments owned by these same firms decreased the number of products it made by two-thirds (U.S. Congress, 1988).

Balancing Competition and Cooperation. Ours is an economy based on competitive relationships. Yet in the networks of the new economy, cooperation is at a premium. Individuals, work teams, and organizational partners in networks are relatively autonomous. Each has access to the same information base and flexible technologies. Each is in control of work effort and quality of output. Moreover, in these networks, the focus of control over work is constantly shifting. In the product design phase of manufacturing, for instance, authority is shared by design engineers, manufacturing personnel, and sales and marketing professionals; the focus of leadership shifts with the aspect of the product up for consideration. Similarly, in a production work team, authority shifts as the primary expertise required shifts during the work process. In such an environment, fixed authority systems discourage the necessary flexibility. Moreover, the relative autonomy of network partners makes authority a poor lever for improving performance. As a result, structures and processes for cooperation are emerging within and among organizations. The growth of cooperation within firms is signaled by increasing team-oriented work processes and new labor-management efforts that emphasize joint agreements in response to strategic change. Partnering among organizations, the integration of suppliers, and the search for cooperative linkages between public and private institutions are examples of increased cooperation among institutions.

The need for balancing conflict with cooperation extends beyond the immediate partners in a network to more external partners, including customers, suppliers, financial backers, local and national communities, and governments. Cooperative relations with customers focus the network on their preferences and needs. Cooperative relations with suppliers assure a flow of timely and high-quality inputs in the good or service delivery process. A more hands-on relationship between institutions and their financial backers can encourage more sustained and informed capital commitments. Involvement with the community can foster understanding and support. Community and political institutions that understand a network's strategic agenda can provide useful information and sensible regulatory procedures. Most important, the community and its political representatives can supply complementary assets to assist the network in realizing its developmental goals. Public infrastructure—from roads and bridges to energy, research and development, and a ready workforce—is critical to economic networks.

Institutional Learning

The importance of organizational learning is obvious. Since 1929, when national productivity data were first available, the ability of organizational structures to learn to make better use of the available human and machine capital has accounted for more than half of productivity improvements (Denison, 1974). These so-called process improvements in productivity are what enable organizations to move up the learning curve—to make more with the same or fewer human and machine resources.

Learning has always been important, but it is even more important in the new economy. It is the common currency of growth and decline in economic institutions. The ability of organizational structures to capture and apply knowledge has become a decisive factor in meeting the expanded set of competitive standards and the key that unlocks the flexible potential of new technologies and organizational networks.

The new standards for competition increase the importance of learning. The constantly changing variety of goods and services and the need to customize them accelerate the pace of change, and organizations need to learn in order to adapt. The race to market innovations requires organizations to learn even faster. The subsequent race to make incremental productivity and quality improvements and to develop new applications after major breakthroughs also increases the value of an organization's ability to learn while making the good, delivering the service, and interacting with the customer. New information and communications technologies accelerate the pace of change and add to learning requirements by increasing the volume and flow of information.

There are important differences between the old and new economies in the way organizations accumulate and use knowledge. In the old organizations, the emphasis was on learning from the outside in. Major research breakthroughs in theoretical knowledge came from universities and government think tanks. Economic organizations focused on developing basic research into goods and services. In the new economy, there is a greater emphasis on learning from the inside out. External research is balanced with more internal development.

In the old economy, organizations focused on exploiting major breakthroughs. Today's organizations must rely more on incremental learning processes. Our competitors have demonstrated all too well that although prize-winning discoveries are proud achievements, it is continuous incremental learning that results in the workaday improvements that are responsible for most of the commercial success.

In the old economy, learning cascaded from the top down; major innovations were developed from outside the organization and rationalized into rigid production or service delivery processes by white-collar and technical personnel. There were few systematic attempts to organize in ways that would encourage or capture new learning at the bottom of the organizational hierarchy or at the interface with the customer. In the new economy, learning is pervasive in the organizational structure. Institutions balance learning from the top down with

Table 7. Characteristics of Typical Production and Service Delivery Systems.

Characteristics	Typical Systems				The New Economy
	Preindustrial Crafts	Mass Production	Services	Small Business, Craft and Profession	
Competitive Standards	Peer standards for state-of-the-art quality	Productivity: the ability to make more with the same or fewer resources in order to sell cheaper	Productivity, convenience, customization	Peer standards for state-of-the-art quality	Quality, variety, customization, convenience, and timeliness at mass production productivity and prices
Scale of Output	Similar products made one at a time	Maximum volume of standardized goods	Volume and scale limited by the inability to standardize services		Flexible volumes of varied outputs at high rates of productivity
Context for Work	Guild, town, family	Large-scale organizational hierarchies	Organizational hierarchies of varying size	Fragmented craft and professional communities	Interdependent networks of work teams and organizations
Human/Technical Combinations	Tools used to express and extend skill	Narrow-purpose machines matched to narrowly skilled workers	Tools and job aids to leverage performance	Tools, machines, and job aids matched to broadly assigned employees	Flexible information-based technologies matched with adaptable work teams

Source of Control and Integration of Work	Recognized expert status	Hierarchical authority, work rules, and careful differentiation of job assignments		Local business standards, licensing requirements, craft standards and professional prerogatives	Consensus on goals and performance standards
Geographic Reach	Local	National	Local/National	Local	Local/National/Global
Driving Forces in the Workplace	Changing craft standards	The rationalization of work and technical change		State-of-the-art changes	Increasing flexibility of organizations, technologies, and employees
Driving Forces in the External Environment	Urbanization, technical knowledge	Urbanization, technical knowledge, energy (water, steam, electricity), infrastructure (roads, communications, skilled workforce), financial capital		Wealth, the commercialization of home and community functions, the growing complexity of economic activity and community life, technical knowledge	Global wealth, global competition, flexible technologies, the value of time, the diversification of tastes, commercialization of private services

Note: The scale of output varies greatly in different kinds of economic structures. In the preindustrial craft economy, products were similar but made one at a time. In mass production systems, products were made in the highest possible volumes of standardized goods in order to realize scale economies. In services, volume and therefore scale economies were limited because service was difficult to standardize. In the independent crafts, workers like electricians and independent professionals, such as doctors and lawyers, produced relatively unstandardized work in low volumes. In the new economy, volumes are flexible and products are varied and customized at prices generally associated with high volumes of standardized goods.

learning from the bottom up. The responsibility for innovations extends beyond the ivory tower to the workaday world, and beyond white-collar and technical elites to the whole workforce. Learning occurs continuously in all phases of the economic cycle.

Learning has important implications for the structure of organizations and networks. Top-down mass production organizations, for instance, discourage learning from the bottom up. The isolated work structures characteristic of the professions, services, and small businesses also discourage access to knowledge. In contrast, effective internal networks capture new learning and allow it to flow across functional lines to pressure points in the work process. In external networks, suppliers can provide the push and customers can provide the pull necessary to keep learning moving through the chain of institutions. Equipment suppliers have long been a principal source of innovation in manufacturing, for example. Lately, the suppliers of computer-based and communication equipment have begun to play the same role in service industries. Customers, too, provide new knowledge. For instance, the Massachusetts Institute of Technology's (MIT) Commission on Industrial Productivity reports that 75 percent of advances in scientific instruments come from users and that computer chip manufacturers account for two-thirds of the advances in the machinery used to make computer chips (Dertouzos, Lester, and Solow, 1989). Table 7 summarizes these and many other characteristics of typical production systems in the new economy.

Chapter Five

COMPETITIVE PROSPECTS
IN CRITICAL INDUSTRIES

American organizations are changing in response to the demands of the new economy, but progress is slow because of a variety of institutional barriers. Old habits that were once successful are the hardest to break, and American organizations have been the most successful of the modern economic era. American organizations have also found it difficult to trade competition and adversarial relationships for more cooperative habits. Some of the reasons for this are historical and profound. Our society is based on individualism and an explicit rejection of feudal traditions. In contrast, the Europeans and Japanese have a stronger attachment to traditions that emphasize clearly delineated social roles and conventions that provide a strong context for cooperation. In addition, cooperation is all the more difficult when the workforce is multicultural and the economy spans great distances.

The long history of labor-management conflict in the United States has also proven difficult to overcome. Nor have relationships between government and industry moved much beyond arguments over the macromanagement of the economy and the deadly hand of regulation. The Keynesian truce hammered out in the post-Depression era leaves the government with macroeconomic responsibility and private management with total control over microeconomic decisions, including the allocation of human and capital resources at work and the development of organizational structures. The government intervenes from the outside in, but only to encourage capital investments and to promote workers' health and safety and equal protection (Carnevale, 1985).

Internal and external networks in America are in their infancy. The interested observer need not travel far to find organizations where workers and suppliers are still viewed as costs to be reduced rather than assets to be developed. Indeed, much of the overall competitive improvement in many American organizations over the past several years has come from the old-time religion — downsizing and dollar devaluation — rather than from more profound changes in organizational structures and attitudes. American networks are weakest in using assets outside the private economy to complement the competitive efforts of private networks. The nation's research and development (R&D), educational, and governmental infrastructures remain aloof from the competitive fray and are underutilized for private production and service delivery. Further, there is little internal pressure for our educational institutions or governments to change because they are not market driven. Yet there are many examples of homegrown and transplanted foreign institutions that have overcome these barriers. A closer look at how specific industries are coping with new organizational demands reveals at least some of the diversity of response.

The Automotive Industry

The American automobile industry is the largest U.S. manufacturing network. The largest car company, General Motors (GM), employs more than a million people. The auto industry is more than twice as large as any other American manufacturing enterprise and accounts for a fifth of U.S. steel consumption, more than 15 percent of the nation's aluminum consumption, and more than half of the American market for synthetic rubber (Womack, 1989). The industry once dominated world production but has slipped in recent years to third place. The Europeans and Japanese both build more cars than we do now, and the Europeans also buy more cars than we do (Dertouzos, Lester, and Solow, 1989). The last major innovation of American origin was power steering, introduced in the 1940s. Traditionally, the Japanese squeeze us at the low end of the market, while the Europeans squeeze us in the luxury car market. With the Acura, the Japanese have begun their assault on the middle and high-end markets. During the 1990s, an increase in Japanese transplant manufacturing institutions in North America and losses in market share could push one of the "big three" American companies—GM, Ford, or Chrysler—out of business or into foreign hands.

Turnarounds do not come easily in the auto industry because it is large and so is its turning radius. American car companies face enormous historical obstacles to building organizations for the new economy. Mass production matured at Ford and was perfected at GM. The auto and steel industries were the focus of the nation's difficult labor history.

On the other hand, American cars are generally of higher quality than European cars and are within reach of Japanese quality. In 1989, J. D. Power, an independent firm that measures consumer opinion, found that since the early 1980s, consumers have preferred American to European cars, although American cars are still regarded as inferior to Japanese cars (*The Power Report*, 1989). Data on built-in manufacturing quality show a similar pattern. The defect rate per 100 cars is 52 in Japan, 56 in Japanese transplants in the United States, 90 in conventional U.S. plants, and at a high of 173 in some European plants (Dertouzos, Lester, and Solow, 1989).

American car companies are also faster at assembly than their European counterparts and close to the Japanese. To assemble a car, it takes nineteen hours in Japan, twenty hours in a Japanese transplant in the United States, twenty-seven hours in a

traditional American assembly plant, and thirty-six hours in a
traditional European plant (Dertouzos, Lester, and Solow, 1989).
In addition, the American auto industry is one of the industries
that have led the nation's productivity turnaround since the
early 1970s. Its productivity improvements have led U.S. manufacturing; they are superior to European and comparable to
Japanese productivity improvements — even if many of them
have come from downsizing. In the United States, the auto
industry has led the way in team-based production systems, joint
labor-management training, and strategic decision making.

European and Japanese auto industry networks are
stronger than our own. The European craft tradition unites
education, industry, and labor to develop a highly skilled and
flexible workforce. The fundamental strength of Japanese auto
networks begins with work teams on the factory floor and
radiates outward to supplier groups and conglomerate groups
of principal partners and financial backers. Japanese manufacturers have stronger relationships with suppliers than do American manufacturers. GM, for instance, makes 70 percent of its car
components itself but still uses 6,000 buyers to procure components outside the organization and has 1,500 suppliers per
plant. Toyota builds only 20 percent of its own components but
has only 177 suppliers per plant.

The importance of functioning networks outside the organization is demonstrated by comparing the experience of
Mazda and Chrysler in their separate crises during the 1970s.
Mazda stumbled when it attempted to sell the gas-guzzling
rotary engine. Mazda's conglomerate partners decided the
institution was badly led and stepped in with a financial
package that mobilized the company and its supplier group in
the development of a new line of high-performance engines.
In contrast, financial interests and network partners stood by
and watched Chrysler go under. After the fall, the affected
interests did mobilize, but only to collect from the government a
financial package that honored debts and business commitments. Chrysler survived with uncertain prospects and insufficient resources to break through to a new product line that

clearly distinguished its niche among the major car companies (Womack, 1989).

The American auto industry faces daunting prospects in the 1990s. Product and process improvements, downsizing, and a devalued dollar brought on an auto recovery in the latter half of the 1980s (U.S. Department of Commerce, 1989c). After a strong year in 1988, however, markets declined in 1989. More Japanese transplants are arriving as dollar devaluation makes U.S. production more attractive, and world auto production is headed toward a glut. As conditions worsen, American companies will be tempted to reduce costs and boost productivity. Downsizing, a squeeze on suppliers, and trade barriers offer gains in short-term productivity and are far easier to effect than profound changes that offer long-term benefits, that is, changes in organizational formats or cultures. Quick fixes will buy time, but unless that time is used to work through more profound organizational changes, more trouble lies ahead for the American auto industry and its vast network of suppliers and financial partners.

The Food Industry

The network that produces and delivers food to American tables accounts for 15 percent of consumer spending. Food networks promise to become more productive and responsive to demands for quality, variety, customization, and convenience as a result of technical changes on and off the farm. The bar code scanners at checkout counters are the most obvious evidence of the invasion of information technology that will likely integrate food networks from the grocery store all the way back to the farm.

As integration occurs, the scale of organizations in food networks is likely to increase. The number of farms has decreased from a pre-World War II peak of 6.5 million to a little more than 2 million today. Five percent of the nation's farms contribute more than half the nation's farm output (U.S. Congress, 1988). By the year 2000, farms with more than $250,000 in cash receipts per annum will likely account for as much as 90 percent of production (U.S. Congress, 1988). Then, too, food manufacturing has become more concentrated. The number of food manufacturers has declined at a steady rate of 2.5 percent a year since 1947. Recent growth has been fueled by mergers and acquisitions. In 1985 alone, companies spent $14 billion on acquisitions in food manufacturing. R. J. Reynolds bought Nabisco, Philip Morris bought General Foods, Nestles bought Carnation, and Beatrice bought Esmark.

Retail and wholesale outlets are also likely to continue to grow in scale and in the scope of their offerings. The number of wholesalers decreased by half between 1950 and 1980 (U.S. Congress, 1988). The number of small independent specialty stores, such as bakeries, continues to decline, whereas the number of convenience stores that offer a broader array of products with an average sale of $1 to $3 has tripled since the sixties. Although supermarkets still account for more than half of sales, the new "superstores" are challenging supermarkets' dominance. Superstores currently account for only 3 percent of all grocery stores yet garner 28 percent of current grocery sales. Moreover, superstores offer an increasing array of food and nonfood goods and services and are likely to capture an even greater share of the market as they continue to expand into computerized shopping and home delivery.

Already, the mechanization of farming and the use of chemical technologies have increased farm productivity to the point where only 15 percent of every dollar spent on food goes to the farmer (U.S. Congress, 1988). As farm productivity increases because of biotechnology, better integration, and increasing scale, a growing share of value added in food networks will go to providing quality, variety, customization, convenience, and timely delivery to the consumer after food leaves the farm. Currently, losses in fruits and vegetables in transit and storage are estimated to run 30 percent, and packaging accounts for at least a third of the cost of processed foods and even exceeds the cost of food products in beer, cereal, soup, baby food, and pet food (U.S. Congress, 1988). New packaging and preservation technologies therefore promise enormous savings.

These same technologies also promise improvements in variety and convenience. Foods will be more available long after harvest, over great distances, and in a variety of sizes and stages of preparation.

The availability of new information and packaging technologies will allow small producers a role in the food business if they have the technical capability to access networks. The demand for specialty items from domestic and foreign producers has already expanded substantially, and small producers who can find a specialty niche in a larger network will survive and prosper. At the same time, the advance of packaging, preservation, information, communications, and transport technologies opens markets to more competition at home and abroad. Items such as Israeli fruit, German beer, and Swiss chocolate are already traded internationally. As packaging and preservation technologies improve and distribution networks become more sophisticated, we can expect to see more trade in staples.

There is some indication that the quantity and quality of institutional learning in American food processing and manufacturing institutions are not up to the emerging technical and organizational challenges. The middle links in the production chain—those between the farms and the retailers—may be the weakest. Although the learning network that includes the American government, educational system, and farm economy is the envy of the world and is responsible for much of the domestic and worldwide gain in farm productivity, America's food industry, outside of farming, seems to pay less attention to learning than do most industries. The Office of Technology Assessment points out that the food manufacturing industry spends only about 0.4 percent of sales on R&D, an expenditure rate far below the average 3 percent for all manufacturing. The large food manufacturers registered only 10 percent of all patents in the industry between 1969 and 1977. The remaining 90 percent of patents were registered to universities, government, and foreigners (U.S. Congress, 1988).

The Chemical Industry

The production chain in the chemical industry involves the complex process of changing basic elements into economically useful substances. The catalytic agent in the industry has always been learning (Bozdogan, 1989). The modern chemical industry relies on a mix of university-based basic research and large internal programs to develop applications. The industry is very research intensive. Chemical companies spend almost 5 percent of sales on research, and pharmaceutical firms in the industry spend more than 8 percent of sales on R&D (Dertouzos, Lester, and Solow, 1989).

The great chemical and pharmaceutical companies in Europe and the United States were founded on individual laboratory breakthroughs, and the history of the industry and its products is defined by seminal breakthroughs in the laboratory. In 1857, William Perkins developed usable synthetic dyes made from coal tar. In 1867, Alfred Nobel turned unstable nitroglycerin into stable dynamite. In the twentieth century, the industry switched to oil and gas as the basic feedstock for new products. The development of plastics and other substitutes for natural materials launched the chemical boom of the postwar era. Ultimately, the explosion in industrial capacity worldwide resulted in a glut of basic commodities, and the industry began to compete more on price than innovation. The rising cost of oil and gas in the early 1970s reinforced price competition. Product and process innovation fell off as price competition squeezed available resources. In the United States, government licensing, antitrust enforcement, and environmental regulations slowed innovation and reduced R&D still further.

In the late 1970s, the American chemical industry began its successful turnaround by deemphasizing commodity chemicals and diversifying into higher-value-added specialty chemicals, biotechnology, and technical instruments. As a result, products are now more varied, customized, and market sensitive. In both the remaining commodity businesses and the more customized markets, the emphasis is on quality more than on volume. Moreover, the new specialty product lines are even more driven than before by learning and the timely development of new products. Closer customer linkages are required to develop specialty items; the customer is an active participant in the learning network.

The continuation of this successful transformation will depend on the industry's ability to strengthen its internal organizational structures and external networks. It needs flexibility to meet the new requirements of specialty markets and to offer competitive quality and convenience if it is to be successful in oversupplied commodities markets. In addition, the industry requires an exponential increase in R&D resources to provide first-rate quality in more diversified and tailored markets. The industry will need to extend its networks further into universities and the government in order to encourage more R&D and participate more effectively in regulatory, antitrust, and licensing procedures.

The Commercial Aircraft Industry

The U.S. commercial aircraft industry continues to thrive, although a glut has developed in small planes and helicopters (U.S. Department of Commerce, 1989c). The dominance of American producers in this industry resulted from symbiotic relationships between the federal government's military and aerospace infrastructure and the airlines. The demand for military aircraft and aerospace equipment provided revenue, and the military was a principal source of flight and repair personnel. Also, government funding of basic R&D was particularly important because of its enormous cost. It takes $2 to $4 billion to launch a new aircraft and $1 billion to develop new engines. Mistakes are disastrous in the commercial aircraft industry. Boeing, Pratt and Whitney, and Pan American were almost sunk by their investment in the design, development, and production of the 747 until the airplane began to make money. Lockheed's losses on the L-1011 eventually caused the company to drop its production of commercial aircraft. McDonnell Douglas was almost ruined by the DC-10 and DC-8 (March, 1989).

The major threat to American commercial aircraft comes from Airbus, a government-owned aircraft company jointly sponsored by Britain, France, and Germany. As the strength of Airbus grows, the American commercial aircraft network falls into disrepair. Deregulation has shifted the focus of U.S. airlines from technical superiority to price competition. Military and aerospace technologies are no longer transferable in the development of commercial aircraft. Boeing, the major civilian aircraft producer, no longer does any substantial business with the government (Dertouzos, Lester, and Solow, 1989). American commercial aircraft companies are now on their own, while their major competitor reaps the advantages of governmental support in technical development and price subsidies.

The Consumer Electronics Industry

The United States dominated the consumer electronics industry from 1877, when Thomas Edison invented the phonograph, to the early 1960s. During the television boom of the 1950s, the United States had almost total control over domestic and foreign markets in consumer electronics; less than twenty years later, we were in a complete withdrawal. Virtually all the producers of consumer electronics in the United States, including RCA, the single largest producer, are now foreign owned. Zenith, a large producer of television sets, remains the last standing homegrown company in the industry (U.S. Department of Commerce, 1989c).

The collapse of the American consumer electronics industry was caused by its failure to shift from the competitive habits of mass production to the competitive standards and organizational formats of the new economy. American producers sought quick returns from major innovations. As a result, the industry focused on breakthroughs and paid little attention to incremental improvements and new applications. Production systems were driven by cost. Foreign competitors were allowed to capture market niches and to surpass us in production quality, efficiency, and new applications development. As markets matured and price competition squeezed profits from original innovations, American companies got out of the business—first for components, then for individual products, and eventually altogether.

The American abdication of consumer electronics also resulted from a failure to develop strong networks for institutional learning. The unwillingness of American companies to invest in continuous improvements after major breakthroughs was paralleled by our universities' and government's general disinterest in consumer applications for electronics. Our Japanese competitors, in contrast, had developed a cadre of technical professionals interested in applications. MITI targeted consumer electronics early in the postwar era, and Japanese institutions leveraged themselves up the learning curve by extending their networks to include consumers, unlike American companies (Dertouzos, Lester, and Solow, 1989).

The videocassette recorder (VCR) provides a case in point. Equipment for commercial video recording was first produced by Ampex, an American firm, in 1956. The machinery was large and clumsy and intended for commercial and professional uses. The market was relatively small, and development costs to build a mass market product were judged to be prohibitively high. American companies were not interested. The Japanese learned their way into the business, however, by making components and eventually video recorders at relatively low profit margins. The Japanese finally built a cheap and usable VCR, and the market exploded after 1982 (U.S. Department of Commerce, 1989c). American firms unable to manufacture a competitive VCR for mass consumption attempted to hijack the new market in the early 1980s with a breakthrough technology—the videodisc and videodisc player. Videodisc equipment was cheaper to manufacture and simpler, but RCA, its principal backer, could not get it to the market in time. The Japanese improved the VCR so that by the time the videodisc was ready for market, the VCR was cheaper and superior, especially because the videodisc could not record but the VCR could (Dertouzos, Lester, and Solow, 1989). Since then, the Japanese have moved into the market with a complementary camera, the camcorder, and sales of the two products continue to grow.

In the 1990s, the new battleground in consumer electronics will be high-definition television (HDTV). New HDTV technology promises to revolutionize the industry, spawning a whole new array of products. American companies say they will fight for control over the pivotal technology. The challenge is not only to make the breakthrough and win the technical battles but also to develop the generations of commercial products necessary to win the economic war.

The Chip Industry

Chips no bigger than the tip of your little finger are the basic building blocks of information technology. They store, process, and control information in goods ranging from computers to video games. Memory storage chips are information technology's muscle; processors and controllers are the brain. The circuitry on each chip may include as many as 70,000 transistors. As Motorola points out in its ad for one of its chips, in the not too distant past, this much circuitry would have taken up as much space as a large refrigerator and required the refrigerator's cooling capacity.

The $50 billion American chip industry is an odd mixture of reluctant giants and eager smaller firms. The two largest producers, IBM and AT&T, produce chips only for their own uses. The commercial chip makers include Motorola, Texas Instruments, Intel, Fairchild, AMD/MMI, and a third tier of short-lived companies that tend to arise in order to take commercial advantage of a specific technical change and then disappear when the state of the art moves beyond them. A similar fragmentation is characteristic of the companies that make the equipment that makes and tests chips. A few stalwarts, including Teledyne and Perkin-Elmer, are in competition with a constantly changing set of quick start-up companies that tend to come and go with technical and market changes. Moreover, relationships throughout the American network, especially between manufacturers and suppliers, have emphasized cost-based competition over cooperation.

The U.S. share of world chip production has fallen from a peak of 60 percent to 40 percent at present; in comparison, the Japanese have a 47 percent market share. The American industry suffers a trade deficit of roughly $1.5 billion. The decline of our position has resulted from an inability to compete in the new economy. Indeed, up until the late 1970s, American productivity was exemplary. The industry managed a productivity rate of 10 percent per year between 1967 and 1979 and more than 4 percent per year thereafter (Clausing, 1989). By 1979, however, American quality was an issue with buyers. American mass production institutions emphasized the commercial exploitation of breakthroughs and paid less attention to incremental improvements derived in the production and utilization of chips.

Moreover, the highly decentralized structure of commercial production in the United States and the relatively small size of commercial producers diminished the benefits of scale and integration, a big disadvantage because in this industry, downturns are frequent and technical changes are rapid and profound. The smaller American producers had less to spend on R&D than their larger competitors overseas and were hit harder during downturns. Companies have not coalesced for development purposes until recently. Furthermore, government R&D focuses on defense and aerospace needs in chip design and manufacture. Although there are important spin-offs from government R&D, civilian needs are quite different. The government seeks peak performance and durability. Volumes are low and cost is no object. Commercial producers need to offer variety, customization, and timely delivery at relatively low prices.

The Japanese chip industry, in contrast, has both advantages of scale and effectively integrated networks. The Japanese industry developed as a complementary offshoot of firms involved with large computers, consumer electronics, telecommunications, and electronic equipment (for example, Sony, Hitachi, and NEC). The size of Japanese firms allows greater resources for R&D and sustained development and capital investment despite the roller coaster of market cycles typical of the fast-paced semiconductor market. The MIT Commission on Industrial Productivity reports that between 1975 and 1982, the American share of patents in the semiconductor industry fell from 43 percent to 27 percent, while the Japanese share rose from 18 percent to 48 percent. By the early 1980s, the Japanese semiconductor industry was spending 28 percent of revenues on capital, whereas its American counterpart was spending 20 percent. Japanese chip manufacturers spend 12 percent of revenues on R&D compared with 9 percent spent by their U.S. counterparts (Clausing, 1989).

The Japanese networks are also stronger externally. Large manufacturers own or have substantial financial interest in their principal suppliers (Clausing, 1989). MITI, the governmental partner in these networks, has played an integral role and focuses its efforts on civilian, not military or aerospace, applications. Japanese financial institutions, now the world's richest, hold substantial equity positions in several of the major semiconductor companies. The strength of the Japanese networks provides staying power over the market cycle, financial strength to drive capital and R&D investments, and a level of interaction that encourages continuous incremental learning, which is critical to meeting the new economy's competitive standards.

Because of the centrality of information technology, the chip industry is leading the way into the new economy. After two good years, there was a slowdown in demand in 1990. Although the downturn was not as severe as it was in 1985 and 1986, it strained available resources for renewed market expansion in 1991. Thereafter, the demand for chips with memory, processor, and control capabilities tailored to the uses of individual customers will accelerate (U.S. Department of Commerce, 1990). The need for stronger customer contact will increase. Product life cycles will shorten. By the mid to late 1990s, superconductivity devices will be important because of increased efficiency in the use of power and higher speeds. At the moment, the Japanese seem better positioned to make the technical transition. In 1988, they outspent American chip makers on research by $1.7 billion, and they are likely to expand their research and capital investment margin. The American hope is that Sematech, an industry consortium focused on military needs, will provide the necessary technical breakthroughs and develop American networks in the industry.

The Computer Industry

Computers are the pivotal hardware in the new information technology, and the United States continues to dominate this $160 billion industry. Indeed, this is one of only a few manufacturing industries in which the United States still enjoys strong, although declining, trade surpluses. (Our trade surplus in computers has been more than halved since the early 1980s.) America owes its strong position in computers to an early lead in developing state-of-the-art products. As in the case of the commercial aircraft industry, which also has a significant trade surplus, this lead was due to a strong partnership between industry and government, which was pursuing defense and aerospace objectives. The early American mainframes dominated world markets, and the enormous investment in compatible hardware and software has made consumers reluctant to shift to new computers that would require whole new generations of complementary software, hardware, and human capital. The early success of the industry also stemmed from its institutional strength. The industry enjoys the combined benefits of scale and strong networks. It is dominated by large, well-financed firms and is organized into networks of suppliers and customers clustered around these firms.

The immediate future of the American computer industry looks promising, although the pivotal position of computers and other information technologies in the new economy will draw increased competition from abroad. The United States lost some ground in the shift from mainframes to more distributed networks of personal computers (PCs), yet Apple and IBM more than held their own in the PC market boom of the 1980s. During the 1990s, the market for distributed data processing will grow apace with the development of organizational networks. Demand will increase for expert systems customized for individual networks. Thus, products will become more varied and customized, and sales will shift away from hardware to software and network services (U.S. Department of Commerce, 1989c; Verity, 1990). These changes, as well as the need to develop new applications of existing technology, will challenge the industry.

Longer-term prospects for the American computer industry are more tenuous. Artificial intelligence and supercomputers more than a hundred times as powerful as anything on the market today may be ready for the market by the mid 1990s. If the history of the industry is a guide to the future, then the ability to make, develop, and disseminate breakthroughs first will be critical. The American consortium at Sematech and a similar Japanese consortium are hard at work developing and designing the new technologies.

The Machine Tool Industry

Machine tools are the mechanisms, such as drills, lathes, punching machines, and stamping machines, that cut, shape, and form material to manufacture final products. The makers of machine tools constitute a small but critical industry. Although there are no more than 500 companies in the business, they are essential in the manufacturing network because they are the principal purveyors of technical change.

American manufacturers do not make their own machinery, they buy it. And increasingly, they buy it from foreign companies. In the 1960s, the United States was a net exporter of machine tools. By the end of the 1980s, most machine tools were imported from Europe, especially Germany, and Japan. The American industry owes its failure directly to its fragmented structure and the relatively small scale of individual producers. These factors left the industry unprepared to adapt to the demand for flexible information-based machinery. In contrast, MITI was pivotal in building an effective network of relatively small scale Japanese producers; strong partnerships between government and industry in combination with a robust tradition in the craft occupations allowed Germany to overtake the American industry (March, 1989; U.S. Department of Commerce, 1989c).

After a difficult decade, the American machine tool industry is revitalizing. Growth in the trade deficit has slowed and domestic business has improved as a result of a devalued dollar and industry protections provided by the Reagan administration in the late 1980s. As in the case of aircraft and computers, the government drives the machine tool network toward defense and aerospace applications, so the continued revitalization of the industry will depend on its ability to develop civilian applications.

The Wholesale and Retail Industry

Wholesale and retail institutions operate at the interface of American economic networks and their customers. The United States has almost half a million wholesalers, who employ more than 6 million workers and reported gross profits of $349.2 billion in 1988. Retailers post annual sales of more than $1 trillion and employ almost 20 million Americans.

Wholesalers and retailers face a challenge in the 1990s: More aggressive integration of networks and a slowdown in consumer buying are likely to result in a shakeout (U.S. Department of Commerce, 1989c; Duncan, 1990; Weber, 1990). Both wholesalers and retailers will compete on the basis of their ability to get closer to their suppliers and their customers. As networks tighten to meet the new standards of quality, variety, customization, convenience, and timely delivery, partners are becoming more dependent on one another. And as dependency increases, each partner has a growing interest in the competitive ability of partners up and down the network chain. Wholesalers and retailers become most dependent of all.

Wholesalers are being squeezed by falling profit margins and by manufacturing and retail networks that increasingly bypass wholesaling. In response, most wholesalers are using new technology to tighten just-in-time networks and developing new relationships with manufacturers and customers. McKesson Corporation, a large wholesaler of drug and health products, is typical of the wholesale institutions of the new economy. McKesson began losing business to the large drugstore chains and responded by using intensive information technologies to track inventory, packing, and shipping. The company then integrated its own information systems with those of the independent druggists. The resultant network has given the independents capabilities they could not afford individually and a stronger position against the chain druggists. At the same time, the network has preserved McKesson's client base (Johnston and Lawrence, 1988).

A similar scenario is building in retailing. Specialty stores are successfully taking on large department stores, which are unable to provide comparable quality, variety, customization, and service. The larger stores are responding by strengthening internal departments and building stronger relationships with suppliers and customers. The future of retailing is likely to include a mix of large and small institutions integrated into networks that balance large scale and flexibility. The critical competitive factor in retailing is no longer scale but the ability to use new technologies and organizational formats to meet new competitive standards.

The Health Care Industry

Health care spending in the United States increased from less than 5 percent of total spending in the mid-1950s to more than 11 percent in the late 1980s (U.S. Department of Commerce, 1989c). The nation's health bill jumped more than 10 percent in 1989 to a whopping $615 billion. The increase is due to a variety of factors, including an expansion in available services and technologies, an expansion of clients as a result of government programs and employer health plans, a greater intensity in the use of the nation's health system, and increasing prices. Health care markets are also expanding, especially in care for the elderly, as previously unpaid care is commercialized.

Despite the remarkable growth of health care as a proportion of the nation's consumer budget, health care needs are not being satisfied. Moreover, attempts to increase the quantity and quality of service by spending more money on health care has resulted in inflated prices without a corresponding increase in supply or quality. As a result, the increase in demand tends to encourage unacceptable inflation, shortages, and unsatisfying quality of care. The response to the health care problem has been to install cost controls and experiment with health care networks. The future of health care promises increased demand and more aggressive attempts to control costs.

As the health care industry moves ahead, it will be forced to develop more carefully integrated networks, a process typical of the service sector's response to the new economy. New information-based technologies are cutting paperwork costs, integrating service delivery, and allowing more time with patients. More and more professionals are on staff rather than operating as private entrepreneurs. Health care organizations are sorting out their roles in the service network. Hospitals are becoming specialists in critical care, and other services are shifting to ambulatory care facilities, nursing homes, specialized testing and technical facilities, and private homes. Consumer participation in service delivery is increasing, especially in preventive care and use of user friendly health care gadgets.

The Housing Industry

Americans consistently spend about 20 percent of their income on housing. As incomes rise, the cost of housing rises, too. New residential construction was valued at almost $200 billion in 1988 (U.S. Department of Commerce, 1989c). Although housing markets have slowed, the demand for housing that is high in quality and affordable exceeds the available supply. As a result, as in the case of health care, market expansion efforts are focused on improving efficiency in production. Housing production in the United States is not efficient, and productivity is actually declining. Only mining has a worse productivity record. Although the decline in mining productivity is traceable to improved safety regulation and therefore justifiable, the productivity decline in housing is due to excessive fragmentation of the industry itself. A house has 15,000 parts, the same number of parts as a car, but houses are assembled almost entirely by hand on-site. Because of the industry's excessive fragmentation, it has impressive flexibility, but it has not been able to mobilize long-

term capital or provide the R&D necessary for long-term economies of scale.

Many observers believe that the U.S. industry needs to
emulate the housing industries in Sweden and Japan. There
housing construction is integrated in manufacturing institutions that utilize more machine capital than is the case in the
United States, and the workforce resembles that of high-tech
manufacturing. Advocates for manufactured housing argue that
a marriage between manufacturing organizations and new flexible technologies such as computer-based design would result in
cheaper, higher-quality, and more customized housing. In the
future, the American housing industry will likely evolve toward
large-scale housing manufacturers that will employ more white-
collar and technical professionals, fewer craft workers, and
more on-site housing assemblers.

The Apparel Industry

New technology and organizational networks pioneered by the
Italians provide stronger linkages between retail outlets and the
chain of institutions that produce fiber, cloth, and apparel. Over
the past two decades, networks of small firms have replaced all
but one of the large Italian apparel companies. The Italian
networks are the leaders in just-in-time production and delivery
of high-quality clothing (Johnston and Lawrence, 1988).

The worldwide apparel industry appears to be evolving
toward a structure and technology that will allow the conversion
of fiber to finished apparel, tailored to individual tastes and
measurements, in a matter of a few weeks. Moreover, industry
analysts argue that this quickly produced tailored clothing will
be no more expensive than current mass-produced items. Eventually, customers' measurements will be stored electronically,
customers will select cloth and style alternatives at the retailer,
and the clothing will be made and delivered within days. In
the space of a few hundred years, clothing markets will have
gone from tailoring to mass production and come full circle
back to tailoring, only this time with streamlined efficiency and
economy.

The Financial Services Industry

Financial service markets grew from 4 percent of purchases in 1955 to more than 6 percent in 1985 (U.S. Congress, 1988). The growth in market size resulted from an explosion in the variety of goods and services available, the use of information technologies to provide variety and tailored financial packages, and improved quality and convenience. From the post-World War II era to the 1970s, profits in banking were made by selling checking and charge card accounts to families and businesses through a growing network of branch offices. By the late 1970s, upward of 80 percent of the estimated checking account market was taken (Noyelle, 1988a). The competitive pressures stemming from the saturation of existing markets in combination with new, flexible information-based technologies resulted in an explosion of new products. Market expansion also resulted from the utilization of the new technologies to deliver high-quality customized services conveniently. Electronic transfers, tailored financial packages, and automated teller machines were some of the more commonplace advances in the industry.

Since the 1970s, growing market potential and deregulation have drawn a motley set of institutions into the competitive fray, accelerating the pace of change and increasing overall volatility. Lately the industry has been shifting from a highly fragmented structure to a complex one that emphasizes both global and local market development. Small institutions are focused on geographic, industry, or functional niches—but often under the umbrella of partnerships or parent enterprises.

Part Three

JOB AND SKILL DEMANDS
IN THE NEW ECONOMY

Chapter Six

THE CHANGING QUANTITY, DISTRIBUTION, AND QUALITY OF JOBS

The new economy is affecting jobs in three ways. First, it is altering the overall quantity of jobs created. Second, it is influencing the distribution of jobs among industries, occupations, geographic areas, and organizations of different sizes. Third, it is affecting the quality of jobs, as measured, for example, by wages, job security, and opportunities for career and personal development.

Quantity of Jobs

The American economy is expected to add 1.5 million new jobs each year between now and the year 2000 (Personick, 1989). Whether this expectation is realized will depend on a variety of factors. The overall quantity of jobs is determined by a combination of macro- and microeconomic factors. In the short haul, the macroeconomic factors are dominant. Low levels of consumer demand, tight money, and high interest rates squeeze economic activity, inhibiting human and technical investments and job growth. Why hire more people to make more and better widgets if you already have too many widgets at the warehouse? Restrictive business environments also encourage an exaggerated attention to cost savings. Because personnel costs run as high as one-half to three-quarters of total costs, attempts to reduce costs will inevitably focus on reduced hiring, especially in full-time positions. In the worst-case scenario, a sustained downturn in the business environment can discourage demand for human development and reduce an economy's potential job growth. In the new economy, sustained slowdowns in demand will reduce job opportunities, whereas sustained growth will provide a robust context for job creation.

Demography, too, drives the overall quantity of work. More people create more demand for goods and services and more willing hands to make and deliver these products. In the 1970s, American job growth was 2.3 million jobs per year. During the 1990s, it is expected to decline to 1.5 million jobs per year, principally because of the slowdown in population growth in the wake of the baby boom (Fullerton, 1989). This reduced growth, however, is not necessarily bad. Economies with fewer people tend to invest more in the people available and to arm them with more capital at work. The result is increased economic potential. In contrast, when there is an ample supply of workers, it is tempting to substitute muscular for mental power, a practice that reduces economic potential as human capital essential for technical and organizational development decays.

America's present macroeconomic prospects are mixed. Large budget deficits and the natural ups and downs of the business cycle suggest there will be some retardation of job growth in the near term. The longer-term macroeconomic prospects are more favorable. Budget deficits as a proportion of GNP are declining slowly, freeing up private resources for investments in the domestic economy. Worldwide demand should continue to increase as the United States and other nations develop formal mechanisms and informal conventions for mobilizing and responding to global demand.

Our demographics are equally mixed. As the baby

boomers move into their high-productivity years, the quality of human capital on the job should improve markedly. Similarly, more financial capital will probably be available to buy technology as the baby boomers move into their high-savings years and as the demographic demand for housing declines. The combination of a seasoned workforce and more available capital for investments in human resources and machines should ultimately bring more robust growth and create more jobs.

The demographic wild card in America's competitive hand is the declining quantity and quality of human capital at the entry level. Cohorts that follow the baby boomers are much smaller and belong disproportionately to groups in which our developmental investments have been grossly insufficient. In some respects, the declining quantity and quality of entry-level employees is a happy problem. The scarcity of entry-level workers will guarantee work for those who are prepared, inspiring better preparation among people whose prospects have traditionally been limited and a greater willingness among governments and employers to invest in young students and workers. For the first time in memory, the nation's cultural and political commitment to economic opportunity will coincide with emerging economic necessities.

Distribution of Jobs

Although the new economy will likely create jobs in the aggregate, the processes of economic change will inevitably distribute new jobs unevenly. New technologies, the globalization of economic activity, and organizational changes will create good jobs for the majority, result in bad jobs for some, and take away jobs from a few. Moreover, the new jobs created by technology, trade, and competitive changes almost never go to the people who have lost their jobs because of these forces. In the 1970s and 1980s, the typical job loser was a midwestern male who was over thirty years old, had a high school diploma, and worked in manufacturing. The typical job gainer was an East Coast or West Coast female who was in her early twenties, had a two- or four-year postsecondary degree, and worked in services.

The unequal distribution of burdens and benefits as we move into the new economy is being exacerbated by concentrated technical and economic changes in specific occupations, industries, and geographic areas. Computers and modern communications technologies have reduced entry-level job opportunities in office settings. Automated manufacturing is rapidly eliminating low-skill entry-level jobs in manufacturing as well as jobs for laborers, material handlers, machine operators, and craft workers while creating jobs for technicians, mechanics, and repairers. In the future, manufactured housing may devastate the construction trades while creating new jobs in housing that are akin to the white-collar and technician jobs found in manufacturing.

In addition, as economic activity globalizes and trade advantages shift, recessions are becoming more specific to particular industry networks. Industry recessions begin in organizations that supply final goods, then move through the chain of suppliers. For example, auto recessions that begin at General Motors, Ford, and Chrysler eventually roll through supplier institutions in the steel, rubber, and electronics industries.

As a community, we are challenged to redress the unequal benefits and burdens characteristic of the new economic environment. Those who benefit from technical change and free trade need to share their good fortune with those who are victims of machines and foreign competition. The employed majority must be sensitive to both the poor and the dislocated. A new social compact will be required. The development of such a compact will not be easy in a polity accustomed to responding to majority concerns. In the current political context, the dislocated employees are the forgotten constituency. They are neither an effective political majority nor a truly needy minority.

The first step toward building a new social compact will be for Americans to recognize that ours is a society based on work. A job is the price of admission to this individualistic culture and participatory polity. People unable to find work eventually disappear from the community, drop out of the American political system, and fall into the underground economy. These same destructive processes are at work for both the poor and dislocated workers. There is no fit measure that allows us to choose between the suffering of these two groups. The chronically poor tend to start out and end up at the bottom of the economic heap. Dislocated employees experience an economic loss that rarely results in persistent poverty but probably involves an equal amount of suffering. In the case of dislocated employees, it is not so much where they land that hurts, but how far they have to fall.

Looking beyond the aggregate numbers to the kinds of jobs the new economy is generating reveals a pattern fitted to the emerging demands of the new competitive standards and networks. Indeed, understood in this context, the changes begin to make sense and provide less cause for alarm. The concern over the relative job growth in manufacturing versus services is a case in point. To equate the growth of service jobs with a decline in the quality of jobs available is misguided. The phenomenal growth in service jobs is not a result of competitive failure. Instead, it reflects the growing service content all industries require to meet the new competitive standards and maintain networks. We are not abdicating basic industries. Indeed, manufacturing output continues to grow. The loss of jobs in basic industries can be understood, at least in part, as a result of competitive restructuring of jobs. Production workers are being displaced by a smaller number of technicians, who use more technology to produce vastly greater levels of output per worker. Meanwhile, manufacturing jobs in management and other service-oriented functions are growing. In fact, even though there are fewer manufacturing jobs, they are more important than ever because they are located at the generative core of our most advanced and critical competitive networks.

The Critical Role of Natural Resources, Construction, and Manufacturing

Not all jobs are created equal in the new economy. Economic activity in natural resources, construction, and manufacturing has the generative power to create jobs in other industries. Only a quarter out of a dollar spent on natural resources stays in the industry. The rest goes to other industries: a dime to construction, almost thirty cents to manufacturing, sixteen cents to transportation and wholesale and retail trades, eleven cents to transactional activities, and eight cents to services. Similarly, the construction industry keeps only about thirty-six cents on the dollar; low-wage manufacturing keeps forty-eight cents; medium-wage manufacturing keeps forty-five cents; and high-wage manufacturing keeps only forty-three cents.

Service-oriented industries are more self-contained. They operate at the periphery of networks centered on manufacturing, natural resources, or construction. Money spent directly on services creates fewer jobs elsewhere. Thus, sixty-two cents of every dollar spent on transportation or wholesale and retail trade stays in the industry, and the transactional services industry retains fifty-seven cents of every dollar. Fifty-five cents of every dollar spent on personal services stays with the provider, and no one industry gets more than a dime's worth of the remaining forty-five cents. Social services are the most insulated of all, with seventy-five cents of every dollar retained (U.S. Congress, 1988).

The Service Revolution

The most noticeable trend in the kinds of jobs typical of the new economy will be a continuation in the shift toward service work. During the 1990s, manufacturing employment will decline by an estimated 300,000 jobs, and extractive jobs in agriculture and mining will decline by a similar number. In contrast, service jobs are expected to increase by almost seventeen million (Personick, 1989).

There are many reasons for the increasing share of service jobs. One is that people satisfy their material wants early as they climb the income ladder. A consumer can eat only so much food, drive only one car at a time, and sleep under only one roof. As a result, a declining share of rising income goes to material goods, and a rising share goes to services such as education, personal services, health care, recreation, and environmental services (U.S. Congress, 1988).

The share of jobs going to services is also increasing

because more and more extracted and manufactured goods are being made with fewer and fewer workers. Productivity in manufacturing and extractive industries has outstripped productivity in services for hundreds of years and continues to do so. The cost of a television set was equivalent to four days' work in 1950, one day's work in 1972, and only four hours' work in 1986 (U.S. Congress, 1988). Between now and the next century, manufacturing output will increase by 2.6 percent per year, while the number of manufacturing jobs will decline by 0.1 percent per annum (Personick, 1989). Production workers in manufacturing will be replaced by a smaller number of technicians, who will work with more technology. The number of technicians will increase by almost 100,000 but the number of operators and laborers will decline by 700,000 by the year 2000.

The competitive requirements of the new economy are a third reason for the increasing proportion of service jobs. A substantial number of new service employees will be required to design, develop, and market a variety of timely, state-of-the-art products in a complex global environment. In manufacturing, for instance, there will be a loss of production jobs but a gain of almost a million jobs for managers, professionals, and marketing and sales personnel (Personick, 1989; Silvestri and Lukasiewicz, 1989).

The increasing number of transactions among complex economic networks also encourages demand for service workers ranging from sales and customer service personnel to lawyers and accountants. Compared with 1972, in the mid 1980s, an additional nickel out of every dollar spent in all economic networks went to pay for transactional activities (U.S. Congress, 1988). As economic networks become more integrated, individual employers will need more employees in service occupations. Business services such as personnel, computer, research, and consulting services will account for one out of every six new jobs between now and the beginning of the next century. As the number of transactions in networks increases, the number of jobs for people doing the buying and selling will increase as well. Retail trade jobs are the fastest growing category of service jobs, and their number will grow by more than three million between now and the year 2000 (Personick, 1989).

The number of jobs in information services will increase dramatically to integrate economic networks. The demand for electronic engineers will grow by more than 40 percent, and we will need half again as many computer scientists in the 1990s as we did in the 1980s. The number of mechanics and installers and repairers of technology will increase by 13 percent overall, with a 60 percent increase in computer equipment repairers (Silvestri and Lukasiewicz, 1989). Computer services are the fastest growing of the business service industries. Demand for all computer-related occupations will grow by almost 5 percent a year in the 1990s compared with an average total job growth in the American economy of 2.3 percent a year in the 1970s and 1980s.

The Geography of Jobs

Contending technical and competitive forces are at work in the emerging geographic distribution of jobs. Technical changes are freeing work from traditional geographic restraints, while competitive realities are concentrating jobs in networks of metropolitan areas.

A variety of forces are encouraging this dispersion of jobs. As raw material becomes a less important ingredient in every production recipe, proximity to raw materials becomes less important. In addition, location near major transportation nodes becomes less important as networks are connected more by information and communications technology and less by physical transport. Moreover, advances in air transport reduce the importance of location near natural overland and water transport sites. Finally, the technical ability to reach far-flung domestic and global markets has resulted in a self-propelled extension of competitive networks beyond local markets.

At the same time, however, the new competitive requirements tend to concentrate job growth in population centers. The increasing service content of economic competition encourages proximity to allow personal contact both inside and outside the organization. The high concentration of customers in urban areas and access to rapid transportation also increase the attractiveness of metropolitan locations. Moreover, the centrality of learning in the new economy encourages location in population centers with access to educational and research and development infrastructure. Therefore, most new jobs are being created in the extensive networks of the densely populated metropolitan areas (U.S. Congress, 1988). Most jobs are being created on the two coasts, where population density is greatest. In the South and West, most new jobs are in urban areas. The urbanization of job creation does not preclude rural or small-town development. The ability of smaller communities to develop their economies, however, depends more on their ability to find a niche in a broader network and less on their ability to develop independently.

Institutions Big and Small

Are most jobs created by big or small employers? It all depends on what one means by "big" and "small." Currently, five out of six American employees work in institutions with fewer than 1,000 employees. This group is divided almost equally among institutions with fewer than 20 employees, with between 20 and 99 employees, and with 100 to 999 employees. The share of new jobs created by firms with fewer than 100 employees has increased to 40 percent, although these firms' share of economic output has declined (U.S. Department of Commerce, 1989c: U.S. Congress, 1988). The fastest growth in jobs is occurring in establishments owned by larger enterprises—a fact that is not surprising in an era when organizations are trying to balance scale, scope, and focus by utilizing organizational networks (U.S. Congress, 1988).

In the final analysis, the debate over job creation in big versus small institutions misses the mark because it ignores the central organizational reality of the new economy. That reality is the growth in networks that integrate large and small institutions in order to capture and balance the benefits of large scale and the flexibility and focus of smaller organizations.

Quality of Jobs

Measuring the quality of jobs is complex because they provide a variety of benefits. Work provides wages and independence in a culture that values both; and in a society based on work, job security is critical to family life. For most of us, work is also the crucible for our personal and career development. The pages that follow assess the jobs of the new economy on the basis of their ability to provide good wages, job security, and career development.

Wages

Importance of Learning. Wage growth in the United States has been flat since the early 1970s (Bound and Johnson, 1989). Principal among the reasons for this stagnation is our poor productivity performance, but there are other reasons as well. Labor productivity has outpaced wage increases in part because an increasing share of the productivity dividend has gone to pay for the capital requirements of the new economy (U.S. Congress, 1988). Another portion of the productivity dividend has come out of wages to pay for the increased cost of benefits, especially health care benefits. Yet another share of the meager productivity dividend has gone to retirees. In addition, the pressure of international wage competition, especially for well-paid manufacturing jobs, has held wages down (Murphy and Welch, 1989). Moreover, as female participation in the workforce rose from 39 percent in 1973 to 45 percent in 1988, overall wages declined because the average wage level for women is only 64 percent of the average wage level for men (Kosters, 1989).

Despite flat overall wage growth, there have been dramatic shifts in earnings among different groups of Americans. Wage increases in the new economy are rationed with an increasingly uneven hand, resulting in a growing maldistribution of income in the United States. Now more than ever, learning is the rationing hand that distributes earnings in the American economy. People with the most education and access to learning on the job are doing best; those with the least education and least access to learning on the job are doing worst.

Formal education, especially college education, boosts earnings greatly in the new economy. People with a good education have always had an advantage, but they are doing better now than ever before. In fact, statistics show that the returns to education declined between 1973 and 1980 but made a phenomenal comeback in the 1980s. In 1973, a college graduate with ten years' work experience earned 49 percent more than a high school graduate with ten years' work experience. By 1980, the college graduate's advantage had declined to 31 percent for males and 37 percent for females. After 1980, however, the advantage of college graduation over high school graduation began to rise again, reaching 86 percent for males and 60 percent for females by 1988 (Kosters, 1989). In a telling analysis of available data, Levy (1987) has demonstrated that postsecondary graduates will ultimately exceed their parents' earnings but high school graduates will not.

The returns to postsecondary education for both two-year and four-year schools are substantial in every occupational category. In 1987, managers with high school diplomas earned $23,306 on the average, but managers with college degrees earned an average of $37,252. Technicians with high school diplomas earned $21,358, technicians with some postsecondary education earned $23,830, and those with four years of college earned $28,004. In service occupations, workers with high school diplomas, those with one to three years of postsecondary schooling, and those with four-year college degrees earned $13,093, $16,937 and $21,381, respectively (Silvestri and Lukasiewicz, 1989).

The returns to postsecondary schooling are reinforced by the synergy between schooling and learning on the job. People with the most schooling have access to the jobs with the most formal and informal training. College-educated managers and technical professionals get substantial formal and informal training on the job. Employees who have high school diplomas plus some formal postsecondary training (for example, supervisors, technicians, and technologists and craft, skill, data-processing, and sales employees) also get substantial formal and informal training on the job. In general, workers who get formal training have a 30 percent earnings advantage over those who do not (Carnevale and Gainer, 1989a).

These data understate the demand for learning in the new economy. What is most remarkable is that the returns to education and learning on the job have remained high and grown even while the supply of educated workers has been constantly on the rise. It is surprising that the dip in the 1970s was not deeper. Since the turnaround, the supply of high school and postsecondary graduates has continued to increase. The proportion of college graduates among males in the workforce has grown from 20 percent to 24 percent since 1980. The proportion for females has increased from 16 percent to 21 percent.

Why are the returns to postsecondary schooling increasing so rapidly? The principal reason is that the competitive demands of the new economy require more learning both in preparation for work and on the job. As a result, employers are using a higher educational standard to sort among job seekers at the entry level, and the fastest growing job categories require postsecondary schooling (Silvestri and Lukasiewicz, 1989). At present, the distribution of American jobs can be divided roughly into thirds: One-third require elementary schooling, one-third require a high school education plus two years of postsecondary schooling, and one-third require a college degree. Since the early 1970s, the proportion of jobs requiring only a grade school education has declined, whereas the proportion of jobs requiring postsecondary schooling has increased steadily. Other reasons for the growing returns to postsecondary schooling are a shift by students toward technical and business subjects and a general tightening of college entry standards in the late 1970s (Bishop, 1989).

Sex, Race, and Ethnicity. Job opportunity and wages in the new economy have not been neutral with respect to sex, race and ethnicity. The new configuration of occupations and earnings tends to favor progress in women's wages. The shift away from natural resources and the factory floor to service functions in all competitive networks reduces the proportion of male-dominated occupations in the workforce. Also, women have been more aggressive than men in pursuing schooling and in utilizing learning to leverage career development. In 1963, 34 percent of eighteen- and nineteen-year-old men and 23 percent of eighteen- and nineteen-year-old women were enrolled in college. By 1975, the figure for both sexes was 34 percent, and in 1988, 48 percent of eighteen- and nineteen-year-old women and 37 percent of eighteen- and nineteen-year-old men were enrolled in college. Although women have lower status than men in most organizations, women participate in formal training programs at work in rough proportion to their participation in the workforce (Carnevale and Gainer, 1989a). These factors, among others, account for an increase in women's average earnings from 59 percent to 64 percent of men's average earnings during the 1980s (Bound and Johnson, 1989).

The new economy has not been nearly so kind to minorities. For instance, in 1963, the average African American male earned 63 percent as much as the average white male, and by the early 1970s, the percentage was up to 75. These earnings gains then stalled, however, and in the 1980s, the earnings differential between African American and white men widened. By the late 1980s, the average African American man was earning less than 70 percent as much as the average white man. The earnings differential between Hispanic and white males has widened also—from 73 percent in 1979 to 65 percent at the end of the 1980s. Moreover, if benefits and earnings other than wages are included, the differential between white males and their African American and Hispanic counterparts is even greater. A similar pattern is evident in the economic progress of other minorities.

A principal cause of the stalled progress of minorities has been the increasing value of education in providing access to good jobs and learning on the job (Juhn, Murphy, and Pierce, 1989). Minority educational attainment has not kept pace with the increase in years of schooling among the majority population, nor have minorities had access to jobs with formal or informal training.

Minorities are concentrated in jobs that pay the least,

provide the least formal and informal learning, and show the least improvement in wages. For instance, in 1988, African Americans made up 10 percent of the workforce (Fullerton, 1989) yet had only 6 percent of the managerial jobs and 7 percent of the professional jobs. African Americans are disproportionately represented in dead-end clerical jobs. About 22 percent of mail clerks and messengers are African American. African Americans are similarly overly represented among low-wage service workers, holding 18 percent of all service jobs. Specifically, 23 percent of private household workers and 23 percent of cleaning service workers are African American. Finally, African Americans are overly represented in manufacturing jobs at risk in the new economy, with 18 percent of operator, fabricator, and laborer jobs (Silvestri and Lukasiewicz, 1989).

Yet African Americans are positioned well in some occupational areas that will survive and provide career ladders in the new economy. African Americans make up 14 percent of technicians and technologists in health care, 28 percent of health care workers in general, and 14 percent of the nation's computer operators.

Hispanics made up 7.4 percent of the workforce in 1988 but had only 4 percent of managerial jobs, 3 percent of professional jobs, and 4 percent of technician jobs. At the same time, Hispanics made up 10 percent of the nation's service workers, having the highest concentrations in low-wage food, cleaning, and private household services. In addition, Hispanics have an inordinate share of low-wage agricultural jobs (13 percent) and, like African Americans, are overly represented in operator and laborer jobs at risk in manufacturing. Still, Hispanics, too, are positioned well in some areas that are likely to grow and prosper. Hispanics make up 5 percent of engineering and scientific technicians, 5 percent of marketing and sales workers, 6 percent of computer operators, and 8 percent of mechanics, installers, and repairers.

Job Security: Shifting Loyalties from Employers to Skill

The characteristic signature of the new economy is flexibility. The fast pace of change within networks and the volatility of markets, especially global markets, require flexible responses. Flexible institutions need flexible workforces. Most employers have reacted by building a workforce in layers: a core workforce with permanent status and a peripheral workforce of part-timers, temporaries, consultants, and suppliers who are accorded varying degrees of commitment. Employers utilize this peripheral workforce for varying purposes: to manage changing workloads, to save money on benefits and other costs associated with full-time employees, and to access expertise not available in-house.

About one in ten American workers is now in the peripheral workforce (Abraham, 1988). For example, the number of workers classified as temporary help has multiplied threefold since 1978, increasing from a little more than 300,000 to a million. And temporary help agencies provide more than clerical support. As of 1982, almost half of temporaries were non-office workers (Abraham 1988). The projected growth in business services reflects the increasing importance of outside suppliers. Only retail and health care will contribute more new jobs between now and the end of the century. Employment in business services will increase from the 5.6 million in 1988 to 8.3 million in the year 2000.

Institutions and employees that do not seek flexibility often have it forced on them. The pace of change in the world economy and the intensification of competition can dislodge even the most secure workers. At best, a worker can hope to work for one employer for a lifetime but cannot realistically expect to hold one job all those years. In fact, although some institutions can guarantee employment in the fast-paced new economy, others, despite good intentions, cannot. Moreover, when dislocation does occur, it tends to affect whole industries or occupations, making the job search particularly difficult for employees whose skills and experience are heavily invested in one job or one industry.

Perhaps there is employment security for workers at the very core of institutional networks, yet the volatility of the new economy suggests that even these workers, as well as those at the periphery of institutions, are best advised to become more loyal to their skills and less loyal to individual employers. Happily, as skill requirements become less job specific, both skill and experience are becoming more transferable from one job to another.

Ultimately, because of the growing importance of skill and its general applicability across institutions, workers who pay attention to education, training, and work experience can increase their control over their working lives. Skill, especially accredited skill, can provide employment security in a particular industry or occupation, even if not in a particular job with a particular employer. Moreover, demography will favor workers who pay attention to skill development in school and at work. As demographic trends lead to shortages of skilled workers, especially entry-level employees, employers will compete aggressively for skilled workers and build stronger relationships with part-timers, temporary workers, and suppliers of business services. The trend toward more carefully integrated networks will also encourage employers to build more permanent relationships with suppliers.

The new demands for flexible employees raise some troublesome complications. First, as skills become more generalized, individual employees will be more interchangeable, and the bargaining power of individual workers may decline (U.S. Congress, 1988). The loss of bargaining power would likely be smallest among core workers and technical specialists and greatest among nontechnical generalists. Peripheral workers would be more mobile but have less bargaining power than core workers. Nurses are an example. They are highly skilled and highly mobile but relatively interchangeable and vastly underpaid. Second, as skill becomes more pivotal, issues surrounding access to learning arise. Postsecondary schooling is more expensive than ever, and college enrollments have flattened, especially for males. Less than 15 percent of Americans get any formal or informal training on the job (Carnevale and Gainer, 1989a). Moreover, training and experience at work are not certified or recorded and are therefore difficult to prove. Finally, if we are to have a truly flexible workforce, American workers will need a whole set of expensive new benefits geared to workers on the move, including portable training, portable pensions, and portable family services like day care and parental leave.

Career Development

Career development prospects in the new economy are a crazy quilt of possibilities. Individual prospects depend on the industry, the occupation, and managerial decisions as to how work will be organized. There are some typical patterns, however.

From Bosses to Brokers. Managers, professionals, and business service workers will prosper. These bosses from the old economy will become brokers in the new economy, easing transactions in internal and external networks, communicating new information and learning throughout networks, and leading and developing other employees.

More Technical Specialists. Technical specialists will do well whether they are manufacturing engineers, health technologists, or specialized bond traders in banking. Some technical specialists (for example, radiologists, CAD and CAM operators, and repair persons) will be attached to particular technologies. Computer and communications workers will grow in importance. Already there are as many jobs for data entry clerks in the food and health care industries as there are jobs for farmers and health care professionals (U.S. Congress, 1988).

Other technical specialties will be associated with particular product lines. The international bond trader is an example. In most cases, technical specialists will substitute for less skilled labor. The manufacturing technician, for instance, works in combination with a powerful and flexible technology that substitutes for a variety of workers—including laborers, material handlers, machine operators, repair workers, and even supervisors—who in combination made up the work team in old-line manufacturing. In services, customer service professionals armed with computer technology will substitute for a host of service personnel who used to be charged with information recording, sales, clerical functions, and final service delivery.

From Craft Workers to Manufacturing Personnel. New jobs will be created and others restructured as networks in some industries evolve. One pattern is a shift in some industries from a preponderance of craft workers to a greater share of white-collar workers and technicians. For example, packaging and processing technologies in the food industry will eliminate local craft workers, who will be supplanted by a mix of managers, professionals, and technicians at the processing factory. Boxed beef has already stolen a march on the local butcher. A similar shift from craft to manufacturing will occur in housing construction. Houses will increasingly be designed and tailored indoors by a typical manufacturing workforce and assembled outdoors by assembly workers and craft laborers.

Partitioning of Professional Jobs. In many cases, the stand-alone professional's job is being partitioned into a job for a team of technical specialists and paraprofessionals who work with a professional generalist. With the assistance of flexible information technologies, technicians are assuming functions previously performed by scientists and engineers. Senior bank managers are being assisted by specialized bond traders and currency experts. Paraprofessional occupations are growing in medicine and law. And in the new school, "master teachers" and apprentice teachers are joined by teachers' aides, media specialists, curriculum developers, and a host of others.

The relationships among the members of the new occupational teams vary. Sometimes the craft model applies. For example, the apprentice teacher can one day become the master teacher. More often than not, the generalist has the biggest paycheck and the senior role, but in other cases, the relationships are ambiguous. The bond trader often makes more money than the bank president, for instance.

More Lateral Entry. The growing importance of learning, especially schooling, has resulted in a multiplication of the lateral ports of entry into institutions. As skill requirements become more generalized and skills become more transferable, employees with the same education and experience become more interchangeable between institutions. Managers, service workers, and nontechnical professionals are gaining mobility, but the skills of technical workers and other specialists are even more transferable. For instance, bank managers may have some difficulty transferring from one bank to another because much of a bank manager's experience and learning on the job are peculiar to the culture and competitive niche of the bank. Data-processing experts and specialized bond traders can move more easily from one institution to another because their experience and learning on the job are attached more to products or technologies than to the institutions in which they work.

Shortened Career Ladders. The increasing salability of education and experience in the new economy is also shortening career ladders inside employer institutions (Noyelle, 1989). A person cannot start out in the mail room and end up as a technician, bond trader, or senior manager because career ladders are tightly tied to education and the experience it leverages. To advance in an industry or occupation, a worker must acquire the credential necessary to get the job. Once on the job, his or her experience leverages the individual up the career ladder.

The shortening of career ladders has important implications for employers and employees. Employers who want to bring their own employees up through the ranks need to make substantial investments in education and build strong linkages with educational institutions (Bailey, 1988b). And workers who want upward mobility need to know that hard work is not enough; upward mobility requires educational investments.

Convergence of Work Life. As technology takes on repetitive physical and mental tasks, employers have an increasing amount of discretion in combining tasks into jobs. If employers choose to do so, they can continue to use mass production techniques, rationalizing jobs into ever more discrete tasks and utilizing traditional occupational hierarchies and information technologies to monitor the work of production and service workers down the line. Because the new technology allows geographically dispersed networks, employers can use cheap, unskilled labor pools for repetitive work while reserving more critical functions for central offices. This "respatialization" of work segregates good and bad jobs geographically (Baran and Parsons, 1986).

For markets that demand highly standardized goods or routine services, specialized hierarchies and information technologies for electronic monitoring may be appropriate. But the sale of routine services and standardized goods is declining as demands for variety, customization, convenience, and higher quality increase. Moreover, organizing work in mass production formats reduces the flexibility necessary to adapt and survive in the new economy. Often, the urge to specialize work is a throwback to the simplistic competitive standards of the old economy and can be self-defeating. The separation of clerical, analytic, and customer service functions is a case in point. Jobs can be upgraded by combining in a single job the tasks of entering customer information, analyzing the information, and tailoring the good or service. This combining of functions improves customer service, decreases response time, encourages organizational learning, and generally brings the entire competitive network closer to the customer.

Job responsibilities are becoming more generalized and overlapping. Employees are spending more time interacting with colleagues and customers. Employees and work teams in top-down hierarchies are becoming more autonomous, yet professionals and entrepreneurs are integrated into more tightly knit networks. The emerging result is an overall convergence of job structures that offer both increased individual discretion and greater interdependence.

Chapter Seven

THE INCREASING NEED
FOR COMPLEX AND
WIDE-RANGING JOB SKILLS

The new economy has profound implications for the way we use people on the job. New competitive requirements demand new job designs, new organizational structures, and more skilled workers. New flexible technologies are beginning to change skill requirements and the context in which skills are used in the workplace. Ultimately, a whole new set of skills will be required, and those skills will be both deeper and broader than currently required ones. This section discusses some of the factors affecting skill requirements and then elaborates on the skills needed in the new economy.

Skill and the New Competitive Framework

Employees need to be flexible in order to live with the ambiguity that is inherent in the new competitive framework. Every organization must find its unique strategic balance of competitive standards, and ambiguity results from the fact that the chosen strategy may seem to be internally inconsistent. For instance, at times, the pursuit of productivity and timeliness may seem to be at odds with the simultaneous pursuit of quality, variety, customization, and convenience.

The competencies, knowledge, and skills required of employees depend on the mix of competitive standards the organization has embraced. At the same time, however, every organization needs to pay attention to each of the new standards. Every organization, for example, must focus on the skill requirements necessary to achieve productivity increases. In the old economy, productivity was generally achieved by automating and instituting rigid control of work processes. Using more machinery meant that fewer workers were needed, and narrow-purpose machinery and rigid work processes reduced skill requirements. These changes drove down personnel costs, which increased the value of output relative to input costs, thereby increasing productivity. The pursuit of productivity was a matter of simple arithmetic. In the new economy, however, a productivity strategy based on deskilling work and reducing personnel costs will not work. New, more flexible technologies and organizational formats require more flexible and skilled employees. Moreover, automating or deskilling work reduces the organization's ability to deliver on other competitive standards. In the new economy, the simultaneous pursuit of productivity and other competitive standards requires that people be treated as assets to be developed in order to add value rather than as costs to be reduced.

Employees capable of improving quality must have a solid grounding in the hard competencies and job knowledge, but the softer skills of communication and good interpersonal relations are equally important. Well-prepared people can do shoddy work or allow shoddy work to go on around them. Quality ultimately depends on the way people use their basic and technical competencies and job knowledge and the way they interact with one another. High quality begins when people take responsibility for more than their own work effort in their assigned responsibilities. They must accept responsibility for the product before it arrives at the workstation and after it moves on in the work process. As a result, the keys to high quality are personal management skills, such as the ability to achieve self-esteem by setting personal goals and motivating oneself, and skills for communicating with, influencing, and working with others in previous and subsequent phases of the production process.

New standards for variety, customization, convenience, and timeliness require, above all, flexibility. To customize goods and services and provide convenience for customers, workers need both the communication and interpersonal skills necessary to interact effectively with customers and the adaptability and influencing skills necessary to direct the organization to the customers' demands.

The Roles of People and Machines

Changing skill requirements in the new economy are also driven by changes in technology. The impact of technology on skill requirements is best understood by analyzing human-machine combinations on the job. There are many facets to the relationship between people and machines at work, and various typologies exist to assess these different dimensions (Baran and Parsons, 1986; Blackburn, Coombs, and Green, 1985). R. M. Bell (1983), an engineer writing for the British Engineering Industry Training Board in 1972, constructed what is perhaps the most useful one. In his study of the metalworking industry, Bell concluded that every work activity is composed of three different work processes: *transformation*, the changing of shapes or states of raw materials or work pieces; *transfer*, the flow or movement of materials or work pieces from one part of the production system to another; and *control*, the responsibility for and physical control over the transformation and transfer functions. Each of these three work processes may be automated to a different degree.

Bell's model is most relevant to manufacturing and extractive industries, but it has broader applicability as well. A parallel typology can be constructed for service industries. In such a typology, the three work processes are *performance*, the act of providing the service; *delivery*, the process of organizing the service and getting it to the client; and *control*, the responsibility for and physical control over performance and delivery.

In the context of Bell's model, the history of human-machine combinations is characterized by two trends: (1) a sequential extension of machine capabilities, first in the transformation of material, then in the transfer of material between workstations, and finally in the control of the transformation and transfer functions; and (2) an often overlooked complementary extension of the complexity and scope of the human role in economic activity.

Extension of Machine Capabilities

In the craft economy, technology was subordinate to the worker in all aspects of the human-machine relationship. The processes of transformation, transfer, and control were unified in the worker. The transition from crafts to early manufacturing in the late eighteenth century to the middle of the nineteenth century took place as individual workers in cottage industries began substituting machines for tools in the transformation process. In the early days of industrialism, the transfer and control functions were still in the hands of people, usually working cooperatively in small groups (Blackburn, Coombs, and Green, 1985). As energy sources progressed from water to steam and then to internal combustion and electricity, machine power was increasingly used for functions such as lifting, cutting, and grinding, further substituting mechanical apparatus for human strength and dexterity in the transformation of material.

Eventually, as the mechanization of manufacturing matured, the new energy sources and the more powerful machines they drove increased the speed of operation and the volume of output at individual workstations. This created bottlenecks in the flow of materials and parts. As a result, mechanization of the transfer of parts and materials between manufacturing workstations became the focus of technological innovation as well as the principal driving force in the design of organizations and jobs from the mid-nineteenth through the mid-twentieth century.

In the modern manufacturing era, the relative importance of technology and people in the transformation, transfer, and control functions at work varies widely. In manufacturing, for instance, managers and professionals utilize relatively little technology, and technical professionals use only general-purpose technologies. This independence from technology is linked to independence from organizational structure and job design. In contrast, production and other nonsupervisory workers use more specialized technology to transform and transfer material goods and have less autonomy. Technology and the white-collar and technical elites exercise control over other employees working through carefully designed hierarchies and work rules.

The penetration of technology in service work has evolved more slowly. The service sector grew rapidly along with industrialization, but it proved difficult to mechanize the performance of services and even more difficult to mechanize delivery and control. New tools and job aids improved performance, but the rationalization of service work has been achieved less by mechanization than by adopting organizational and managerial practices from the more technology-intensive sectors.

Because service functions are difficult to automate, nonsupervisory workers in services are less subservient to technology, organizational structures, and job designs in the performance and control functions than are manufacturing workers. Yet at the same time, the basic differences between supervisory and nonsupervisory workers in manufacturing are mirrored in service delivery: White-collar elites are relatively independent of organizational structure and restrictive job designs, and nonsupervisory workers tend to work with more job-specific technologies and are more constrained by organizational structure and careful job design.

The Changing Complexity and Scope of Skill

In recent years, we have had to make a qualitative leap in the use of human-machine combinations at work in order to satisfy new competitive standards. As a result, technology has supplanted the human partner in some tasks. For example, in manufacturing, programmable machines have superseded human skill in many aspects of the transformation of materials. The skilled machinist and tool and die maker are being replaced by computer-based machinery because the new technologies improve precision and thereby improve quality. At the same time, the new information technologies allow faster setup and reprogramming and thereby encourage timeliness, variety, and customization. In addition, information technologies have revolutionized the transfer of parts and materials, allowing just-in-time production. Information technologies have also improved control functions because of the programmability of information networks as well as their ability to monitor performance and communicate both within the organization and with suppliers and customers.

The role of technology has also expanded in service industries. In some cases, such as long-distance calling and automated banking, the new technology has almost completely automated performance, delivery, and control.

The broadened scope of economic activity is expanding the roles and demanding more of both machines and people in manufacturing and services. While technologies, especially information-based technologies, have expanded the technical role in all aspects of economic activity, the human partner has taken on higher-order control functions necessary to deploy new technologies effectively and to operate in a more complex work environment.

Therefore, the advance of technology in the new economy does not necessarily represent a growing dominance of machines at work. Substantial evidence to the contrary shows a growing preponderance of high-skill jobs in the economy as a whole and increasing skill requirements in existing jobs (Johnston and Lawrence, 1988; Spenner, 1985; Kutscher, 1989; Baran and Parsons, 1986).

In part, confusion over the impacts of new technologies at work stems from our inability to understand the dynamics of skill change. The combination of human and machine capital is not a zero-sum game, in which winners can gain only at the expense of losers. Jobs are not fixed sets of tasks to be divided between machines and people. Both the complexity and the scope of jobs change over time. An expanded technical role in economic activity does not necessarily signal a reduction in human contributions. Instead, when the complexity of work is increasing, as it is now, a commensurate increase in the quality of both technical and human elements is usually required. In theory, the advance of information technologies permits employer institutions to operate effectively with small elite corps of white-collar and technical employees and even smaller groups of workers who have been reduced to passive machine tenders monitored by video surveillance and computers. Such a strategy can speed up production or service delivery and reduce costs, thereby increasing productivity, and is consistent with the market demands and organizational structures of mass production. However, there is growing evidence that this strategy does not fully exploit technical potential and is inappropriate to the new competitive requirements (Adler, 1988; Hirschhorn, 1988).

Typing pools and other kinds of electronic sweatshops are examples of inappropriate use of the new technology in services. In manufacturing, the recent introduction of numerically controlled machine tools is a particularly instructive example. Numerically controlled machine tools were originally sold as labor-saving substitutes for mass production technologies to increase productivity and save on labor costs. Employers have since discovered that having more skilled workers use these tools more flexibly increases the ability to provide high-quality, small-batch, varied, and tailored products and eventually improves productivity, quality, speed, and convenience (Piore and Sabel, 1984; Adler, 1988).

The dynamic of automation is entirely different in the new economy than it was in mass production. Employers wedded to old habits of mind are tempted to deploy the new technology to reduce labor costs, not realizing the importance of the new competitive standards. These employers are competing in the old economy, not the new one, in which flexible technologies are raising the ante on general skill requirements. Generally, the new automation eliminates or subsumes repetitive intellectual tasks in much the same way previous mechanization eliminated or took over repetitive physical tasks. For every task surrendered, however, new responsibilities are generated for exploiting the flexible capabilities of the technology. Moreover, the more flexible and powerful the machinery, the more employees, work teams, and organizations must increase their skills to deploy it.

Of course, not all employees benefit from the new technology. Some existing tasks and responsibilities are eliminated, some are subsumed, and others are added. Typically, technical change in manufacturing has harmed middle-aged machine operators in the Midwest and has helped younger technicians and service personnel in trade-sensitive coastal economies. In services, the new technology has reduced opportunities for office personnel who record, store, update, and transmit information and increased opportunities for front-office service workers. Moreover, the progress of technical change is rarely smooth. Partial automation can create low-skilled jobs that offer little opportunity for upward mobility while they last and little transferable human capital when they are eliminated. For instance, the partial automation of phone service has reduced skill requirements for operators and increased electronic monitoring of their work.

Our inability to appreciate and respond fully to the skill requirements of new technologies in the new economy is compounded by our limited definitions of skill. Skill is not a homogeneous commodity. Work skills can be sorted loosely into two broad categories: skills related to technical complexity and skills related to scope of action.

Technical Complexity. Skills associated with the technical complexity of work are the hard bits of knowledge and physical movements necessary to perform specific tasks. The machinist, for instance, combines a basic knowledge of computation and hand-to-eye coordination, deepening these skills over long periods of time until achieving the expert status of tool and die maker.

Skills associated with technical complexity are those most immediately affected by automation. The mass production economy reduced dexterity to simple physical movements to be mimicked by machines. Information technology goes a step further, reducing repetitive thought processes or branching logic to software. In the new economy, the role of technology is increasing in a broad array of jobs. At the same time, however, this economy seems to be demanding a higher level of technical complexity in the human role in a growing proportion of jobs. For instance, in the traditional mass production workplace, the machinist had to have depth of skill, principally in hand-to-eye coordination. In the manufacturing workplace of the new economy, the technician who substitutes for the machinist needs skills involving much greater technical complexity. He or she also needs better reading and writing skills to learn and communicate in an environment where the pace of change is faster, products are more varied, and there is a premium on speedy innovation and response times. Finally, the modern technician needs broader math skills than the traditional machinist in order to work with flexible technologies based on arithmetic and branching logic and to monitor the quality of output with mathematically based readouts.

Some increases in the technical complexity of human work result from learning requirements peculiar to particular employer institutions. Each employer's technologies, human-machine combinations, and products are unique. Technical changes resulting in new work processes and procedures require constant updating of employer-specific technical knowledge. Variety in a product requires greatly expanded product knowledge. The proliferation of computer-based technology also increases the need for understanding in-house software.

Scope of Action. A job's scope of action is usually indicated by the range of activities involved in getting the job done effectively. The growing technical complexity of a job generally requires a greater depth of skills, whereas the expanding scope of action of a job requires greater breadth of skills. To continue the previous example, the manufacturing technician has assumed an expanded scope of responsibility for productivity, quality, and speed not only at his or her assigned workstation but also upstream and downstream in the work process. The technician has also assumed responsibility for deploying technology flexibly to produce a greater variety and a more tailored set of products. In order to manage the greater scope of action on the job, the technician needs a broader set of skills than the machinist. To operate beyond his or her work station, for example, the technician needs a new set of interpersonal and organizational skills. To cope with change and variety, he or she needs learning and problem-solving skills.

The human scope of action, which can expand or contract as a result of technical change, can usually be measured by the extent to which a job unifies the design, execution, and control of the work. Scope of action was extensive in the jobs of the craft economy. In the mass production economy, scope of action was extensive for white-collar and technical personnel but not for workers down the line. The mass production economy shattered the unity of work for the sake of efficiency. In the new economy, scope of action is expanded to exploit more flexible technologies and to satisfy more intense and expanding competitive requirements. The unity of design, execution, and control is returning.

Other Changing Dimensions of Skill in the New Economy

Depth and breadth are not the only dimensions of skill that are changing. The context in which skills are used is changing too. Skills in the emerging economy are increasingly peripheral to hands-on work. Moreover, this context is shifting skills from repetitive applications to more sporadic and exceptional uses. In addition, it is shifting skill requirements from job-specific to more general capabilities, from "harder" concrete skills to "softer" more abstract skills, and from objective capabilities to more personal skills. Finally, skill requirements are beginning to converge as they become less job specific and are utilized in more fluid contexts. More and more of us spend our time at work doing the same sorts of things.

From Hands On to Hands Off

As technology subsumes more and more of the hands-on and repetitive aspects of work, human labor becomes more peripheral to the actual fabrication of goods and the delivery of services. In manufacturing, for instance, our traditional team on the factory floor included a machinist, a maintenance person, a laborer, a materials handler, an assembler, and a supervisor. Each of these workers had a hands-on relationship with materials as they moved through the production process. The machinist transformed the shapes or states of materials or parts. The maintenance person adjusted and maintained the machinery by manipulating its parts. The laborer and materials handler transferred work pieces from work site to work site. The assembler put the pieces together. The supervisor monitored the work flow, balancing output at sequential workstations to avoid bottlenecks.

Today a single technician who works with more powerful automated technology can replace all these employees. The technician works through control boards and software in a hands-off relationship with the product. He or she programs and maintains information-based technologies that have taken over all the other hands-on tasks of the old working team, with the possible exception of maintenance.

As technology subsumes hands-on tasks, manufacturing institutions shed direct labor. Fewer employees are involved in hands-on production, but more are dedicated to service functions peripheral to the production process. The challenge to manufacturing skill in the new economy is not so much to make the widget but to make it with quality and variety, to tailor it for the consumer, to deliver state-of-the-art versions of it quickly and conveniently, and to win the race up the learning curve to improve the widget. The labor and skill involved in these processes have less and less to do with hands-on production.

The peripheralization of labor is also characteristic of services in the new economy. Labor-intensive tasks associated with collecting, recording, analyzing, and communicating information are increasingly subsumed in information-based or communications technology. As a result, service employees spend more time face-to-face with co-workers or clients, designing and performing an expanded variety of services tailored to clients' needs and delivered conveniently.

The banking industry is a good example. In the bank of the 1950s, most of the human capital was utilized to collect, analyze, and process information. Frontline personnel, principally tellers, were ciphers who passed customer information back to mainframe data-processing centers. A complex hierarchy of administrative control and work rules ensured the integrity of financial information and bank services. At the middle and top of the hierarchy were bank officers, who sifted and assessed financial information to make deliberate and responsible decisions. Face-to-face customization of services was rare apart from the essentially passive role of the tellers and was provided by officers located only in the middle and upper ranges of the bank hierarchy.

In the financial services institutions of the new economy, in contrast, frontline personnel armed with new information and communications technology work face-to-face with customers to fashion tailored financial service packages. The central collection, recording, analysis, and communication of financial information that so preoccupied the bank of the 1950s has changed radically. Information technology has been "distributed" throughout the organization. The traditional flow of information from the customer to the back room data-processing operation and up the organizational hierarchy has been deemphasized. Instead, a shared information network moves information to the interface with the customer or other operational pressure points as necessary. The bank's varied products have been incorporated in user friendly software that is invisible to the financial service worker and customer, who work together to tailor offerings to the customer's specific needs.

From Specific to General

As new technology automates the tedious and repetitive physical and mental tasks of nearly every job and work becomes more peripheral to hands-on functions, skill requirements become less job specific and more general. At the most personal level, the ability to adapt to a changing variety of products and situations requires self-possession born of self-esteem and the ability to set goals and motivate oneself to achieve them. Flexibility in the varied and changing environments of the new economy also requires a solid foundation in reading, writing, and computational skills, as well as the capacity to learn, solve problems, and be creative. The expanded scope of action on the job requires an ability to juggle a variety of responsibilities and tasks.

Organizational formats typical of the new economy also require general skills. The substitution of flexible networks for top-down hierarchies means employees need interpersonal skills to get along with customers and co-workers, listening and oral communication skills to ensure effective interaction, negotiation and teamwork skills to be effective members of working groups, leadership skills to move work teams forward, and organizational skills to utilize effectively the work processes, procedures, and culture of the employer institution (Carnevale, Gainer, and Meltzer, 1989; Carnevale, Gainer, and Meltzer, 1990). More flexible organizational formats in combination with more powerful and flexible technologies also grant individual employees greater autonomy at work. Employees need sufficient self-management, goal-setting, and motivational skills to handle this new autonomy.

The more flexible organizational formats also tend to reduce job security. At best, employers can guarantee employment security but not job security. At worst, employees will have to change employers and jobs frequently throughout their careers. As a result, employees need the general skills necessary to move among jobs and to take responsibility for their own personal and career development.

From Concrete to Abstract

Skill requirements are also shifting from the concrete to the abstract (Bailey, 1988b; Adler, 1988; Zuboff, 1988). Increasingly, jobs require workers to spend more time sitting in front of computer screens grappling with abstractions or interacting with colleagues, suppliers, or customers.

As the scope of responsibility expands and work becomes more of a hands-off affair, the individual worker must be able to conceptualize goods and services and understand the impact of his or her work on production and service processes. In such an environment, former physical tasks become mental tasks and thinking becomes procedural. As work becomes more abstract, higher-order conceptual skills become more important, as do communication skills for making the abstract more concrete.

From Self-Sufficient to Social

In the mass market economy, employees were largely responsible for their own work effort and the technical quality of their own output. In the new economy, human responsibilities are being reintegrated at higher levels: Individual workers are responsible for the integrity of whole work processes and final goods and services (Adler, 1988). Employees now need specialized competencies but also more holistic skills such as self-management and interpersonal skills.

In the new economy, jobs are more social. The decline of hierarchy and the growing importance of informal networks, the substitution of continuous processes and shared information for sequential work processes, the increasing interaction with co-workers and customers all increase the importance of social interaction at work. Like craft workers, employees in the new economy are concerned with broad aspects or the totality of the work process. But unlike autonomous craft workers, employees in the new economy are members of working teams. Both the shoemaker and the computer programmer have highly developed technical skills, but the context in which these workers operate is entirely different. For the computer programmer and a growing share of workers, work is a collective process. Each individual's effort has a reciprocal effect on the efforts of others. In tightly integrated just-in-time manufacturing or extractive industries, one technician's mistake can affect all other workers. In service functions, incorrect data entry by one employee pollutes the data base for everybody else.

As employees become more interdependent, social skills become more important. The technical knowledge necessary to perform a task must be accompanied by the more complex capability for assuming roles in the context of a group. The fundamental social skill is the ability to manage oneself. Self-esteem is the taproot to effective management and successful interaction with others. Self-awareness is also critical to self-management. Employees need to understand their limits, ability to cope, and impact on others. The ability to set goals and motivate oneself to achieve is critical to being a team member; lack of motivation or goal-setting skills can create an undercurrent that undermines team accomplishments.

As the frequency of personal interaction with co-workers and customers increases, the ability to communicate also becomes crucial: Employees must be able to listen and to express themselves orally and in writing. If individuals are to be effective in groups, they need good interpersonal, negotiation, and teamwork skills. Interpersonal skills include the ability to judge the appropriateness of behavior and to cope with undesirable behavior, stress, and ambiguity. Negotiation skills include the ability to manage and to defuse potentially harmful disagreements. Teamwork skills include the ability to cope with and understand the value of team members' different work styles, cultures, and personalities and to provide and accept feedback constructively.

As work becomes more of a social process, the ability to influence co-workers also becomes more important. Influencing skills include both organizational effectiveness and leadership skills. Each organization is a bastion of implicit and explicit power structures. To be effective inside the organization, the employee needs to understand both. Without this understanding, leadership skills are misplaced; they can even be counterproductive if they become barriers to strategic organizational goals or positive change processes. At its most elementary level, leadership is the ability to influence other people. As group processes increase in importance, leadership skills become critical for every employee from the chief executive to the line worker.

From Repetition to Exceptions

Because the reach of technology is taking over repetitive work functions, human capital is used more and more to handle exceptions to routine production and service delivery. People are called upon less often, but the technical complexity of the required work can be extensive. For this reason and because of the expanded scope of action characteristic of work in the new economy, workers must have technical expertise they can apply as needed in exceptional circumstances. Like the sentry, the employee in the new economy uses this expertise rarely, but if the skills are not there when needed, the consequences are disastrous. For example, as explained earlier, the modern manufacturing technician in combination with more powerful and flexible technology replaces several other employees who used to make up the old assembly-line team in low-tech manufacturing. The technology actually performs most of the tasks, but the technician is responsible for deploying, monitoring, and problem solving when necessary. As a result, the technician needs a greater breadth and depth of skill than did the traditional manufacturing employee, whose work was more routine and repetitive.

White-collar and technical elites, on the other hand, have always been required to have reserve skills that are more highly technical and broader than everyday skills. Amply educated and assigned to jobs that demand competence in a constantly changing variety of situations, they learn to juggle changing assignments, adapt to changing demands, and tailor actions to the specifics of the situation at hand. Although managers neither hire nor fire very often, they need to be able to perform these functions flexibly and competently when called upon to do so. Technical elites are not asked for new ideas very often, but they need a reservoir of skills to dip into when creative leaps are required. The critical difference in the new economy is that both elites and nonsupervisory workers need a reservoir of skills that are more highly technical and broader than those routinely required on the job.

The industrial worker, for instance, often spends long periods of time monitoring abstract representations of work processes on computer screens or electronic control boards. Yet the industrial sentry is asked to do much more than stand, watch, and wait. He or she needs sufficient reserve skills to adapt to technical and work process changes, recognize and respond to anomalies, maintain and repair the equipment, and occasionally reprogram technologies to produce variety and customize products. Moreover, the industrial sentry must be alert and able to capture quality and efficiency improvements and to develop new applications.

Service workers, like industrial workers, need robust reserve skills in order to cope with change, tailor service, handle exceptions, and use their experience on the job to develop ideas for improving the company's performance. They also need to interact closely with customers. For example, it is relatively simple to operate a cash register, but providing good customer service requires more. In the financial, real estate, and insurance markets, every customer is an exception to the rule in terms of marketing, selling, and packaging. Similarly, education workers must respond to students' different learning styles, and health care workers must treat a wide variety of medical problems.

What kinds of skills do employees need to handle a growing list of unprecedented situations at work? First, they need the intellectual and emotional flexibility necessary to adapt to change and dissimilar situations. Central to flexibility is the ability to learn — to keep abreast of changes, to know what needs to be learned, and to learn it without disrupting performance. Second, because of constantly changing situations, employees must be able to cope with ambiguity. Finally, problem-solving ability and creativity also are important because novel situations are constantly arising (Carnevale, Gainer, and Meltzer, 1989).

Skill Convergence

In the new economy, both jobs and the skills they require are becoming more alike. As the preceding discussion indicates,

Table 8. Characteristics of People at Work in Typical Production and Service Delivery Systems.

Characteristics	Preindustrial Crafts	Typical Production and Service Delivery Systems					Independent Sector	New Economy
		Mass Production			Service			
		White-collar workers, technical professionals	Skilled trades people	Blue-collar production employees	White-collar workers, service professionals	Nonsupervisory employees		
Typical Workers	Artisans	White-collar workers, technical professionals	Skilled trades people	Blue-collar production employees	White-collar workers, service professionals	Nonsupervisory employees	Small business craft and professional workers	Teams of individuals alternating expert, brokering, and leadership roles
Independence at Work	Autonomous, self-employed	*Discretion dependent on assignment in organizational hierarchies*					Independent and often self employed	Individuals and work teams autonomous but mutually dependent in networks
		Broadly assigned	Broadly assigned in technical domain	Narrowly assigned to specific tasks	Broadly assigned	Narrowly assigned		
Source of Rewards	Membership in the guild community	Time and grade in job assignment					Certification and entrepreneurial ability	Performance of teams and networks
Source of Job Security	Membership in the guild	Longevity with a particular employer in a particular job category					Certification and entrepreneurial ability	Skills, experience, and career development

Skill Require-ments	Deep occupa-tional skills	Deep occupational skills, as well as broad group effectiveness, adaptability, and organizational skills	Deep technical skills, problem-solving skills	Narrow job-specific skills	Broad adaptability skills, inter-personal and organi-zational skills	Narrow job-specific skills, inter-personal skills	Deep occupational skills, personal management and adaptability skills	Deep technical skills, as well as learning, com-munication, adaptability, personal management, group effective-ness, and influencing skills
Use of Skills at Work	Hands on/concrete; specific and repetitive skills	Hands off/abstract; reserves of technical and nontechnical skills for handling exceptions	Hands on/concrete; reserves of technical skills for handling exceptions	Hands on/concrete; job-specific and repetitive skills	Hands off/abstract; broad and deep reserve skills	Hands on/concrete; job-specific and repetitive skills	Mix of hands-on and hands-off skills; reserve skills for handling exceptions	Hands off/abstract; general skills, reserves of technical and nontechnical skills for handling exceptions

there is a trend for required skills to be hands off, general, abstract, personal in content, and applied in the context of groups and unusual situations. In addition, the expansion in service functions in manufacturing and natural resource industries, in combination with the increasing dominance of the service sector, ensures that a growing proportion of employees need the broad, abstract, flexible skills typically required in service jobs.

Skill convergence is driven from the top down and the bottom up. There is a compression of skills as supervisors, managers, and technical personnel surrender autonomy to nonsupervisory workers and as nonsupervisory employees take on more general assignments. The need to provide tailored goods and services conveniently and to design and install incremental improvements and new applications drives elite managerial and technical functions down the line because frontline workers are best situated to perform these functions. The more flexible and powerful technologies also free up nonsupervisory labor for more general responsibilities. Moreover, to take advantage of these technologies, employers are developing more flexible work processes, resulting in further increases in autonomy down the line. Table 8 summarizes characteristics of people at work in typical production and delivery systems.

Chapter Eight

SIXTEEN JOB SKILLS
CRUCIAL TO SUCCESS

The discussion thus far has enumerated a variety of skills required of workers in the new economy. This chapter discusses these skills one by one, in each case defining the skill and answering these questions: Why is the skill important in the new economy? What is its curriculum? What constitutes competence in the skill?

Learning to Learn

Foundation Skills. Knowing how to learn is the most basic of all skills because it is the key that unlocks future success. Learning to learn involves knowing the principles and methods that allow us to perform in three domains: (1) in the cognitive domain, we need skills to collect, know, and comprehend information; (2) in the psychomotor domain, we need skills to control our bodies in order to accomplish tasks; and (3) in the affective domain, we need skills to know, understand, and respond to feelings and behaviors.

Once an individual learns how to learn, he or she can achieve competency in all other basic workplace skills. Learning skills are required in order to respond flexibly and quickly to technical and organizational change; to make continuous improvements in quality, efficiency, and speed; and to develop new applications for existing technologies, goods, and services.

Learning to learn curricula include procedures for self-assessment, exposure to alternative learning styles, and training specific to the work context in which learning needs to occur. Specifically, these curricula should do the following:

- Identify personal learning styles, capabilities, and sensory preferences (seeing, hearing, or feeling) with testing instruments such as the Myers-Briggs Type Indicator, the Learning Styles Inventory, or the Memorize, Understand, and Do
- Develop awareness of cognitive, psychomotor, and affective learning strategies and tools
- Match the employee's job content and career trajectory to his or her learning needs by means of an instrument such as the Instructional Systems Design and Job Learning Analysis

Competence in learning includes demonstrated ability to assess what needs to be learned, to apply learning techniques, and to use new learning on the job. Employees must be able to conduct a learning needs assessment and demonstrate personal learning skills such as understanding their own learning styles and capabilities. Individuals must be able to demonstrate skill in the cognitive domain by organizing, relating, recalling, and evaluating knowledge; moving from knowing to understanding and applying knowledge; understanding how to think logically, divergently, critically, and intuitively; understanding alternative learning strategies and tools; and understanding how to mobilize and organize learning resources.

The learning process is ultimately cognitive and individual; but because learning in applied settings often involves interacting with others, employees must have a complementary set of interpersonal learning skills, including giving and receiving feedback, learning collaboratively, and using others as learning resources.

The Academic Basics: Reading, Writing, and Computation

Reading Skills. Workers need three levels of reading skills for success on the job: (1) basic literacy, the ability to decode and comprehend written material; (2) reading to do, the ability to utilize basic reading skills, short-term memory, and information processing to locate printed information for immediate use; and (3) reading to learn and reading to do, the ability to use basic literacy skills in conjunction with long-term memory and writing, computation, learning, adaptability, and job-specific skills in order to decode, problem solve, or troubleshoot.

On average, American workers spend from one and a half to two hours every working day reading forms, charts, manuals, electronic display screens, and general literature. In the new economy, reading skill requirements are increasing and deepening because the growing complexity and scale of global economic activity require more written communication. The expanding reach and complexity of electronic and organizational networks also require workers to have better reading skills to stay abreast of change, foster incremental improvements, and accelerate innovation. In addition, the infusion of information technologies requires more reading from operating and repair manuals and electronic screens.

A curriculum for reading on the job should be specific to the workplace in which the reading skills are to be used and in general should do the following:

- Develop basic literacy skills such as recognizing and understanding common job-related words and comprehending sentences and paragraphs
- Develop reading-to-do skills such as identifying details and specific actions in context, locating relevant information in context, and using charts, diagrams, and schematics

- Develop reading-to-learn skills such as synthesizing written information from several sources and inferring meaning from texts that do not explicitly provide the required information

Every American must be able to read at fourth-grade level to decode the simplest written information, such as warnings and traffic signs. Reading skill beyond this level provides improvements in comprehension and expands the number of words that the reader can decode. Whereas a fifth-grade reading level is the minimum necessary to qualify for military service, substantial evidence suggests that a fifth-grade reading level is less than adequate for work.

About one-third of American workers— frontline employees working at the point of production and service delivery and at the interface with customers, machine operators, and service workers— need to read at the eighth-grade level to comprehend work orders, forms, and manuals.

Another third— skilled workers, craft workers, manufacturing technicians, health care technologists, secretaries, and computer programmers— need to read beyond the eighth-grade level, probably at the average level of people with two years of postsecondary education. These workers must be able to master complex manuals and other materials associated with their responsibilities at work and necessary for keeping up-to-date in their areas of technical expertise.

Another third of American workers— professionals, managers, and scientists— must be able to read at the college-graduate level. These employees need a higher level of reading competency to stay abreast of changing professional and technical information.

All workers must be able to apply their reading skills in the context of their task or job responsibility, for competency is measured by performance of a task rather than by direct tests of reading ability. At work, people decode forms, phrases, and abbreviated technical language, not the fully developed information they learned to read at school. Comprehension at work requires the ability to understand written cues. Therefore, standards for reading skills at work should be set after an assessment of the context in which these skills are to be applied. Evidence shows that individuals who participate in performance- and competency-based instruction achieve mastery when they demonstrate correct performance 75 percent to 80 percent of the time.

Writing Skills. Writing on the job involves a two-stage process: (1) prewriting, or selecting the topic, preparing, accessing, and organizing information; and (2) writing, including spelling, penmanship, reading, editing, and revising.

Rapid change and the growing complexity of information networks inside and outside organizations require better writing skills from a growing share of American workers. Although the average employee spends only 8.4 percent of his or her communicating time writing, he or she most often uses writing at critical junctures in the work process. Written communications become part of a relatively permanent information base; they are shared and used to inform and guide people inside and outside organizations over time. Inaccurate or unclear writing can pollute the shared information base and affect the quality and efficiency of work upstream and down.

Work-related writing curricula are unlike those of the traditional classroom, which focus on creativity and full development of thoughts in essays. Curricula for writing at work emphasize a distillation of information in formats that sometimes ignore the academic standards for quality and grammar. An effective work-related writing curriculum should do the following:

- Develop writing skills oriented toward applications and job performance
- Provide exercises on transferring information, such as writing key words and standardized sentences and entering information on forms
- Provide exercises on recording actions and transactions, identifying the intent of the writing and understanding the

reading audience, outlining sequences and structures, and providing brief, accurate, and clear descriptions

The essential standards for writing at work are brevity, clarity, and accuracy. Most writing on the job involves transcribing key terms and standard sentences: 42 percent involves filling out prepared forms; 25 percent requires recording, summarizing, or using language peculiar to specific occupations and jobs; 23 percent involves writing memos and letters; and only 10 percent is dedicated to writing academic-style reports and articles. An individual's mastery of writing on the job, therefore, is tied to work-related competencies.

Computational Skills. Five elements of computational skill are required at work: (1) quantification, or the ability to read and write numbers, put numbers in sequence, and recognize whether one number is larger or smaller than another; (2) computation, or the ability to add, subtract, multiply, and divide; (3) measurement and estimation, or the ability to measure time, distance, length, volume, height, weight, velocity, and speed and to use such measurements; (4) quantitative comprehension, or the ability to organize data into quantitative formats; and (5) quantitative problem solving, or the ability to recognize and set up a problem and compute the answer.

New organizational, competitive, and technical requirements at work require higher computational skill levels. Flexible and decentralized organizations and networks are becoming integrated by complex, shared information systems that rely on quantitative measures of markets, performance, and quality. Goods and services are increasingly customized, requiring employees to constantly reset quantities and dimensions for production and delivery. New flexible technologies and software require mathematical skill if one is to utilize their logically patterned capabilities fully.

Almost 75 percent of Americans are computationally literate. They know how to quantify, compute, and measure, but many cannot apply what they know. As a result, workplace computational skills are best taught in an applied fashion. In school, mathematics is taught as an end in itself, as a sequence of operations from the simplest to most complex, followed by drill and practice on the mathematical operations themselves. Tests are standardized and emphasize proficiency in separate operations. At work, computational skills focus less on the correct performance of mathematical operations and more on using math to solve problems. An effective curriculum should therefore emphasize selection and use of mathematical operations to solve particular work-related problems and contextual examples of possible job situations.

Although computational skills for work do not correspond neatly to academic grade equivalents, there are some rough rules of thumb. Most workers must be competent in basic operations—addition, multiplication, subtraction, and division—at about the eighth-grade level. This group includes managers, nontechnical professionals, health care workers, machine operators, and service workers—about 80 percent of all American workers. Another 15 percent—including technicians, technologists, and craft and data-processing workers—need computational skills roughly at the level of a few years of postsecondary schooling. The remaining 5 percent—technical managers, accountants, engineers, economists, and other technical professionals—need computational skills at or beyond the college-graduate level.

Ultimately, grade equivalents are only clues to job-related needs. The requirements vary by occupation, although all employees should be able to organize information into quantitative formats, select appropriate computational tools, and recognize errors resulting from inappropriate use of quantitative operations. Competency standards and assessments should be based on performance standards and reflect current and future job needs.

Communication: Speaking and Listening

In the new economy, workers spend most of the day engaged in some form of communication. Reading and writing are essential communication tools, but it is through listening and speaking that people interact most frequently at work. The average worker spends 8.4 percent of his or her communication time at work writing, 13.3 percent reading, 23.0 percent speaking, and 55.0 percent listening (Carnevale, Gainer, and Meltzer, 1990).

The competitive standards of the new economy require effective communication skills. For instance, to ensure high quality, employees must take responsibility for final goods and services, which means they must be able to communicate with others throughout the work process. New standards for speed and reduced cycle time require quick and informal communication. Variety and customization require adaptable communication to switch from one good or service design to the next. Improvements in customer service also require effective communication skills, as do new organizational formats and technologies. Flexible networks rely on communication in order to integrate work efforts effectively. As new technologies take on repetitive physical and intellectual tasks, employees will spend more time communicating with co-workers and customers.

Speaking Skills. The speaking skills needed on the job can be broken down into three areas: (1) nonverbal skills, or body language and appearance, which deliver 55 percent of the meaning in face-to-face communication; (2) vocal skills, or rate, pitch, and loudness, which transmit 38 percent of the message in face-to-face communication and 70 percent to 90 percent of the message over the telephone; and (3) verbal skills, or language, which transmits only 7 percent of the message but tends to be worth more later, when the listener gets past nonverbal and vocal characteristics in the communication process.

A curriculum for speaking should accomplish the following:

- Build awareness of individual communication style by using the Myers Introduction to Type (MITT), Performax's Personal Matrix System (PPMS), and the Communication Skills Self-Assessment Exam (CSSAE)
- Develop the ability to value different communication styles by participation in group exercises

- Develop the ability to adjust speaking style to meet the demands of different work situations by participation in group exercises and role playing

Competence in speaking includes (1) the ability to get a point across in a way that has a desired impact on others; (2) the ability to use available instruments (MITT, PPMS, CSSAE) for tracking individual progress, setting performance goals, and deepening self-awareness; and (3) the ability to obtain and use formal and informal feedback from superiors, peers, and customers as a means of measuring competence and progress.

Listening Skills. Listening skills on the job involve receiving and assigning meaning to aural stimuli.

There is a distinct curriculum for listening skills:

- Develop awareness of alternative listening styles by means of the Sequential Test of Educational Progress (STEP), the Watson-Barker Listening Test (WBLT), the Attitudinal Listening Profile System (ALPS), or the CAUSE for Listening (CAUSE)
- Assess individual listening style
- Develop the ability to reduce environmental and interpersonal barriers to effective listening at work
- Develop the skill of listening actively

Competence in listening can be measured by means of formal and informal feedback from superiors, peers, and customers and from listening tests such as the STEP, WBLT, ALPS, or CAUSE.

Adaptability: Problem Solving and Creativity

An organization's ability to overcome barriers to achieve productivity and quality improvements, to develop new applications for existing technologies and goods and services, and to manage variety and customization of goods and services depends on the problem-solving and creative abilities of its employees. New flexible organizational formats require equally flexible workers and work teams capable of solving problems on their own. Moreover, as technology takes over repetitive work, employees spend more of their time using their problem-solving and creativity skills to handle exceptions to routine mental and physical tasks.

Problem-Solving Skills. Problem solving is the ability to bridge the gap between what is and what ought to be. Problem-solving skills include the ability to recognize and define problems, invent and implement solutions, and track and evaluate results.

The curriculum for problem solving includes developing knowledge of one's own problem-solving style and capabilities, exploring alternative problem-solving styles, and learning problem-solving techniques to be used individually and in groups. A typical curriculum must do the following:

- Assess individual styles by means of the Myers-Briggs Type Indicator and the Herrmann Brain Dominance Instrument
- Teach the employee how to recognize, define, and organize problems by using (1) order, or the sequence and arrange-ment of things and ideas; (2) structure, or the connections between things and ideas; (3) relation, or how things and ideas interact; (4) level, or depth of focus; and (5) point of view
- Explore the types of thinking necessary for problem solving, such as (1) deduction, or moving from the general to the particular; (2) induction, or moving from the particular to the general; (3) lateral thinking, or thinking intuitively; (4) dialectical thinking, or holding conflicting points of view; (5) unfreezing (reframing), or accepting new points of view; and (6) critical-reflective thinking, or reflecting while doing
- Explore group processes and techniques, including (1) brain-storming, or sharing ideas; (2) synectics, or following a leader's directions; (3) nominal group techniques, such as working with a facilitator and peers; (4) systems and force field analysis, or reviewing a problem's context; (5) orienta-tion, or analyzing group problem-solving styles; and (6) con-

trolled orientation, or developing a group consensus on the statement of the problem

- Teach problem-solving processes, such as the Juran Model, the Friedman and Yarborough Comprehensive Model, the Workplace Basics Model, problem analysis, investigation of assumptions, and the sequence of identifying tentative solutions, evaluating alternative solutions, selecting and implementing a solution, and using feedback to modify that solution

Competence in problem solving requires an awareness of alternative problem-solving styles; the ability to recognize, define, and analyze problems; and familiarity with problem-solving tools as well as systematic individual and group processes for solving problems. Any test for problem-solving ability should be performance oriented and competency based. Ultimately, competency is measured by performance on the job.

Creativity Skills. The ability to solve problems involves a significant measure of creativity. Creativity is a continuum of thought and application that begins with creative thinking, which produces an untraditional or novel idea; moves on to inventiveness by turning a creative idea into a practical one; and ends with innovation by actually applying the idea to some facet of the work process.

Creativity curricula presume a depth of knowledge and experience in a particular subject area and teach the ability to reframe traditional patterns of thinking and doing. A curriculum for creativity should develop rational thinking skills as well as the ability to escape logical, sequential thought patterns by relying on intuitive knowledge.

Measures of competency in creativity should span the creativity continuum, covering creative thinking, inventiveness, and innovation.

Developmental Skills: Self-Esteem, Motivation and Goal Setting, and Personal and Career Development

Self-Esteem Skills. The self-esteem skills needed in the workplace are based on one's ability to maintain a realistic and positive self-

image. A positive self-image gives an individual a firm foundation from which to reach his or her maximum potential both on
and off the job. New standards for organizational performance,
increased personal autonomy, employee responsibility beyond
the formal work assignment, and the accelerating pace of
change in the workplace demand a strong, positive sense of self.
At the same time, self-esteem is necessary to manage the growing
amount of interaction with co-workers and customers.

A curriculum for self-esteem uses experience, reflection,
and counseling to help the employee build self-awareness—
including awareness of his or her own skills and abilities, impact
on others, and emotional capacity and personal needs—and a
positive and realistic self-image.

The skills that lead to greater self-esteem are highly personal and diverse. Therefore, competence can be only partially
measured by norm-referenced scales. Workers demonstrate
competency in self-esteem skills when they are willing to take
risks, assume responsibility and leadership, function successfully in an ambiguous and flexible environment, and follow
through on tasks.

Motivation and Goal-Setting Skills. Motivation at work involves
the ability to translate work into an instrument for the development of the self and the realization of one's potential. Goal
setting is the ability to set performance targets that are consistent with goals for personal development. Motivation and goal
setting are inextricably intertwined. Motivation inspires goal
setting, and goal setting clarifies and augments one's deepest
motivations.

Given the characteristics of the new economy already
outlined, employees are coming to realize that they must become more personally and actively engaged on the job and must
assume responsibility for motivating themselves and setting
goals. A curriculum for teaching motivation and goal setting
begins with individual self-assessment and ends with application in the work group. The usual curriculum sequence is as
follows:

- Develop an awareness of personal motivations and cognizance of appropriate goals
- Structure a hierarchy of goals (integrating short- and long-term goals as well as job-related and personal goals)
- Define strategic steps to reach goals
- Measure progress
- Develop an ability to negotiate goals with others
- Identify resources for setting goals
- Revise goals in light of new information and experience

A person demonstrates competence in motivation and goal setting in the ability over time to envision, set, and meet defined objectives; to become motivated by personal goals rather than goals set by others; to set realistic goals and understand obstacles; and to find the resources to overcome obstacles.

Personal and Career Development Skills. Personal and career development skills allow individuals to adapt to changing work requirements in a way that ensures employment security and fulfills personal potential.

As noted earlier, new requirements for competitive, organizational, and technical flexibility have reduced job stability. Employees should expect to have to change as job requirements change. Because lifetime employment in the same job or even with the same employer is no longer a realistic expectation, self-conscious personal and career development is central to employment security as well as individual development and career success.

The sequence of learning goals in personal and career development usually begins with a grounding in self-assessment and concludes with the development of a career strategy:

- Develop skills useful for finding a job, including self-assessment, reality testing, goal development, and job search competencies such as résumé writing
- Develop maturity skills for career development, such as integrative skills (reconciling self-assessment with work assign-

ments) and self-development skills (marketing oneself and using workplace resources for personal career development)
- Develop a career and personal development plan that includes a hierarchy of short- and long-term goals

Ultimately, competence in career development is demonstrated by the ability to take personal responsibility for career progress. To control and direct one's own career progress requires other competencies as well, including such skills as résumé writing and interviewing. A variety of instruments are available to test generic career skills. One such instrument is the Career Mastery Inventory.

Group Effectiveness: Interpersonal Skills, Negotiation, and Teamwork

Work is a group activity. Throughout the postwar era, economists have observed that a majority of productivity improvements result from the ability of work groups to use their human and technical capital more effectively to move up the learning curve. Meeting competitive standards other than productivity also depends on the effectiveness of work groups. For example, high quality is more than the sum of individual excellence. It requires successful interaction throughout the organization. Similarly, flexible and fast responses to customers also require effective teamwork. Flexible organizational formats and technologies increase the intensity and importance of group interactions at work. Whenever people work together, successful interaction depends on effective interpersonal skills, negotiation to resolve conflict, and teamwork.

Interpersonal Skills. Workers need interpersonal skills such as the ability to judge the appropriateness of behavior, cope with undesirable behavior, absorb stress, deal with ambiguity, share responsibility, and interact effectively with others.
    The curriculum for interpersonal skills is a sequential learning program delivered in a group setting and designed to accomplish the following:

- Assess interpersonal needs and styles through instruments such as the FIRO-B Scale
- Establish interpersonal credibility by conducting training in areas such as cross-cultural awareness and communication skills
- Encourage familiarity among group members and provide personal sharing exercises involving interviewing, active listening, values clarification, and nonverbal communication
- Build skills needed for forming attachments, such as skills in disclosure, process observation, giving feedback, and oral communication
- Develop role clarification skills through exercises in role negotiation and goal setting

Competence is generally measured by the subjective evaluation of people who interact with the employee. Assessment should focus on the extent to which the employee is positive and proactive in group settings.

Negotiation Skills. Negotiation skills enable employees to overcome disagreements by compromising with, accommodating, and collaborating with others.

A curriculum for negotiation uses a variety of group exercises and techniques to do the following:

- Develop awareness, problem-solving, and communication skills by separating subjective personalities from objective problems
- Explore problem-solving techniques for establishing individual and common interests among stakeholders involved in negotiation
- Develop problem-solving, interpersonal, and creativity skills to invent options for mutual gain
- Show how to develop objective criteria for evaluating personal interests and available options

Competency in negotiation skills includes the proven ability to assess individual negotiation styles and demonstrated knowledge of negotiation techniques. Peers, supervisors, and customers can provide assessments of an employee's negotiation skills and effectiveness.

Teamwork Skills. Teamwork skills relate to the ability of groups to pool human talents to pursue common goals.

The curriculum for teamwork concentrates on individual abilities usually learned best in structured work groups. It uses exercises focused on the needs of the group to accomplish the following:

- Assess individual and team capabilities
- Establish, clarify, and communicate team goals
- Develop the ability to plan and set performance standards
- Provide feedback, coaching, and motivation

A competent team makes maximum use of the human talents available to pursue shared goals. Competence includes both awareness of team concepts and teamwork skills. It can be assessed by outcome measures of team efforts, including productivity, quality, flexibility, and speed, and review of team performance by peers and customers.

Influencing Skills: Organizational Effectiveness and Leadership

Organizational Effectiveness Skills. Organizational effectiveness skills needed on the job include the ability to work productively in the context of explicit and implicit organizational cultures and subcultures.

An organization is a maze of explicit and implicit power structures and cultures. Understanding how to operate within this maze is the key to peak performance in the new economy. Networks driven by common goals and information are supplanting both rigid hierarchies and fragmented structures, and workers need strong organizational skills to participate effectively in such networks. Because of increasing independence on the job, workers also need organizational skills to align their own efforts and goals with those of the organization and thereby minimize friction and wasted effort.

The curriculum for organizational effectiveness teaches an appreciation of institutional cultures, explores organizational limits and opportunities, and actively includes the trainee as a member and owner of the organization. Specifically, the curriculum should do the following:

- Provide the employee with an understanding of what organizations are, why they exist, and how one can navigate in the complex social waters of varying types of organizational structures
- Expose the employee to the organizational structure of his or her employer and industry network, discussing goals, values, culture, and traditional modes of operation
- Train the employee in interpersonal, group effectiveness, and communication skills

Competence in organizational effectiveness includes a demonstrated awareness of organizational types and of skills and behaviors that encourage alignment between the organization and employees and a demonstrated awareness of the implicit and explicit structures in the employee's own organization and industry network. Competence further includes a knowledge of relevant skills, such as communication, personal management, and group effectiveness skills, and how to use them. Mastery is best measured by performance-oriented, competency-based instruments. More generic instruments such as the Career Mastery Inventory can be useful for making initial assessments and charting progress. Assessments by co-workers, customers, and superiors are also useful.

Leadership Skills. Leadership skills in the workplace involve influencing others to serve the strategic purpose of an organization or the developmental needs of an individual.

The pace of change and the competitive standards in the new economy require workers to assume leadership roles beyond their own formal assignments. Moreover, the new economic environment requires adaptability in leadership roles; every person at every level of an organization may need to assume a leadership role at one time or another, depending on the requirements of the task at hand. In addition, the growing utilization of more flexible technologies and organizational networks is creating more fluid work processes that demand spontaneous leadership.

A curriculum for leadership should do the following:

- Develop an awareness of leadership approaches
- Develop leadership skills, such as personal management, group effectiveness, adaptability, and influencing skills
- Develop leadership behaviors, such as developing and communicating a vision, developing commitment, inspiring effort, and modeling appropriate behaviors (for example, taking risks, being consistent, being trustworthy, showing respect for others, and tolerating ambiguity)

At its most elementary level, leadership is the demonstrated ability to influence others to act. Competence is demonstrated by an awareness and application of leadership theories and associated skills and is subjectively assessed by peers, customers, and superiors.

Part Four

STRATEGIES FOR
COMPETITIVE SUCCESS

Chapter Nine

ORGANIZATIONAL STRATEGIES
FOR MEETING THE NEW
COMPETITIVE STANDARDS

Both the popular and the professional media resound with a clarion call to the new economy. The new competitive standards are already embedded in our everyday imagery and vocabulary. Winners of the Malcom Baldrige National Quality Award remind us of their worthiness with pomp and circumstance normally reserved for royalty. The public is bombarded with organizational claims to variety, customization, convenience, and timeliness. Both business and professional literature champion methods for promoting elusive goals such as excellence, product integrity, teamwork, and multicultural awareness. The simple "great power" arithmetic that governed America's involvement in the world since the end of the Second World War has given way to a more complex ideological, cultural, and military equation driven by the calculus of the new standards of economic competition.

We judge all our organizations—public, private, and military—according to the new set of competitive standards. Gov-

185

ernmental institutions once preoccupied with expanding access to public services are now being measured by the new standards, which emphasize results. In public education, the focus is no longer on the right to free education through high school but on demands for high-quality education flexibly tailored to the learning styles of individual students. Even our military institutions are not exempt from the new competitive standards. Flexibility and speed of deployment in response to global crisis challenge our accustomed view of the American military as the bastion of waste and inefficiency.

The words differ but everywhere the music is the same. We share a common vision of the new economy and its competitive standards. We all know the organizations and goods and services of the new economy when we see them. We all know where we need to go. Our difficulty is in getting there. The remainder of this book provides perspectives and advice on how to get beyond the embattled standard of the old economy in order to embrace the new competitive reality. This chapter provides an analysis of requirements for meeting the new competitive standards.

Productivity: The Old-Time Religion

The pursuit of productivity has been the driving force in economic history to date. Ultimately, productivity performance determines a nation's ability to generate wealth. In the year 700, productivity rates produced material wealth at subsistence levels—about $200 per capita in 1980 dollars. Productivity improved at less than 0.1 percent annually over the next ten centuries. By 1700, productivity in European nations generated about $600 per capita in material wealth measured in 1980 dollars. Although productivity accelerated after 1700, the most dramatic improvements occurred after 1870, when industrial nations consistently averaged productivity improvements of about 2 percent per annum. The cumulative effect of the improvements between 1870 and 1980 increased output per worker by a multiple of seven in Britain, twelve in the United

States, and twenty-six in Japan (Baumol, Blackman, and Wolff, 1989).

Minor variations in productivity performance can have an enormous impact on relative economic standing if the differences accumulate over the long term. Over the past hundred years, British productivity increased slightly below trend. The British were able to increase living standards fourfold and cut working hours almost in half, yet they lost ground relative to the productivity leaders. British workers began the period earning one and a half times as much as workers on the Continent and in the United States and ended the period earning two-thirds the wages of other industrialized nations (Baumol, Blackman, and Wolff, 1989).

Just as productivity performance determines the absolute and relative economic welfare of nations, it is also the original free lunch. Productivity improvements allow a nation to use the same or fewer resources to create new wealth that can then be used to pay for social improvements, income redistribution, and other cultural and political goals without making anyone worse off. Arguably, the ability of market economies to mobilize the productivity dividend to create the modern welfare state accounts for the victory of liberal democracies first over monarchies and lately over fascist and communist forms of social organization.

Productivity is both the emblem and the measure of economic status and progress. But productivity statistics by themselves are just another way of keeping score. They tell us how we are doing and who is winning the economic competition but reveal nothing about how to improve our performance. The United States has not maintained its productivity lead since the midnineteenth century entirely by accident. Yet the perspectives, strategies, and tactics that have made us the world's longest-running productivity leader are becoming shopworn and outdated, especially in the face of the new economy's more stringent and complex competitive demands.

An assessment of the implicit and explicit elements of the American productivity strategy suggests two basic weaknesses: First, our accustomed perspectives on productivity overemphasize short-term cost savings over long-term investment. All too often, we meet our productivity goals with "lean and mean" tactics that leave us too anemic to meet the new robust competitive standards. Second, our financial strategies overemphasize the manipulation of aggregate levels of savings and investment and pay too little attention to complex innovative processes in the workaday world of the real economy. Money helps, but it cannot buy productivity. Innovation at work assures productivity and attracts savings available for investment worldwide.

Gaining Perspective. The first step in building a successful productivity strategy is the most difficult. We need to change the way we think about productivity. We need to change our perspective on productivity goals from the short to the long run. Productivity makes all the difference but only in the long run. Short-run fluctuations are impressive but transitory. Recent negative productivity rates in the United States and double-digit improvements in Japan are cases in point. However, over time productivity moves at a snail's pace and even the double-digit productivity performance of the Japanese over the past decade will not allow them to catch us soon.

Minor variations in productivity performance make all the difference in the long haul because productivity gains are cumulative. Sustained productivity growth is the gradual process of building productive capacity. It is an evolutionary process that gathers momentum over time. Properly nurtured, a nation's or an organization's productive capacity will generate increasing productivity returns as capacity increases and advantage creates still greater advantage.

What accounts for the evolutionary changes in productive capacity? The first crucial ingredient is innovation, the ability to get more out of the existing stock of knowledge and other assets. Economists have consistently demonstrated that the ability to make process improvements that utilize the current stock of human and machine capital more effectively accounts for a persistent 60 percent of improvements in productive capacity (Denison, 1974; Baumol, Blackman, and Wolff, 1989).

The second critical ingredient in the evolution of productive capacity is investment, which embodies innovative gains in the productive base of whole economies and individual organizations. Investment allows for the accumulation and dissemination of innovations. Innovation without subsequent investment and dissemination will at best lead to short-lived improvements in productive capacity. Thus, it is commonly argued that Britain's industrial decline is due to the failure of the British to invest in their workforces and organizations after securing an early lead in the industrial revolution with a burst of innovation (Baumol, Blackman, and Wolff, 1989; Mokyr, 1990).

The third crucial ingredient in the evolution of productive capacity is the mutual attraction between innovation and investment. The two appear to be mutually reinforcing. Investment encourages innovation. Conversely, innovation and an impressive productive capacity tend to attract investment. This opportunistic flow of investment occurs both within and among nations.

The dynamic relationship between investment and innovation encourages wide divergence in productivity in the short run and long-run stability and convergence in the productivity performance of nations. The evolutionary processes that account for convergence in productive capacity are reasonably well understood: Leaders secure an initial productivity edge through innovation. Innovation increases productivity and wealth beyond the historical experience and expectations of the consuming public. The result is a lag in consumption and an increase in savings available for further investment. Increased investments embed innovations in productive capacity. With high levels of innovation, low consumption, and high savings and investment, productive capacity continues to accumulate. As it does so, momentum builds and the leader surges ahead of the productivity pack. At some point, workers decide they want to consume a higher proportion of the fruits of their labor. Available savings and investment decline as workers pursue the good life, and work effort and innovation may also decline. Meanwhile the pack is always closing in. Followers are constantly converging on leaders by copying their innovation and investment patterns. Playing catch-up is easier than leading because copying is less wasteful and less risky than forging ahead. As a result, the rate of productivity improvement is usually greater among followers although their overall productivity levels are lower than those of the leaders. Eventually, the convergence process reduces the difference in overall productivity rates between leaders and followers and results in a more level playing field. Ultimately, productivity standards among nations begin to lose their meaning. Advantages in productive capacity become more specialized by industry and organized across national boundaries.

Strategic Implications. The fact that productive capacity evolves over the long term suggests that short-term productivity strategies are usually ineffective or transitory and possibly harmful. First, productivity changes too slowly to leverage other goals. We cannot hope to fight a spike in the rate of inflation with productivity improvements. Second, we cannot expect sustained productivity improvement from splashy inventions or sudden surges in investment. Invention is relatively useless unless it is embedded in productive capacity through continued innovations and sustained investment. Third, our accustomed habit of kiting productivity statistics with downsizing and other forms of cost cutting are risky if they cross the fuzzy line that separates simple efficiency improvements from real reductions in productive capacity.

We should be careful when eliminating fat that we do not cut into the meat and bone of our productive capacity. "Lean and mean" private strategies and public policies are characteristic of short-term productivity thinking. They are a staple of mass production organizations, where the instinct is all too often to increase volumes and lower costs by automating and by using cheaper, less skilled labor and rigid organizational formats. As touched on earlier in this chapter, organizations that pursue productivity through cost cutting usually end up too anemic and rigid to meet the new demands for quality, variety, customization, convenience, and timeliness. Public policies that promote slow growth or recession, usually in the interest of price stability, have a similar destructive effect on long-term productivity growth if they are allowed to last too long. Incentives for innovation and investment, the two-stroke engine of productivity, are nowhere to be found in economies where no growth or slow growth is the rule. Why innovate or invest when the warehouse is full with inventory and sales are always flat?

The role of innovation in the long-term development of productive capacity has profound implications for public policies and private strategies. Increased investments in education and plant and equipment consistently account for only 40 percent of increased productive capacity. Applied learning processes, the stuff of the workaday world, account for the remaining 60 percent. Unfortunately, our understanding of applied processes is deficient, and in this arena our productivity performance appears to be lacking. At first, everyone tried to explain America's alarming productivity free-fall in the early seventies as the result of the energy crisis. The theory was that the energy crisis raised prices and forced new investments in more efficient technologies. But in the eighties, energy prices fell back to their 1973 levels with no corresponding productivity improvement, and the theory fell flat.

The current wisdom, especially in Washington, is that the United States is losing its productivity lead in an orgy of consumption. The argument is that because we consume more, we save less. The shrinking pool of savings increases interest rates, which in turn discourages investment. The absence of investment accounts for our competitive failure. Therefore, so the story goes, we need to fix the budget deficit and build tax incentives that discourage consumption and encourage saving.

There are two flaws in the current wisdom. First, it exaggerates the strength of the relationship between savings, investment, and the development of productive capacity. Productivity declines in the United States date to the early seventies, and the savings rate did not fall until the early eighties. Historically, savings, investment, and productivity growth have been loosely associated rather than linked in direct sequential order. Second, the current wisdom ignores the dominant role of innovation in the development of productive capacity. In fact, innovation and the availability of productive opportunities drive savings and investment as much as and perhaps more than the other way around (Baumol, Blackman, and Wolff, 1989). Be innovative and build a strong productive base and the savings and investment will follow, especially in today's global market for footloose capital.

The appropriate metaphor for the productivity competition is not a relay race in which savings hands off to investment and investment hands off to the development of productive capacity, which runs the last lap. A more appropriate metaphor is a basketball game in which savings, investment, innovation, and existing productive capacity are all players moving forward simultaneously in a complex dynamic toward a common goal. Each player depends on all the others. Each controls the ball at some point. Anyone can score but the smart money is on innovation.

Thus, the principal lever for productivity improvement seems to be located in the inner workings of the economy itself rather than in the regulation of financial flows, which has been a principal preoccupation of governments and organizational leaders. Growing recognition of the importance of innovative processes in generating sustained productivity improvements is refocusing both private strategies and public policies. Private elites traditionally concerned with investment decisions and financial flows are showing a new interest in innovative strategies involving new forms of work organization both within and across institutional boundaries. Government elites are struggling with new roles that provide technical support and targeted tax incentives; in some cases, these elites are also becoming directly involved in innovative processes and allocating investment capital to promote economic performance.

America's Prospects. The long view gives us some cause for optimism. Our current performance is likely to allow us to continue to double our living standards every thirty years, or about once every economic generation. We may have to do better, however, if we are going to remain the world's productivity leader. If present short-term trends continue, we will have to improve our productivity performance by about 30 percent—that is, from our 1950–1980 annual average of 2.1 percent to about 3.1 percent—or as many as eight other countries will beat our productivity rates in the next century (Baumol, Blackman, and Wolff, 1989).

While we are still ahead, our competitors are running faster, and if present trends continue, they are bound to catch up soon. But will they? According to the convergence hypothesis our competitors' productivity advances will slow as they approach our own productivity performance. This hypothesis asserts that follower nations make faster productivity gains by copying and borrowing from the leader. As the distance between followers and the leader narrows, however, there is less for the followers to copy, and left to their own resources, the followers begin to fall back. It may be that the copycat nations can match short-term productivity gains in specific areas but do not have the depth or breadth of productive capacity to match the United States over the long haul. The Japanese, for instance, are coming up fast in manufacturing but cannot match our productive capacity in agriculture or services. Nor can they contend with the size of our domestic market, population, or global military and diplomatic presence. Finally, the corollary to the convergence hypothesis suggests that initial productivity spikes create wealth that consumers are unable to capture and spend and is therefore plowed back into productive capacity. Eventually, many argue, consumers demand the right to spend the proceeds of their efforts, thereby reducing savings and investment capital available to build more productive capacity. Japan watchers eagerly await the rebellion of Japanese consumers as a means of leveraging access to Japanese markets and encouraging a more level playing field between Japan and the West.

Another good sign for the United States is the fact that innovation and a high-quality productive capacity are more important to productivity growth than short-term fluctuations in saving rates. Thus far, the American economy has been a magnet for investment driven by the savings of other nations. If over the long haul the productivity returns from foreign borrowing exceed the costs of repayment, we will have had it both ways: We will have been able to spend our own money and money borrowed from our competitors to make the United States an even stronger base of innovation and productive capacity that will act as a magnet for the world's savings.

There are more reasons for optimism. The American workforce is aging and becoming more experienced and productive with each passing year. Capital drawn down to bear, educate, feed, and house the baby boom generation is now becoming available for productive investment. We have only just begun to realize the returns to the seminal information and communications technologies of the new economy. Moreover, whenever two or more economic experts are gathered together, you can get an honest argument as to whether our productivity data do us justice, whether the deficit matters, whether our savings are in fact high or low, and whether we really invest too little.

In truth, the long-term view of productive capacity is more a challenge than a comfort. If we are in the productivity game for the long haul, a higher commitment will be required. We will need to sustain momentum in innovation and investment up and down the business cycle. Our organizations built for high volumes and low prices seem too inflexible and anemic for the new economy's innovative requirements and competitive standards. Our existing workforce is becoming more experienced and productive, but new entrants to the labor force are smaller in number and increasingly drawn from populations in which our prior investments have been woefully inadequate. We are a magnet for international savings, but are we distributing our resources in productive endeavors or wasting them in an orgy of consumption, buyouts, and militaristic hubris?

We should also recognize that the productivity game as we have known it may already be over. The convergence process may have taken the economic game to another level. Once rough parity is achieved among Western industrial nations and Japan in the early decades of the twenty-first century, the notion of national productivity competition is likely to break down in the advanced economies. Instead, highly integrated productive networks are likely to compete across national boundaries. Second, the dynamic of convergence in productivity rates among nations is likely to focus on the divergence in productive capacity between the advanced economies and the less developed portions of the world left behind after 1700.

In the final analysis, productivity itself is likely to be displaced as the monolithic measure of economic performance. The miracle of productivity—the ability to produce higher volumes at lower prices—may be reduced to the status of an economic parlor trick, especially in advanced economies. Already, quality, variety, customization, convenience, and timeliness have joined the old-time religion of productivity as legitimate standards for competition in the new economy.

Quality: The New Emblem

Quality subsumes productivity as the cumulative standard for competition and differs from the productivity standard in ways that are both subtle and profound. In a sense, quality is not different from productivity; it is just more. Henry Ford did not set out to make a low-quality car; he set out to build the best-quality car at the lowest possible price, with the emphasis more on price than quality. Moreover, he operated under the assumption that there is an inverse relationship between quality and price. He was able to achieve low prices by making fewer dollars in profit on each car. Ford could keep his markup relatively low because he sold high volumes. The rigid organizations, technologies, and work practices of mass production produced a reliable standard of quality at low cost. Eventually, new technologies, the growth in worldwide productive capacity, and richer, more demanding consumers, upped the ante in automobile competition. The Ford Motor Company responded with even higher productivity levels. The ratio of outputs to inputs improved dramatically, as is evident in the radical downsizing of raw muscular power in the auto workforce and the dramatic infusion of skill and machine capital. In addition, with new flexible production technologies, price no longer varies directly with volume. The new technologies allow flexible volumes at mass production prices. As a result, Ford provides greater variety and customization in its cars today. In Henry's day, you could get a Ford in any color as long as it was black. Ford has also made dramatic increases in convenience to customers and in the speed of its development, production, and delivery of state-of-the-art improvements. For Henry Ford, "price was job 1"; in the modern-day Ford Motor Company, "quality is job 1," but quality means variety, customization, convenience, and speed at mass production prices.

Although, quality was always part of the productivity equation, the equation was structured toward solutions that lowered prices. Because quality was perceived to have an inverse relation to volume and prices, it was the constrained variable in the productivity equation. The new economy has a new economic equation, however, and now quality contends with and perhaps displaces price as the variable to be maximized. Increasingly, the economic equation is solved for higher quality more than lower prices. Moreover, there is a change in the perceived relationships between quality and the other variables in the new economic equation. With greater flexibility in technologies, organizations, and workforces, the strength of the inverse relationship between quality on the one hand and volume and price on the other has been greatly weakened and perhaps destroyed. Finally, the quality variable has been articulated into a growing set of component variables, including variety, customization, convenience, and timeliness, each with its own internal dynamic.

Perceptions and Values. The shift to quality as the focus of economic calculation has profoundly changed perceptions and values in the economic domain. Productivity is a quantitative standard. Quality is a measure that judges economic output by more than its volume. The notion of quality presumes that goods and services include attributes other than their gross number. In the new economy the quality standard is the doorway through which other nonquantitative standards are likely to enter into the economic equation. Some of these standards may even reflect value judgments about the way goods and services are made and used. One can already envision markets where products are judged for their environmental purity and whether their production or use engenders exploitation or violence. In its most profound sense, the addition of the quality standard is a shift in the way we value goods and services. If productivity was the historical emblem of economic growth, quality is the new emblem of economic progress.

With the new prominence of quality, we are shifting the way we experience the goods and services we produce. Productivity takes the bean counter's view, asking how many. Goods and services are seen from the outside in; they are made, counted, and then checked against an average standard. The quality perspective looks at products and services from the inside out, focusing on the characteristics that define the ideal good or service. When quality is job 1, the first task is to define the basic characteristics of the good or service, and the second task is to create structures and processes that encourage excellence in each of those attributes and their cohesion, or "integrity," in the final good or service (Clark and Fujimoto, 1990). A family car, for example, is roomy, reliable, safe, and durable. Building family cars with bucket seats, sensitive racing engines, and aesthetics for dating mixes elements and destroys basic integrity.

The quality perspective is organic and evolutionary, whereas the productivity standard is mechanical and static. According to the productivity standard, improvement is a matter of making the same object or service in higher quantities and at lower prices. Knowledge of the good or service is mechanical, analytic, and objective. In contrast, the quality perspective views goods and services as evolving entities that change over time. Moreover, the quality perspective presumes that understanding a good or service and its changing character and attributes comes from the experience of making or using it rather than the more aloof mechanical, analytic, and objective kinds of knowledge characteristic of productivity measurement. Productivity statistics ignore the value added when quality is improved. They fail to capture the value of increased variety and customization and improved customer service. They ignore the intrinsic value of up-to-the-minute, state-of-the-art engineering, aesthetics, and built-in convenience and the overall integrity of the product.

Productivity and quality also encourage different values

and beliefs, which in turn lead to different behaviors and patterns of interaction. Mass production structures emphasize the no-nonsense values of mathematicians, "hard" scientists, engineers, and economists. They believe in the efficiency of the machine and in progress through the sublimation of all human urges except the urge to rational calculation. If you cannot objectively measure or count something, it does not exist. Such structures hold to the convictions that rational calculation requires analytic objectivity and that involvement encourages counterproductive, irrational biases. The intellectual roots of the productivity standard can also be traced to a corollary conviction that truth is tempered by the rigorous process of competition and proved through objective measurement.

The quality standard calls for an ineffable "excellence" in a variety of tangible and intangible features of a good or service and integrity when all the parts are experienced as a whole. The attendant values tend to come from the biology and the behavioral sciences. The quality standard invokes an organic version of efficiency, not the machine efficiency implicit in the pursuit of productivity. The quality standard spawns organic structures and processes that value involvement over neutral objectivity. Organic entities are inherently democratic. The body will not work properly if the toe does not. Organizations serious about quality tend to move away from top-down authority structures and to integrate themselves into the external structures that constitute their environment. Survival requires a complex structure of cooperation and competition rather than the foxhole mentality of mass production. There is no one right way to pursue quality. Organic entities evolve into unique forms with developmental requirements that are equally unique.

Every denomination in the quality movement preaches quality programming in the same three areas: (1) building perspective, commitment, and responsibility; (2) setting standards; and (3) creating processes for conformance to standards. Similarly, all the quality gurus tend to focus effort, explicitly or implicitly, on two aspects of quality: built-in quality and customer satisfaction.

Building Perspective, Commitment, and Responsibility. To meet the quality standard, people must change their perspectives. They need to understand the quality of each aspect of a good or service and the quality of the good or service as a whole. Building a quality perspective is most difficult in productivity-oriented organizations, where employees are more accustomed to counting goods or services than truly seeing and experiencing them. The psychological difference is what sociologist Max Weber called the difference between "rational" and "substantive" knowledge. Rational knowledge is the ability to identify and count things. It is knowing from the outside in. Substantive knowledge is usually gained experientially. It is knowledge from the inside out, that flash of recognition or the "aha!" that comes when one truly understands something one has always known.

Developing a quality perspective is crucial to improving quality. Unless one understands the quality aspects and overall integrity of a good or service, one will find it difficult to make improvements, especially improvements consistent with the product's essential integrity. In addition, because quality improvements are evolutionary, they tend to occur incrementally along a constant developmental path. Many of these improvements are initiated as people produce, deliver, or use a good or service. Consequently, employees throughout the organization and individuals in the network of customers, suppliers, and other institutions that affect intermediate inputs or the final good or service need to acquire the quality perspective.

Commitment and a willingness to take responsibility are also important psychological and normative requirements for quality improvement. Commitment to quality is necessary to free up discretionary effort. Without commitment, employees are likely to respond with ritual compliance to work standards, providing the minimum effort and involvement to get the job done. The ability to take responsibility is crucial. Competence alone will not guarantee quality. We all know highly competent employees who do shoddy work. Neither is hard work any longer good enough. Organizations that produce quality products need employees who take responsibility not only for their own job assignment but for the final good or service of the organization in which they work. And that means taking responsibility for the good or service as it comes to them and after it leaves them.

These psychological aspects of building quality performance are the most difficult. Guru calls for new perspectives, commitment, and responsibility sound more like the pious homilies normally found on samplers than part of any previous business plans. In his "Fourteen Points" toward quality, W. Edwards Deming (1982), the grand old man of quality, directs his followers first to "create constancy of purpose" and second to "adopt the new philosophy." The Malcom Baldrige National Quality Award gives a full 100 of its 1,000 points for "leadership in creating quality values." As is true for most psychological or value-laden aspects of human endeavors, words fail to communicate the depth and difficulty inherent in the normative aspects of quality. Deep-seated changes in human perspectives and commitments and a willingness to take responsibility are easily advocated but not easily done. Just for starters, quality standards require higher levels of interpersonal and organizational skills, more egalitarian organizational structures, and radical changes in selection, rewards, and evaluation systems to encourage and utilize new skills. Yet even these changes will not be sufficient to guarantee that employees will change the way they perceive work and be more willing to commit to their work and take responsibility for its outcomes.

Setting and Conforming to Standards. A new perspective, deeper commitment, and the acceptance of broader responsibility provide the foundation for developing standards and processes to assure conformance to quality goals. Standards are necessary to encourage built-in quality as well as to measure up to customers' expectations for quality.

Built-in quality standards tend to mirror the perspective of the producing organization, to emphasize the objective and quantifiable, and to focus separately on the various aspects of quality as well as the overall quality by means of a multiplicity of indicators. In manufacturing, built-in quality standards tend to emphasize measurable characteristics important to scientific, engineering, and managerial elites, such as purity of final products (as, for example, in the manufacture of energy products, chemicals, foods, and pharmaceuticals), statistically measured defect rates (as in the manufacture of consumer durables, including cars and refrigerators), and conformance to state-of-the-art standards of performance, reliability, and durability. In services, built-in quality standards also reflect the biases of organizational elites, but unlike the case in manufacturing, the standards often center on the way the service is delivered and by whom. The quality of medical care or legal services, for instance, is often judged by whether the service is delivered by qualified personnel and according to established procedures.

The customer views quality from outside the organization, looking inward. In this case, standards are more subjective and focus on the customer's overall perceptions. Customer standards for quality and built-in quality standards tend to coincide most when organizations or professionals are selling to each other. For instance, auto suppliers and auto manufacturers tend to have the same kinds of quality standards because both take the technical perspective of the engineering profession. Doctors, hospitals, and medical suppliers have similar biases on quality. Even in these cases, however, the two sets of standards diverge. Buyers are likely to emphasize such things as choice, through variety and the ability to customize; convenience, both built in and in the form of good customer service; and timeliness, in the form of state-of-the-art goods and services available faster than the competition can provide them. Built-in and customer standards of quality diverge even more in consumer markets. For instance, organizational elites tend to measure performance against the technical state of the art, but consumers' sense of performance is purely experiential, adding aesthetics, image, and reputation to the list of quality standards.

The various denominations of the quality movement endorse a variety of processes to assure conformance to standards and continuous quality improvements. In the design phase, conformance to standards is encouraged by processes that attempt to create involvement and simultaneous information flows integrating the perspectives of technical and managerial elites, employees at the point of production and service delivery, suppliers, employees at the interface with customers, and the customers themselves. Subsequent production and service delivery utilizes processes for quality assurance and statistical techniques to minimize deviations from standards. Continuous quality improvement is fostered by processes and benchmarking techniques that constantly assess and capture new knowledge by scanning the external environment, drawing on internal technical and managerial elites, accumulating incremental improvements at the point of production and service delivery, working with suppliers, and listening carefully to customers.

Ritual observance of techniques for conformance to quality standards is no substitute for bedrock changes in perspective, commitment to quality, and a willingness to take on responsibility for quality beyond one's own work effort and assigned responsibility. It is all too easy for American managers schooled in the rigid Taylorist standards and work processes of mass production to pursue quality standards and processes with an authoritarian fervor that honors the letter but not the spirit of the laws of quality production and service delivery. Deming's (1982) point no. 10 in his Fourteen Points demands that organizations "eliminate slogans, exhortations, and targets" that will "only create adversarial relationships. . . as the bulk of the causes of low quality belong to the system and thus lie beyond the power of the workforce." In point no. 12, Deming admonishes those in pursuit of quality to "remove barriers to pride of workmanship."

Whether they ascribe to the principles espoused by W. Edwards Deming, Joseph Juran, Philip Crosby, Armand Feigenbaum, or David Garvin or to the ecumenical Baldrige standards, followers and leaders in the quality movement all agree that the pursuit of quality is not consistent with productivity-based management style and organization. Standards crafted by established technical and managerial elites at the top of the organizational structure are likely to emphasize technical and managerial biases for low-cost production or service delivery, technical performance, reliability, and durability. They are likely to ignore customers' performance standards and desire for choice and timeliness. They are equally likely to ignore consumers' valuations of aesthetics, convenience, image, and reputation. Organizations that successfully create viable quality standards, processes for conformance, and structures for continuous quality improvement eschew top-down values, structures, and work processes. Ultimately, the lion's share of quality standards must be agreed to and met down the line, and a significant proportion of continuous improvements must be captured at the point of production and service delivery and at the interface with the customer. Moreover, organizations that intend to foster quality must share power, resources, and information not only with customers and employees who deal directly with customers but also with suppliers, governments, external sources of research and development, and other external institutions that affect the quality of the final products.

Changes in organizational and personal perspectives, stronger commitments, and a willingness to take on broader responsibility are the preconditions necessary to quality innovations. Ultimately, if quality innovations are to be exploited fully and embedded in organizational capacity, investments are also likely to be required, as with innovations directed at any of the new competitive standards. Institutions and communities cannot escape the need for resource commitments to foster, capture, and disseminate innovations in work processes, machine technologies, human capital, tools, and methods.

Variety, Customization, Convenience, and Timeliness

To a large extent, variety, customization, convenience, and timeliness are simply new recruits that march under the quality banner. They are an articulation of the quality standard, which is subject to change and further articulation. Yet although all these more specific standards share a common set of needs for innovation and investment, each is distinct and each requires a strategic approach to effect its realization.

Variety and Customization. Customization is the more aggressive alter ego of variety. Both respond to the consumer's desire for choice and the convenience of products that are tailored to group or personal needs. The principal lever for promoting variety is innovations and investments that encourage flexibility. Robust organizations with flexible technologies and workforces are capable of handling the exceptions inherent in tailoring goods and services to particular group or individual needs. Flexible organizational structures are integrated by consensus on visions and goals. Flexible technologies tend to utilize information and communication capabilities. Flexible organizations and technologies require flexible workers to exploit organizational and technical capabilities.

Convenience. Convenience is the competitive standard most focused on the interface with the customer. Ultimately, convenience is about serving the customer. It can be built in or delivered in the form of customer service. Built-in convenience can be achieved through meeting other competitive standards of the new economy. High-quality goods and services provide built-in convenience because they satisfy customers' needs and expectations when consumed. Variety and customization guarantee built-in convenience because goods and services are tailored to satisfy the particular needs of certain groups or individual customers. Timeliness builds in convenience because it guarantees access to state-of-the-art products.

Customer service, the second aspect of convenience, has become a more important and more complex function in the new economy. Employees at the interface with customers must be sufficiently competent to represent the built-in conveniences of the organization's goods and services, tailor an expanded array of varieties to meet customers' needs, serve as a listening post to transmit customers' expectations back into the organization, and supply traditional customer service by providing personal attention, dependability, promptness, and competence. Customer service functions are far less demeaning in the new economy than they were in the old because of increased reliance on the built-in features of goods and services. In many cases, built-in convenience leaves the service and customization functions to the customers themselves, reducing the overall volume of transactions in which one person is asked to be servile to another. For example, with do-it-yourself medical kits, automated teller machines, and home-based entertainment centers, customers provide more of their own services. In an egalitarian society such as our own, this change is one of the fortuitous side effects of competition in the new economy.

Timeliness. Time has emerged as a universal solvent in the competitive machinery of organizations. Being the first to get ideas off the drawing board and into the hands of customers guarantees market share. Being the first to improve the efficiency and quality of goods and services and to develop new applications sustains competitive performance. Timeliness is joined to other competitive standards in a seamless weave of interrelationships. Speed reduces costs by saving carrying costs on inventory. Speed leverages profits and convenience to customers because products are available when consumers are ready to buy—thus avoiding stockouts and losses due to unsold items that are overstocked when demand recedes. Speed forces quality: Just-in-time systems eliminate the organizational slack traditionally relied on to compensate for inconsistent quality.

Time has also emerged as a constraining element in the economic equation. In the new economy, the trick is to provide variety, customization, quality, and convenience while maintaining both the productivity levels that allow low prices and the overall speed of operations. Maintaining the balance between low cost and high speed on the one hand and quality, variety, customization, and convenience on the other requires ever higher levels of innovation and investment, which bring more flexibility in organizations, technologies, work processes, and workforces. Flexibility is the key to meeting the new competitive standards while maintaining low prices and speed of operations.

In the long run, speed, like cost reductions, may bring diminishing returns. Organizations need to be careful that they do not accelerate speed beyond the point where it harms their ability to deliver on quality, variety, customization, and convenience. Moreover, product and technology cycles may accelerate beyond the point where organizations can recoup the costs of their initial innovations and investments. The life cycle of products has declined precipitously compared with the average life of products fifty years ago. Life expectancy has gone from twelve to four years in cosmetics, from fifteen to about four years in games and toys, from almost twenty to about five years in tools, from almost twenty-five to about eight years in pharmaceuticals, from about seven to less than three years in automobiles, and from almost a decade to a year in consumer electronics.

The average age of the spectrum of products offered by individual companies is also shortening. One study shows that between the mid seventies and the mid eighties, the proportion of an average company's products more than ten years old declined from 27 percent to 15 percent; over the same period, the proportion of products introduced in the preceding six to ten years declined from 33 percent to 29 percent, and the proportion of products introduced within the preceding five years increased from 40 percent to 56 percent (von Braun, 1990).

In most cases, the returns to improvements in speed are far from exhausted. In some markets, however, the rapidity of technical and product cycles has begun to force unacceptable trade-offs with quality and other competitive standards or the pace of change does not allow organizations to recoup returns to innovation and investment. In these cases, strategies that are alternatives to a continued acceleration of change become more important. Such alternatives tend to focus on making it difficult for competitors to enter preferred markets. One strategy is to focus innovations and investments in areas that will build cumulative competitive capacity that is difficult to duplicate except at huge costs and with long lead times for learning. Investment requirements and learning curves can be powerful barriers to entry in whole industries as well as in specific product lines within them. The human, organizational, and technical infrastructure necessary to enter the auto or electronics industry is a formidable barrier as is the know-how necessary to produce quality. The same is true for a switch from cars to trucks and vans or from computer chips to consumer electronics.

Additional barriers that can be erected include intellectual property rights and patents, especially in industries such as chemicals or pharmaceuticals, where the relationship between invention and applications is most direct. In markets where the fast pace of technical change does not allow an organization to recoup a sufficient return on innovations or investments, competitive advantage stems from competitive features other than state-of-the-art technology. Organizations can emphasize quality, variety, customization, or convenience as a competitive difference.

New Organizational Structures

The new economy's competitive standards require equally new kinds of structures to house them. Such new structures must be more egalitarian and participatory to foster the commitment and acceptance of responsibility necessary to quality. They need to be flexible enough to allow variety and customization at ever higher rates of speed. And the new structures need to be open to customers, suppliers, and others who affect their ability to meet competitive goals.

The new competitive standards have spawned a new organizational format: flexible networks integrated by information and consensual goals and energized by a set of dynamic processes that emphasize synergies from communication, learning, and collaboration. The top-down behemoths of big business have switched to network formats in order to encourage flexibility and exchange their bureaucratic anonymity for the common touch of convenience. Small and fragmented structures are forming networks that allow them the productivity advantages of bigness and consistent quality in goods and services.

Building Work Teams. The networks of the new economy exist simultaneously and fluidly at several levels. They are nested in a hierarchy extending from the work site to whole organizations, groups of organizations, and finally global networks. The primary network in this complex structure is the collection of individuals that make up the work team. A work team can consist of as few as three or as many as thirty people. It is defined by shared commitment to meeting an agreed upon outcome that directly affects overall efficiency or the competitive quality of the final good or service. In this regard, work teams are fundamentally different from highly rationalized mass production work structures, in which each worker is responsible only for some narrow function that is rarely tied to the final product.

Work teams vary greatly in functional responsibility and autonomy. A quality circle is a work team responsible for sharing knowledge and discussing problems, but it generally has limited operational responsibility. More powerful work teams demarcate a sphere of operation, set goals, and control functions, including priority setting, scheduling, purchasing, inventory control, personnel, and relations with other teams upstream and down.

The governance structure of a team tends to evolve in a way that increases relative autonomy and effectiveness. At first, the team is led from the outside by a manager or supervisor. As commitment and a common sense of responsibility increase, the team selects its own leader, usually someone who has adapted well to the team concept and is highly trusted by others. When commitment, responsibility, and trust become widely shared, the team becomes independent and self-directed, with leadership shifting according to task and skill.

Teams have a number of competitive virtues. Teams organized around outcomes cut straight to the competitive fore. When team goals have an appropriate customer focus, built-in convenience and customer service are natural results. Teams also discourage bureaucratic procedure and encourage flexibility and speed. Teams are organized for collaboration, assuring synergy in their efforts. The results of teamwork are always more than they would have been had each team member worked separately. In a sense, teams create new shared work space where new learning, the fount of competitive improvements, can be accelerated and captured (Schrage, 1990).

Building teams is not easy; it has both financial costs for those who must pay for teams and psychic costs for those who must surrender power. Team members need cross training if they are to solve problems together, and they need training in communications, interpersonal, and organizational skills if they are to be internally autonomous and effective in their interactions up and down the line. Moreover, team performance and individual acquisition of new skills should be recognized and rewarded. Above all else, organizations need to download authority and resources to teams, especially those teams near the point of production and service delivery.

The Victory of Process Over Function. Networks in the organization as a whole are collections of teams bound together by a common commitment and a shared sense of responsibility. These networks focus on the integration of team efforts and the overall competitive integrity of the final product. They can leave specific functional categories in place and rely on temporary project teams or task forces to achieve competitive goals, or if goals require ongoing efforts, these networks can establish themselves as permanent structures. The distinctive difference between network organizations and traditional organizations is that in the former, competitive goals associated with the final product triumph over functional goals and standards.

Traditional organizations are usually structured by function. As a result, they tend to optimize functional performance and standards. Marketing departments emphasize excellence in marketing; procurement departments emphasize low cost; manufacturing functions emphasize high volumes and low defect rates; engineering departments emphasize technical performance. These functional entities are self-contained. Arranged in the same organization like freestanding silos, they rarely let any light in or out. Employees organized into these vertical chambers rarely communicate effectively or work together, and the organization as a whole is subordinated to function. Outcomes focus more on functions, less on promoting excellence in the various aspects of the final product, and least of all on bringing cohesion and integrity to the good or service as a whole.

Functional organization made sense in the old mass production economy. Workers generally understood and ascribed to the single-minded focus on higher volumes at lower prices, and standards were the province of organizational elites. In process manufacturing industries, such as steel and chemicals, elites designed processes that assured purity. In the manufacturing of durables such as cars and electronics, built-in reliability and low defect rates were emphasized. In services, the elite standards of professional accreditation and established procedure tended to prevail.

Functional organization is not working well in the new economy, however, because the competitive equation has become more complex and demanding. The new economy demands and new technologies allow flexible volumes, quality, convenience, and speed at low cost. Moreover, customers' perspectives have added new dimensions to quality as well as a demand for overall integrity in a given good or service. Functional organizations find it difficult to deliver on the new competitive standards. They tend to ignore the customer's view, even in marketing and sales, where the traditional approach is to convince the customer to buy what is offered rather than to offer what the customer wants. Traditional functional structures also tend to rely too heavily on the quality standards of technical and professional elites rather than on standards that include perspectives from down the line at the point of production or service delivery and at the interface with the customer. In addition, functional structures are too compartmentalized to focus on the overall integrity of the good or service. Finally, traditional functional organizations fritter away energy and resources on functional goals, while the intense competitive environment requires the synergy that comes with a collaborative focus on common competitive goals.

Ultimately, the networks of the new economy are the triumph of the organic over the mechanical, the systematic over the piecemeal, and process over function. But the new networks do not begin with wholesale systemic changes. Instead, they are triggered by incremental competitive challenges and evolve as a result of incremental changes in behaviors and patterns of interaction (Beer, Eisenstat, and Spector, 1990). The development of networks that work in the new economy usually begins with real-world needs to meet new or heightened competitive standards. The process usually evolves from the solving of particular work problems to more systemic changes.

Attempts to meet new standards raise organizational issues. Formal structures and work processes do not get the job done. New behaviors and patterns of interaction emerge. The inappropriateness of current structures becomes apparent, and perspectives on the organizational structure itself change. The organization is viewed less as a machine with functioning parts and more as an organic system of implicit and explicit structures that produce results either at odds with or in conformance with new standards. The static organizational chart begins to lose its meaning as formal and informal networks emerge to encourage conformance to standards. Indeed, the critical path to competitive success is most likely to blaze a trail that follows the white spaces between the functional boxes in the organizational chart (Rummler and Brache, 1990).

During the transition, senior managers may become advocates for specific standards such as quality. Temporary teams, project management, and task forces are other network devices for overcoming organizational barriers. Gradually, more permanent structural changes focused on competitive targets and organized around customers, products, or specific competitive standards develop.

Partners for Profit. Networks in the new economy extend beyond the environs of the traditional organization. Organizations operate as members of value-added chains that deliver final goods and services to customers and clients, and the competitiveness of an entire value-added chain is only as good as the competitive performance of its weakest link. As a result, competitive partners both up and down the chain build networks to improve overall performance. In the end, it is the performance of the network and not of each component organization that determines the competitive quality of the final good or service and the competitive fate of each of the component organizations in the network. For example, the upstream performance of suppliers of rubber, steel, fabric, plastics, and electronic compo-

nents and the downstream performance of dealerships are critical to the competitiveness of the automobile company. The
competitiveness of apparel manufacturers depends on the performance of chemical companies that treat fiber and textile
operations that weave fiber into cloth as well as on the performance of wholesalers and retailers. Restaurants depend on
farmers, food manufacturers, and equipment manufacturers as
well as on the value added by service personnel.

Competitive networks have always existed, if only implicitly. The difference in the new economy is that they have
become more important and explicit, and the relationship
among network members has become more cooperative and
less competitive. The growing importance of networks of organizations is a result of the growing intensity, complexity, and cost
of competition in the new economy. As the extension of productive capacity in the nation and around the globe intensifies
competition for market share, each organization is forced to
add competitive muscle not only inside itself but in upstream
and downstream organizations as well. Moreover, higher standards and improved performance in an organization demand
commensurate improvements among its suppliers and the consumers of its output. Higher performance standards in engines,
for instance, cannot be met if parts suppliers provide components that cannot perform up to standard, and improved engine
components may overwhelm engines built to a lower standard of
performance, resulting in unacceptable breakdowns. Similarly,
higher-performance engines will be wasted on dealers who cannot sell or repair them.

The growing complexity of economic activity encourages
the self-conscious development of networks to capture synergies
in diverse kinds of organizations. In the new economic environment, the extraction of natural resources, manufacturing,
service functions, and the end use of goods and services by
consumers have become more interdependent. Partnerships
between separate organizations that extract basic resources,
manufacture products, and deliver final goods and services to
consumers are more important in the new economy. Moreover,
consumers are becoming active participants in networks. For

instance, as uses for basic commodities extracted from the earth become more specialized, manufacturing and service processes provide more value added. This is true in areas as diverse as specialty steel, specialty chemicals, pharmaceuticals, and foods.

Manufacturing and services are also more intertwined than they were before, encouraging networks that embrace manufacturers, service providers, and customers. As service functions historically performed in the home and community become commercialized, they become more capital intensive. The commercialization of cooking, cleaning, and caring for people requires a richer mix of manufactured equipment and labor than the domestic alternative. User friendly technologies have increased the manufactured content of most services. The use of computers is an example. Growing consumer participation in the consumption of both goods and services has also made traditional services more capital intensive in a variety of activities, from the use of automatic teller machines in banking to the use of more consumer electronics for entertainment and domestic chores in the home.

The diverse standards of the new economy are oftentimes best met by a diverse network of organizations, each with a unique set of behaviors, systems, and technologies. A common partnership is that between organizations that focus on built-in quality standards and organizations that contribute the quality perspectives of customers or clients. The partnership between manufacturing organizations that meet built-in quality standards and service organizations that customize and provide convenience is typical. Partnerships between organizations that supply a basic product line and organizations that provide varieties, alternative applications, and commercialized by-products also lead to such networks.

Time and cost constraints also leverage partnerships that expand networks among organizations. Finding a partner is often less time-consuming or less expensive than starting a homegrown capability from scratch, especially in industries where basic technologies and human capital are expensive and where learning curves require continuous experience over long periods of time. Partnerships in search of cheap labor are more characteristic of the old economy than of the new. It is difficult to meet the new competitive standards with cheap labor. Also, labor is a declining share of costs everywhere, especially in manufacturing, where labor costs have been reduced to about 15 percent of costs overall and 10 percent of costs in high-tech manufacturing (National Research Council, 1990).

As improvements in work processes, technologies, and strategy accelerate and diversify, individual organizations find it prudent to develop partnerships in far-flung networks to capture new knowledge. Scientific and technical developments emanate from a variety of global sources. Furthermore, the geographic dispersion of markets adds new value to a geographically dispersed network of partners, for market requirements differ significantly in Boston, Bombay, and Paris. Networks can provide an organization the opportunity to learn its way into new markets as well as provide access to local resources and a way around legal or more subtle entry barriers.

Networks also provide an added measure of security for individual organizations. As a network, suppliers, financial backers, and customers generate commitments that can hold an organization together in hard times. Networks that provide varied products and geographic reach cushion poor performance in specific product areas and can help an organization withstand the vagaries of the business cycle. Business may be bad in Houston, but the organization can be sustained by better business conditions accessible through partners in Bonn.

Integrating and sustaining useful networks presents formidable challenges. Maintaining the quality and integrity of goods and services requires constant attention to standards. Sustaining networks made up of peers from different cultures is even more difficult. Thus far, our experience with networks inside and outside organizations teaches much the same kind of wisdom that one hears in discussions of more personal relationships: Be clear about common goals, objectives, and expectations. Play to each other's strengths. Build trust. Share risks and rewards. But always protect the heart of the organization's strength. If the organization's core competency is not sustained and protected, the organization will be of little use in the network.

Chapter Ten

CONTINUOUS LEARNING:
THE CORNERSTONE
OF ECONOMIC PROGRESS

What accounts for the ability of some nations and the inability of others to meet the new competitive standards? Does an abundance of natural resources guarantee success? No, natural resources are nice but not absolutely necessary. Bereft of natural resources, the Japanese have enjoyed enormous success in the new economic environment. The Middle Eastern nations, on the other hand, are favored with oil but are unable to expand beyond their oil economies. The Soviets hold the world's largest untapped oil reserve but cannot seem to get it out of the ground.

Is cheap labor, then, the key to economic success? The availability of cheap and plentiful labor is an advantage in Korea, Africa, and other parts of the developing world. Yet labor scarcity after World War II is generally credited with the intensive investments in human and machine capital that led to the current successes of the Germans and Japanese. Natural conditions cannot be the answer either, for the Europeans and Japanese, who have so little arable land, are grossly inefficient in

215

their agriculture, whereas the United States, blessed with vast
expanses of arable land to waste, uses the land very efficiently. A
global military presence is not necessary, or those who lost and
were disarmed in war would not be making economic advances
faster than the winners, who still bristle with armaments. What
about the presence of free markets and the absence of collectivist institutions? This factor is surely part of the explanation
for the failure of fascist and communist economies, but it does
not explain away the success of the gentler forms of collectivism
characteristic of the mixed economies of the West, including the
United States, and the harsher forms of collectivism characteristic of the Japanese and Koreans.

Even a casual glance around the current global economic
community is enough to upset biases on the roots of economic
success. A second and closer look suggests that success in the
new economy is predicated on the ability to understand and
utilize a loosely connected set of economic and social processes,
including the following:

Scientific inquiry
Invention
Innovation
Dissemination
Networking
Investment
Commercialization
Cumulative learning

Taken together, these processes represent a complex interaction between learning and economic enterprise. Science,
invention, and innovation are processes for creating new knowledge. Dissemination, networking, investment, and commercialization embed new knowledge in economic systems and
encourage its continuing accumulation. All of these processes
are driven by the dynamic of learning. The conventional sup-
position is that they follow one another in a natural sequence:
Science produces new knowledge, which begets practical inventions and subsequent innovations. Inventions and innova-

tions are eventually disseminated through networks and resource investments, leading to commercial successes and the
accumulation of economic advantage. This linear stereotype
does not reflect the real economy accurately, however. The eight
processes are only loosely connected, and any one of them can
proceed in the absence of all the others. Moreover, economic
progress can begin with any one of them, and all eight are not
necessary for success. Most often economic progress requires a
synergistic mix of some but not necessarily all the processes.
The flow of influence among the processes is similarly complex.
Inventions, for instance, can and very often do precede the
scientific knowledge implicit in them. Innovation drives investment as much as if not more than investment drives innovation.

In short, the dynamic of economic progress in the new
economy depends on learning, but the processes of generating,
capturing, and accumulating knowledge do not work in a neat
or predictable pattern. As explained in the earlier discussion on
productivity, the proper analogy is not the relay race, in which
each runner hands off to the next in a prescribed sequence, but
the basketball game, in which each player interacts with the
others in a complex set of patterns while moving toward a
common goal. In this case, the goal is economic progress.

Scientific Inquiry

Science is a game played with nature in its purest form. The
object is to understand how to use and manipulate nature in the
interest of human progress. The game is always risky because the
use and manipulation of the natural environment can result in
unintended consequences that ultimately threaten human survival. Science is also a game against society. Science shows no
respect for or allegiance to convention and is more interested in
progress through knowledge than economic progress. Economic payoffs from science are not always obvious in the short
haul. Science is self-interested, risky, rude, and uncertain. It is
little wonder that the history of science shows a pattern of
begging resources by day and fleeing priests and politicians in
the night. The ultimate social questions in the sciences have

always been who will defend science and who will pay for it. The patrons of science have influence over the questions asked, if not the answers given.

Among all the learning processes in the growth dynamic, then, scientific discovery is the most removed from economic and social processes. Prior to the latter half of the nineteenth century, the relationship between science and economics was loose and long term at best. The earliest inventions had little to do with science. Levers, wheels, cams, wheelbarrows, and other tools were invented by people with almost no theoretical understanding. The industrial revolution was driven by tinkerers and talented amateurs, not by scientists. Of course, science did contribute a basic set of beliefs that nature was knowable and manipulable, but beliefs are always a mixed blessing. They point us toward the possible but at the same time tend to set boundaries on human behaviors and inquiries. Some scientific historians go so far as to argue that institutions and societies that value science are unlikely to be innovative, focusing too much in theoretical domains and too little in the realm of the applied (Kuhn, 1970).

Scientific discovery became more important in the latter half of the nineteenth century. Great Britain had built her lead in the early phase of the industrial revolution through the efforts of talented amateurs and craft workers but fell behind in the second phase in part because France and Germany had invested in strong scientific establishments that became more critical after the first wave of industrial growth. Science has become increasingly important in the growth dynamic ever since. Scientific advances often have direct applications, especially in such industries as chemicals and pharmaceuticals. More often, prior knowledge derived from scientific principles eliminates the number of false starts. Moreover, as the pace of change accelerates and the intensity of competition intensifies in the new economy, science becomes more closely linked to economic processes in two ways: First, scientific discovery is applied more quickly and more often. Second, the processes of invention, innovation, dissemination, networking, investment, and commercialization and the overall accumulation of knowledge they foster both accelerate and direct the focus of scientific inquiry.

The increasing importance of scientific inquiry has not eclipsed other processes for obtaining and using knowledge, however. The prevailing view is that practical applications still dominate economic advances. Economists agree that the lion's share of productivity improvements comes from more effective utilization of existing knowledge, and students of technology agree that most improvements come from learning by doing or learning by using rather than from scientific discovery (Rosenberg, 1982). From a purely economic point of view, science still owes more to talented amateurs than the talented amateurs owe to science.

The ability of science to contribute directly and immediately to economic progress always suffers from two inherent problems. First, invention, innovation, dissemination, networking, investment, commercialization, and their cumulative effects often create goods and services beyond the boundaries of scientific understanding. Second, scientific understanding awaits all these other processes before it can be transformed into usable products. The first problem is Dr. Jekyll's dilemma. Jekyll's best intentions, through a process of trial and error, produce a potion that turns him into the loathsome Hyde. Ultimately, he is undone because he does not understand how the potion works and therefore cannot control it. With time, science usually catches up with the goods and services available, but meanwhile, improvements are generated by trying everything in reach until something works.

The second barrier to the integration of science into economic progress is what Joel Mokyr (1990), a student of the history of technology, refers to as Leonardo's dilemma. Leonardo da Vinci imagined helicopters, submarines, and a variety of other modern devices, and his sense of the scientific underpinnings of these devices was essentially correct. His dilemma was that the inventions and innovations necessary to the devices were not yet available. Neither was investment capital available to develop and disseminate the necessary devices, and there was no commercial structure or underlying demand for his fantastic machines. In the new economy, Leonardo's dilemma is evident in our slow progress in areas where real-world processes have been slow to apply scientific knowledge. We understand "cold fusion" as an alternative to our current reliance on oil for energy, but we cannot seem to make it happen. We understand cancer and heart disease but are left with the slow processes of trial and error to apply what we know. Eventually, our attempts at application will bring deeper understanding and more scientific knowledge.

Scientific inquiry has proved to be an effective means for advancing economic progress since time in memory, first as the author of a worldview suggesting the possibility of progress of all kinds and later as a source of tangible improvements in goods and services. Investment incentives, however, have always been weak, especially in market economies. Science does not always pay off, and with the exception of industries that sell the products of science directly, it rarely pays off quickly. Scientific knowledge is generally available, encouraging investments in its application rather than in its development. For these reasons, where science has been most successful, public support has driven it.

Public support for scientific infrastructure is likely to be more neecessary and more difficult to come by in the new economy. Organizations and governments have both learned that there is more money to be made in applying scientific advances than in paying for them, but someone has to pay for basic science. Because the fruits of scientific inquiry are difficult to appropriate and science benefits from open inquiry, the most effective and cost-efficient strategy for promoting science is shared costs and responsibility. Public funding is one way to share costs. Consortia of organizations and even nations are another alternative device to share costs. Happily, the scientific community is already a network that extends beyond the confines of individual organizations and nations. All that remains is to develop the incentives, leadership, and will to maintain its open structure and utilize it effectively.

Invention and Innovation

Science pursues knowledge as an end in itself. Invention is distinct from science in that it applies knowledge in order to create something. Usually inventors attempt to make things that are useful in an economic or social context, but not always. Some inventions result from the sheer joy of tinkering or, like science, from the irresistible human urge to play the game against nature. The history of flight is an illustration: Flight has its uses in modern times, but a fascination with flying gadgets predates any practical need or demand for it. The turning point in the history of flight came when the Montgolfier brothers launched their balloon in France in 1783. Even then, ballooning had few practical uses except for military observation, yet the Montgolfiers' achievements were greeted with worldwide exuberance as an affirmation of human ingenuity and a victory over nature.

Science and invention both operate somewhat apart from current economic and social processes, but in general, scientific inquiry is carried on at a greater distance from the everyday world. Science and invention are complementary processes. Although invention led the way until the closing decades of the nineteenth century, since then science and invention have been connected by a two-way street.

Innovation is the learning process at the core of economic progress. Innovation accounts for the bulk of improvements in productivity and quality and is at the heart of the flexibility that allows for variety, customization, convenience, and speed. It is both a complement to and a substitute for science and invention. It complements by applying both in eocnomic and social contexts. Innovation continuously improves on the products of science and invention until there are no more improvements to be had. But the process of innovation does not necessarily run down when science and invention offer no new raw material; innovation can provide its own raw material for economic progress. Incremental improvements on an original scientific discovery or invention can accumulate into breakthroughs and new applications that set off a whole new round of economic progress. The automobile, for example, is neither a scientific discovery nor an invention. Instead, it is a collection of scientific principles and inventions made whole through innovation.

There are other subtle but important differences between innovation on the one hand and science and invention on the other. The products of science tend to be intangible principles and processes. The products of invention tend to be tangible things or clearly defined processes. The products of innovation usually cover a broader territory, including changes in machinery, materials, work processes, organizational structures, tools, or methods that lead separately or in combination to improved performance.

Ultimately, innovation is distinguished from the other learning processes because it is embedded in the workaday world. In contrast, the norms of science strive to remove the processes of scientific inquiry and its outcomes from real-world influences, even through the economic and social context may affect the focus of inquiry. Even invention is not always driven by social and economic demands. Nor does invention guarantee use in economic or social contexts. The Incas invented the wheel but used it only in their toys.

Innovation results from learning by doing and learning by using at work. It is generally pursued by following one's nose inductively and comes gradually, with great knowledge and long experience. It is much less dependent on careful design, genius, or serendipity than either science or invention. External agents, including governments, consultant geniuses, or the latest cure-all, rarely lead to sustained innovation. More often than not, the spark that ignites the innovation process is an attempt to solve a specific problem by changing values, behaviors, and patterns of interaction. Innovation is usually found in organizations and societies that create rewards and status systems that encourage it, build extensive networks that enrich the possibilities for learning by doing and learning by using, and systematically clear obstacles in innovation's evolutionary path.

Dissemination, Networking, and Investment

Dissemination is the process that embeds advances in learning from science, invention, and innovation in the economic and social structures. There are two complementary dimensions to dissemination: a quantitative dimension best measured by the extent to which innovations are known and used and a qualitative dimension best measured by the gap between best practices and the general practice. Dissemination is both the process of increasing the extent of new learning and the process of reducing the gap between general and best practice.

Dissemination's reach necessarily extends beyond the world of work. New learning needs to be embedded in the educational system, and public institutions need to keep abreast of up-to-the-minute developments in science, invention, and the world of work if they are to be effective partners and provide the complementary assets necessary to economic progress.

Networks at all levels are primary structures for generating as well as disseminating new knowledge. They provide cooperation that expedites new learning and its dissemination, and if network members collaborate, the result is synergy in the learning and dissemination processes. In cooperative networks, learning and dissemination tend to be additive, and dissemination tends to occur sequentially. Collaborative networks, in contrast, effectively create a common work space where learning and dissemination increase exponentially and dissemination is simultaneous.

If learning is the heart of economic progress and dissemination and networks its arterial system, then investment is its life's blood. Resource investments are required to generate, capture, and embed new learning in an organization or a whole society. The generation of new learning in the realms of science, invention, and workplace innovations requires expensive infrastructrure. Investments necessary to capture new learning tend to focus on networks and three kinds of learning: learning by doing, learning by using, and learning by borrowing. For instance, an individual organization should invest in its work teams to accumulate learning by doing and invest at the point of interaction with the customer to capture learning by using. An organization must also invest in the information-gathering capacity of its external networks to capture learning that occurs elsewhere. Investments that focus on embedding new learning in the economic and social contexts are necessary to update and deepen the growth capacity of an organization or even a whole society. New scientific findings, for instance, need to be embedded in workplace practices and education and training curriculums. Innovations at work need to be generalized and fed back into school curricula as well as analyzed and integrated into scientific findings.

Rarely are there enough resources to meet existing demands, including demands for investment, and every individual, organization, and nation must allocate resources among competing claimants. The first difficult choice is how much to invest and how much to consume. The only way to consume and invest beyond the limits of available resources is to borrow, as American families, organizations, and governments are presently doing. Borrowed resources must eventually be repaid with interest, but if the borrowed funds generate more economic gain than the cost of repayment, then the borrowing is worthwhile. Borrowed money can be consumed or invested. Consumption can generate improvements in productive capacity by creating a demand for goods and services, which in turn fuels innovation. Investment generates economic improvements directly by paying for the generation, capture, and embedding of new learning, thus deepening the capacity for further economic progress.

As a general rule, people and organizations are willing to pay for the benefits they accrue. Investments in the generation, capture, and dissemination of new learning are no exception. The difficulty, however, is that neither individuals nor organizations are ever able to capture all the benefits from learning. The reason is relatively simple: We make new knowledge generally available in the interest of economic and social progress. Even patent laws offer only temporary protection to inventors. Moreover, new knowledge will not generate any economic returns unless it is used, but once used it is difficult to keep secret. Learning is a classic case of what economists call market failure, or the inability of a market left to itself to generate a sufficient level of a particular good or service. Individuals and organizations will underinvest in learning that is generally available because they cannot capture the full economic and social benefits of their investment. For similar reasons, individuals and organizations have an interest in restricting the dissemination of new learning.

Investment in learning should follow two rules of thumb. First, costs should be incurred in rough proportion to benefits, which means that individuals, organizations, private networks, national governments, and networks of governments should all pay shares depending on the investment needs at issue. Second, investment decisions should take into account the interests of future generations. Because future generations will benefit from current investment, it is fair to support investment with borrowing that must be paid back in the future. By the same token, those who will repay the debt should get a fair share of the benefits.

Investments by networks are likely to expand as individual organizations find that they can neither afford nor capture the benefits from general, easily appropriable forms of learning. In instances where networks cannot afford or capture returns easily, especially in scientific inquiry, the public role is also likely to expand. Innovation is inherently nested in the workplace, but a stronger public role is likely even for innovation — in the form of incentives. It already seems clear from the tax debates in the industrialized world that general tax subsidies are going to be replaced by more targeted incentives. General forgiveness on capital gains, for instance, is likely to give way to more targeted subsidies for specific kinds of investment, research and development, energy efficiency, and training. Government is also likely to become more integral in networks. At a minimum, governments will become cooperating members of networks by substituting more flexible regulation for inflexible rules. Governments are also likely to play a helpful role in dissemination by inventorying, analyzing, modeling, and disseminating best practices. Whether government participation will extend to a more aggressive collaboration in private networks remains to be seen.

In cases that involve national security or environmental protection, governments themselves are likely to form networks for joint investment, as in the multinational response to Iraq's attempt to annex Kuwait. Simply put, it is no longer sensible for individual nations to handle all their own security needs. Warfare no longer has the payoffs it used to have. In ancient times, military might and the power it conferred were valued for their own sake. Later, military power became a means to economic power. Conquest brought the acquisition of land access to resources or transportation routes over land or water. But in modern times, neither land nor critical resources are worth the destruction of the complex communications, transportation, and social infrastructure necessary to commerce. European liberalism has won its bloody victory over fascism and outlasted communism. Moreover, hot and cold wars have become expensive distractions with little payoff in civilian sectors because military technologies have become too specialized to create civilian spin-offs. In addition, the sheer size and specialized needs of the military make it difficult to shift civilian production to military purposes quickly enough to react to an external threat in time. As a result, the modern military is made up of standing forces and capabilities, and the complementary standing industrial and technical infrastructure competes with the civilian economy for human, financial, machine, and technical capital. Excessive financial commitments to national security can absorb valuable resources better used to promote economic progress.

Fortunately, military adventurism is not only unwise, it is increasingly unnecessary in a world no longer segregated by national boundaries. The substitution of global networks of economic production for self-contained, autonomous national economies both discourages wars of imperial expansion and makes them unnecessary. At the same time, however, this is not the moment to disarm. Nationalism, religion, and ideology still provide some reason to fight, but the greatest spur to war comes from the division of the world into "haves" with little to gain and much to lose and "have-nots" with much to gain and little to lose. This division is especially virulent when combined with frustrated nationalism turned fascist or frustrated development gone communist. The former inevitably leads to dangerous leadership and turns on indigenous minorities. Fanatical leadership and the anti-Semitism of a frustrated Arab culture are only the most evident examples. The potential for similar developments in Eastern Europe, Africa, South America, and Southeast Asia grows daily. The division of the world into haves and have-nots destabilizes economic networks and threatens war over resources. Resource wars are generally difficult to mount and sustain in democratic nations.

The lesson is plain: The developed nations have a stake in the stability and economic advancement of the developing regions of the world. Until the have-nots catch up with the haves, security is still necessary, but sharing security costs through worldwide networks of like-minded nations is the wave of the future.

History demonstrates that the failure to disseminate new learning through the development of networks and wise use of scarce investment capital can undermine economic progress severely. The British provide an instructive historical example. Beginning in 1750, Britain led the industrial revolution, but by 1870, the United States had taken the lead by copying British methods and borrowing their technology. By the beginning of World War I, the French, Germans, and Americans had become the leading innovators in the industrial world. The British failed to hold their lead because they did not embed new learning in their economic and social infrastructure through investment and the development of powerful learning networks. The British never built an effective scientific establishment. In the early days of the industrial revolution, practical innovations dominated and science was of little economic consequence. Beginning in the last quarter of the 1800s, science and innovation became more closely tied, but the British scientific community remained a quaint group of talented amateurs and adventurers. Higher learning in Britain was generally underfunded and dedicated to the classical education of a select elite. The British also failed to invest in elementary and secondary education and continued to emphasize classical curricula over technical subject matter. An enormous share of the wealth of the realm went to war and empire. Eventually, homegrown commercial capital was invested in the United States and other parts of the world where a stronger focus on innovation and the development of a higher-quality productive capacity promised higher returns.

Commercialization

An increase in the overall volume of exchange increases economic welfare. If I make hats and you make shoes and we trade shoes for hats, we are both better off. Gains from the increased volume of trade can accrue to individuals, regions, and nations. The extent and volume of commerce both push and pull economic welfare: Commerce extends the reach and complexity of learning networks and gives a push to both the volume and the rate of learning by doing, learning by using, and learning by borrowing. Commerce also increases the demand for goods and services and thereby encourages investment, pulling economic progress along as well as influencing its direction and focus. Commerce encourages dissemination and provides feedback that influences the levels and the direction of scientific inquiry, invention, and innovation.

The history of commerce is a story of new learning, especially in energy, transport, information, and communications technologies; the extension of networks; and the special role of governments. In the Iron Age, from about 500 to 110 B.C., learning focused on toolmaking, and commerce was local if it can be said to have existed at all. During classical antiquity, from about 500 B.C. to A.D. 500, the Macedonians, Greeks, and Romans extended commerce by conquest and the dissemination of law as well as common coinage and standardized weights and measures. Commerce followed the angry tide of soldiers but ebbed when empires were eventually reduced to warring factions. Commerce grew at a snail's pace in the Middle Ages, from about 500 to 1500.

The Renaissance, an age of exploration from about 1500 to 1750, marked the beginning of international commerce and its dominance by European culture along with its market-oriented economic organization and international norms of open trade. The industrial revolution, from 1750 to 1830, accelerated commercialization and established commerce as a central concern of nations. During the nineteenth century, the Europeanization of commerce continued, with Britain as its anchor.

Since the end of the Second World War, the tide of Western commercialization has continued, with the United States replacing the Europeans as the anchor and new currents originating with the Japanese. As the twentieth century draws to a close, commercialization continues, reaching into Africa, the Islamic world, the ocean nations, and other parts of the world and extending the bounds of economic networks, increasing demand, and accelerating the pace of learning.

The commercialization of the new economy is driven by new information and communications technologies that allow global networks of production and consumption. Networks of governments are hard at work building the fiscal, monetary, trade, and security infrastructure critical to the commercialization of the globe. The rhetoric for a "new order" of mutual security was first sounded at the end of the Cold War and tested in the Persian Gulf crisis. This new order is likely to substitute a more complex and multicentered world for American hegemony, and commercialization is likely to accelerate even faster, emanating simultaneously from European, Japanese, and American sources. The Chinese, eastern Europeans, Soviets, South Americans, Africans, and citizens of Oceana are likely to borrow most of their learning for a time, but the processes of convergence will accelerate if the growing flow of global commerce remains open. International networks will ultimately promote the growth of an international society that is more than the sum of mutual interests among independent nations (Bull and Watson, 1989). We already see the development of a set of common values, norms of behavior, rules, and institutions that will ultimately structure the world community (Inglehart, 1990).

Cumulative Learning

Learning leverages economic progress in the new economy. Moreover, learning has cumulative effects driven by a complex dynamic. In general, the accumulation process gets a kick-start from the application of science, invention, or innovation. Momentum builds when new learning is embedded by investment and accelerates through dissemination, networking, and commercialization. Those who start up and sustain momentum through learning processes will get ahead, stay ahead, and increase their lead over others; the rich get richer and lavish their wealth on others through expanding networks bound by investment and commerce.

The importance of cumulative learning in the new economy represents a shift in emphasis from old-style mass production. In mass production organizations, increased production was valued because it reduced unit costs, thereby allowing lower prices and larger market shares. Design and production of the first unit is expensive, but with each successive unit produced average costs decline. In the new economy, producing additional units of output not only brings greater efficiencies but also contributes more experience and understanding as to how to make the good or deliver the service more inexpensively and better. The more experience is gained and learning is accumulated, the more products—and the processes for making them—are improved. In the new economy, market share is leveraged by continuous improvements not only in efficiency but in quality, variety, customization, and convenience as well. Moreover, given the self-reinforcing processes characteristic of economic progress in the new economy, one kind of learning tends to lead to another. Experience gained and feedback received from expanding networks and commercialization tend to promote new scientific advances, inventions, and innovations. For example, early clock making and the making of navigational instruments provided the precision and work processes necessary to the industrial revolution. Japan's initial investment in building precision instruments eventually led to advances in consumer electronics and integrated circuiuts (Arthur, 1990).

The cumulative dynamic of learning in the new economy tends to confer runaway momentum in the competitive race to those who can jump-start and accelerate learning processes. Once organizations or even whole nations build a lead, it is hard to catch up because an appreciable share of learning can only be acquired through experience. Some learning, especially scientific advances and inventions, can be bought off the shelf. Other learning can be borrowed quickly through reverse engineering and copying best practices (Dosi, Tyson, and Zysman, 1989). However, an increasing share of learning in the new economy is experiential and difficult to appropriate. The fruits of learning by doing and learning by using, both central to innovation, are difficult to separate from experience and package into portable formats. The processes of dissemination exhibit a similar experiential bias. Networks and their extension through commercialization are built on complex behaviors and patterns of interaction refined with practice. Investment processes broaden and deepen learning over long periods and create complementary assets that take time to evolve. For example, the production of automobiles required complementary technologies in steel, rubber, and electronics. The commercialization of automobiles required new financial, legal, and regulatory infrastructure. And the use of automobiles requires roads, bridges, and energy technologies. Long lead times are also required to embody new knowledge in the skills of the workforce. Investments in complementary assets, new infrastructure, and human capital are relatively immobile, especially across national boundaries.

Finally, the new competitive standards themselves require learning that takes place in specific work teams and networks in the incremental process of attempting to satisfy those standards in specific contexts. Because the new learning takes place in groups, is incremental, and is tailored to specific contexts, it is particularly difficult to generalize and transfer. Moreover, the specific kind of learning demanded by each of the standards is difficult to appropriate off the shelf. Quality, for instance, demands a shift in perspective from a one-dimensional valuation of quantity to a valuation of excellence in the various facets of a product and its overall integrity. Quality requires higher levels of commitment and a willingness to take responsibility for final products. Variety, customization, and timeliness require the ability to learn, solve problems, and handle exceptions. These skills are best learned through experience in applied contexts and usually in groups and networks. The ability to provide convenience requires a sensitivity to customers and interpersonal skills that one can only learn experientially.

The cumulative value of learning in leveraging economic progress is not monolithic. In concept, economic progress can peter out in networks that depend on fixed resources (Arthur, 1989). The more of our oil supply that we use, for example, the less we have for future use. Dissemination and commercialization in oil-based networks draw down available supply and bring declining returns to expansion and further investment. In information- or communication-based industries that rely only marginally on scarce natural resources, however, dissemination and commercialization bring only increasing returns and positive feedback. The more that resources in these learning-based industries are used and extended through dissemination and commercialization, the more knowledge accumulates, bringing increasing returns to investment and additional momentum to economic progress.

Even in networks based on natural resources, learning can greatly reduce and at times reverse declining returns to the growth of networks and commercial uses of resources by serving as a substitute for or a complement to natural resources, thus extending their effective supply. Scientific inquiry, invention, and innovation can find ways to get the job done using fewer essentially nonrenewable resources. Oil is a case in point. Despite an absolute decline in the earth's oil supply since 1960, the available supply has doubled as a result of advances in extraction and increased further as a result of recycling (Baumol, Blackman, and Wolff, 1989). Moreover, learning can create a network of complementary assets that rely less on natural resources or use them more efficiently. We can build more fuel-efficient cars, for instance. Oil is not the only example; despite doomsday projections, the world's economic networks have never run out of any critical resource, and careful analysis suggests that the *effective* supply of all natural resources has only increased over the past decades.

The cumulative dynamic of economic progress is not all good news. Accumulation provides momentum for economic progress but also directs the trajectory of that progress along a self-reinforcing path, and the path is not necessarily optimal. Contrary to traditional notions, the path of economic progress is not the guaranteed, gradual revelation of best alternatives in a free market of competing alternatives. Inferior alternatives can be selected, and momentum can lead to dead ends.

In the early stages of invention or innovation, several alternative paths are open, and the existence of many choices can stall progress. For example, uncertainty as to whether Beta or VHS tape or disc would be the technology of choice in home video stalled commercialization until VHS became dominant. Eventually, a particular innovation secures an edge in adoption, and once it is adopted by a critical mass of users, experience and use lead to improvements. Complementary innovations and commercial networks evolve until eventually the process of accumulation builds sufficient momentum and sunk costs to ward off alternatives—even superior ones. It is difficult to change paths once the process of accumulation reaches a critical mass that allows for a self-reinforcing momentum. The British continued to build narrow-gauge railroads long after there was solid proof that a broader track could optimize load and speed. The British still drive on the "wrong" side of the road. The qwerty keyboard persists despite more efficient alternatives. FORTRAN survived long after superior alternatives became available. The world is still divided into 110-volt and 220-volt nations despite the inconvenience. The Irish stuck with potatoes until the potato famine drove them from their homeland. We use VHS because it built a critical mass of commercial distributors, not because it is technically superior to Beta.

How can an organization, a network, or a nation choose an inferior path for economic progress? The basic difficulty is that it is impossible to know enough about the future to always make the right bets. Learning processes usually begin with incremental choices, but accumulation eventually magnifies these small events. Alternatives that are marginally superior now may lock us into inferior developmental paths later. We chose internal combustion over steam at the turn of the century in large part because it was difficult to maintain pressures for steam safely and because it was easy to turn off the internal combustion engine but took a while for steam pressure to subside. Given current standards, steam might have been preferable; it is cleaner, and water is infinitely available and recyclable. Could we have built an effective steam engine for mass transport, flight, and industry? There is almost no way to know. The roads not taken are long since overgrown. And because we did not take them, we do not know where they would have led.

Another reason we may follow economic paths that are inferior or lead to dead ends is that our choices are always conditioned by the path we are already on. Our accumulated knowledge influences our decisions. When trying to increase fuel efficiency, for example, auto engineers had to choose between building aluminum engines and reducing the amount of steel in cars. The engineers had little experience with aluminum and were not metallurgists, but they did know about car designs. They decided to add more composites to bumpers and other auto parts rather than try to build a light aluminum engine (Dosi, Tyson, and Zysman, 1989).

The path-dependent character of learning processes turns economic progress into a game of chance. As a result of our inability to predict the future, we place our bets on the basis of marginal differences among alternatives. Our understanding of those differences in economic potential is conditioned by the current accumulation of knowledge. If our current stock of knowledge, the result of past bets, were different or if we could see farther into the future, we might make different choices. The best we can do is to use the scientific and applied knowledge available to us effectively and place as many bets as we can. Because the multiplication of economic networks worldwide assures that many paths for testing and accumulating new learning will be pursued simultaneously, a strategy of spreading our bets puts a premium on the free flow of scientific and applied knowledge. The greater the number of paths and the more sharing of knowledge, the more economic progress worldwide.

CHALLENGES FACING AMERICA
IN THE NEW ECONOMY

We should not take the path of economic progress in the new economy for granted. Economic progress is always a game against both nature and society and doubly difficult to win. Despite the cumulative momentum inherent in the processes that foster it, economic progress has always been a sporadic and temporary phenomenon in the history of individual societies. Sunk costs and momentum make it difficult to get off inferior paths and to strike out in new directions. Societies also fail to meet new challenges because the tenacious hold of the past is rooted in our inherent limitations as individuals and the complex structures of communities (Kuran, 1988). New beliefs, behaviors, and patterns of interaction do not come easily, especially when the tried-and-true has the cumulative weight of history to recommend it. Even if individuals are willing to change, organizations and societies can remain intransigent. The status quo is always organized to meet the last challenge,

235

not the next one, because the general interest is diffused while special interests are organized and focused.

Ultimately, our success in the new economy will depend on the extent to which we value economic progress. Economic success was short-lived in the past because it was not valued sufficiently. The economic advances of classical antiquity were only by-products of conquest and empire; economic progress lived and died by the sword. In medieval times, economic progress was possible only to the extent that it glorified Christianity or Islam or contributed to the evolution of nation-states. The Renaissance valued discovery more than its application. Industrial Britain enjoyed the fruits of invention, but her chivalrous elite actively eschewed commerce as déclassé.

The best hope for the new economy is that it is the only game in town. In all but the most isolated and backward corners of the globe, economic progress has supplanted war, ideology, and religious fundamentalism as the focus and competitive field of play among nations. Indeed, economic networks have already outgrown nations. Economic networks and the emerging international society are the newest creations of humankind. The extent of networks and the reach of commercialization assure that even the hindmost are aware of progress elsewhere and their relative position in the material world. Isolation, the principal ally of backwardness, is disappearing, assuring an acceleration of economic convergence. Moreover, examples of successes elsewhere challenge the prevailing wisdom at home and provide the necessary feedback in nations pursuing suboptimal or dead-end economic paths. A loss of relative position or unfavorable comparisons with other nations' material progress can inspire populations to break the tenacious grip of the past.

The new economy presents formidable challenges. Its materialism is no substitute for ideology and humankind's transcendental instinct. If it proves a wasteland, it risks awakening the false gods of fascism. Of course, it could also clear away the debris of old ideological and religious arguments and prepare the way for a more positive spiritual revival. To some extent, the new values of environmentalism and social responsibility have already begun the greening of the new economic compeition.

Moreover, these new values are at the heart of an emerging global consciousness (Inglehart, 1990). Honesty, integrity, and service to others are becoming good business. Whether the notion of economic progress will expand to include normative constraints and goals remains to be seen.

REFERENCES AND
SUGGESTED READINGS

Abernathy, W., Clark, K., and Kantrow, A. *Industrial Renaissance: Producing a Competitive Future for America.* New York: Basic Books, 1983.

Abraham, K. *Restructuring the Employment Relationship: The Growth of Market-Mediated Work Arrangements.* College Park, Md.: University of Maryland, 1988.

Adams, C. *The Straight Dope: Answers to Questions That Torment Everyone.* New York: Ballantine, 1984.

Adler, P. "New Technologies, New Skills." *California Management Review,* 1986, *29* (1), 9–28.

Adler, P. "Managing Flexible Automation." *California Management Review,* 1988, *30* (3), 34–56.

Albrecht, K. *At America's Service.* Homewood, Ill.: Dow Jones–Irwin, 1988.

Albrecht, K., and Zemke, R. *Service America!* Homewood, Ill.: Dow Jones–Irwin, 1985.

Allaire, P., and Rickard, E. "Quality and Participation at Xerox." *Journal for Quality and Participation*, 1989, *12* (1), 24–26.

Arendt, H. *The Human Condition.* Chicago: University of Chicago Press, 1970.

Arthur, W. B. "Competing Technologies, Increasing Returns, and Lock-in by Historical Events." *Economic Journal*, 1989, *99*, 116–131.

Arthur, W. B. "Positive Feedbacks in the Economy." *Scientific American*, Feb. 1990, pp. 92–99.

Asaka, T., and Ozeki, K. *Handbook of Quality Tools.* Cambridge, Mass.: Productivity Press, 1988.

Bailey T. "Changes in the Nature and Structure of Work: Implications for Employer-Sponsored Training." Paper presented at Conference on Employer-Sponsored Training, Alexandria, Va., Dec. 1988a.

Bailey, T. "Changes in the Nature and Structure of Work: Implications for Skill Demand." Paper presented at Conference on National Assessment of Vocational Education, Washington, D. C., 1988b.

Bailey, T. *Education and the Transformation of Markets and Technology in the Textile Industry.* Technical Paper, no. 2. New York: National Center on Education and Employment, Teachers College, Columbia University, 1988c.

Bailey, T., and Noyelle, T. *New Technology and Skill Formation: Issues and Hypotheses.* New York: National Center on Education and Employment, Teachers College, Columbia University, 1988.

Baloff, N., and Doherty, E. M. "Potential Pitfalls in Employee Participation." *Organizational Dynamics*, 1989, *26* (5), 51–62.

Baran, B., and Parsons, C. "Technology and Skill: A Literature Review." Paper presented at Carnegie Forum on Education and the Economy, Berkeley Roundtable on the International Economy, Hyattsville, Md., Jan. 1986.

Barra, R. "Motorola's Approach to Quality." *Journal for Quality and Participation*, 1989, *12* (1), 46–50.

Baumol, W. J., Blackman, S. A., and Wolff, E. N. *Productivity and American Leadership: The Long View.* Cambridge, Mass.: MIT Press, 1989.

Beer, M., Eisenstat, R. A., and Spector, B. "Why Change Programs Don't Produce Change." *Harvard Business Review*, 1990, *68* (6), 158–166.

Bell, R. M. *The Coming of Post-Industrial Society: Adventure in Social Forecasting.* New York: Basic Books, 1983.

Berger, P., and Luckmann, T. *Social Construction of Reality: A Treatise in the Sociology of Knowledge.* New York: Irvington, 1966.

Berger, S. "The U.S. Textile Industry: Challenges and Opportunities: In *The Working Papers of the MIT Commission on Industrial Productivity.* Vol. 2. Cambridge, Mass.: MIT Press, 1989.

Berryman, S. "Shadows in the Wings: The Next Educational Reform." Paper presented at the Education Policy Forum, sponsored by the American Educational Research Association and the Institute for Educational Leadership, Washington, D. C., March 1987.

Bertrand, O., and Noyelle, T. *Human Resources and Corporate Strategy.* Paris: Organization for Economic Cooperation and Development, 1988.

Bishop, J. *Achievement, Test Scores, and Relative Wages.* Conference Paper. Washington, D. C.: American Enterprise Institute for Public Policy Research, 1989.

Blackburn, J. *Time-Based Competition: The Next Battleground in American Manufacturing.* Homewood, Ill.: Business One Irwin, 1991.

Blackburn, P., Coombs, R., and Green, K. *Technology, Economic Growth and the Labor Process.* New York: St. Martin's Press, 1985.

Bound, J., and Johnson, G. *Wages in the United States During the 1980s and Beyond.* Conference Paper. Washington, D.C.: American Enterprise Institute for Public Policy Research, 1989.

Bozdogan, K. "The Transformation of the U.S. Chemicals Industry." In *The Working Papers of the MIT Commission on Industrial Productivity.* Vol. 1. Cambridge, Mass.: MIT Press, 1989.

Brache, A. P., and Rummler, G. A. "The Three Levels of Quality." *Quality Progress*, 1989, *21* (10), 28–30.

Brandt, R. "Chips Are Down but Not for Long." *Business Week*, Jan. 8, 1990, p. 100.

Braverman, H. *Labor and Monopoly Capital: The Degradation of Work in the Twentieth Century*. New York: New York Monthly Review Press, 1974.

Bull, H., and Watson, A. (eds.). *The Expansion of Economic Society*. Oxford, England: Clarendon Press, 1989.

Bush, D., and Dooley, K. "The Deming Prize & Baldrige Award: How They Compare." *Quality Progress*, 1989, *22* (1), 28–30.

Carnevale, A. P. *Jobs for the Nation: Challenges for a Society Based on Work*. Alexandria, Va.: American Society for Training and Development, 1985.

Carnevale, A. P., and Gainer, L. J. *The Learning Enterprise*. Washington, D. C.: U.S. Department of Labor; Alexandria, Va.: American Society for Training and Development, 1989a.

Carnevale, A. P., and Gainer, L. J. *Training America: Learning to Work in the Twenty-First Century*. Washington, D.C.: U.S. Department of Labor; Alexandria, Va.: American Society for Training and Development, 1989b.

Carnevale, A. P., Gainer, L. J., and Meltzer, A. *Workplace Basics: The Skills Employers Want*. Washington, D.C.: U.S. Department of Labor; Alexandria, Va.: American Society for Training and Development, 1989.

Carnevale, A. P., Gainer, L. J., and Meltzer, A. *Workplace Basics: The Essential Skills Employers Want*. San Francisco: Jossey-Bass, 1990.

Carnevale, A. P., Gainer, L. J., and Shultz, E. *Training the Technical Work Force*. San Francisco: Jossey-Bass, 1990.

Carnevale A. P., Gainer, L. J., and Villet, J. *Training in America: The Organization and Strategic Role of Training*. San Francisco: Jossey-Bass, 1990.

Carnevale, A. P., and Johnson, J. *Training America: Strategies for the Nation*. Alexandria, Va.: American Society for Training and Development; Rochester, N.Y.: National Center on Education and the Economy, 1989.

Chance, P. "Redefining the Supervisor's Role." *Across the Board*, 1989, *26* (5), 36–37.

Clark, K., Chew, W., and Fujimoto, T. *Product Development in the World Auto Industry*. Brookings Papers on Economic Activity, 3. Washington, D.C.: Brookings Institution, 1987.

Clark, K., and Fujimoto, T. "The Power of Product Integrity." *Harvard Business Review*, 1990, *68* (6), 107–118.

Clausing, D. "The U.S. Semiconductor, Computer, and Copier Industries." In *The Working Papers of the MIT Commission on Industrial Productivity*. Vol. 2. Cambridge, Mass.: MIT Press, 1989.

Coates, J. E. "The Ins and Outs of Quality Circles—Mostly the Ins." *Industrial Management*, 1988, *30* (3), 4–6.

Cyert, R. M., and Mowery, D. C. (eds.). *Technology and Employment: Innovation and Growth in the U.S. Economy*. Washington, D.C.: National Academy Press, 1987.

De Geus, A. P. "Planning as Learning." *Harvard Business Review*, 1988, *66* (2), 70–74.

Deming, W. E. *Quality, Productivity, and Competitive Position*. Cambridge, Mass.: MIT Press, 1982.

Denison, E. *Accounting for United States Economic Growth 1929–1969*. Washington, D.C.: Brookings Institution, 1974.

Denton, D. K. *Quality Service*. Houston: Gulf, 1989.

Dertouzos, M., Lester, R., and Solow, R. *Made in America*. Cambridge, Mass.: MIT Press, 1989.

Desatnick, R. *Managing to Keep the Customer: How to Achieve and Maintain Superior Customer Service Throughout the Organization*. San Francisco: Jossey-Bass, 1989.

Dillon, L. S. "Can Japanese Method Be Applied in the Workplace?" *Quality Progress*, 1990, *23* (10), 27–30.

Dixion, J. R., Nanni, A. J., and Vollman, T. E. *The New Performance Challenge: Measuring Operations for World-Class Competition*. Homewood, Ill.: Dow Jones–Irwin, 1990.

Dosi, G., Tyson, L. D., and Zysman, J. "Trade, Technologies, and Development." In G. Dosi, L. D. Tyson, and J. Zysman (eds.), *Politics and Productivity*. New York: Harper Collins, 1989.

Doz, Y. "International Industries: Fragmentation Versus Globalization." In B. Guile and H. Brooks (eds.), *Technology and Global Industry: Companies and Nations in the World Economy*. Washington, D.C.: National Academy Press, 1987.

Doz, Y., and Prahala, C. K. *The Multinational Mission, Balancing Local Demands and Global Vision*. New York: Free Press, 1987.

Dumaine, B. "How Managers Can Succeed Through Speed." *Fortune*, 1989, *119* (4), 54–59.

Dumaine, B. "Who Needs a Boss?" *Fortune*, 1990, *121* (10), 52–60.

Duncan, A. "It's a Lot Tougher to Mind the Store." *Business Week*, Jan. 8, 1990, p. 85.

Edwards, R. *Contested Terrain: The Transformation of the Workplace in the Twentieth Century.* New York: Basic Books, 1979.

Ergas, H. "Does Technology Policy Matter?" In B. Guile and H. Brooks (eds.), *Technology and Global Industry: Companies and Nations in the World Economy.* Washington, D.C.: National Academy Press, 1987.

Fairbank, J., Reischauer, E., and Craig, A. *East Asia: Tradition and Transformation.* Boston: Houghton Mifflin, 1978.

Feigenbaum, A. "Seven Keys to Constant Quality." *Journal for Quality and Participation*, 1989, *12* (1), 20–23.

Felgner, B. "Consumer Expenditures Study: Specialty Foods." *Supermarket Business*, 1988, *43* (9), 185–207.

Flamm, K. *Creating the Computer: Government, Industry & High Technology.* Washington, D.C.: Brookings Institution, 1988.

Flemings, M. "The Future of the U.S. Steel Industry in the International Marketplace." In *The Working Papers of the MIT Commission on Industrial Productivity.* Vol. 2. Cambridge, Mass.: MIT Press, 1989.

Flynn, P. *Facilitating Technological Change: The Human Resource Challenge.* Cambridge, Mass.: Ballinger, 1989.

Ford, G. W. "Innovations in Post-School Skill Formation Markets." Paper presented at United States Organization for Economic Cooperation and Development Seminar on Technological Change and Human Resource Development, Washington, D.C., June 1989.

Freedman, A. *Productivity Needs of the United States.* Report No. 934. New York: Conference Board, 1989.

Frohman, M. "PM: Participative Management: The Missing Ingredients." *Industry Week*, 1989, *238* (23), 30–36.

Fullerton, H. "New Labor Force Projections, Spanning 1988 to 2000." *Monthly Labor Review*, 1989, *112* (11), 3–12.

Galagan, P. A. "Mapping Its Patterns and Periods." *Training and Development Journal*, 1989, *43* (11), 41–48.

Galvin, R. "Statement on Motorola's Quality Experience." Unpublished speech, National Institute of Standards and Technology, Washington, D.C., Nov. 1988.

Garraty, J. A. *Unemployment in History: Economic Thought and Public Policy.* New York: Harper & Row, 1979.

Garvin, D. "Quality on the Line." *Harvard Business Review,* 1983, *61* (5), 65–75.

Garvin, D. "Competing on the Eight Dimensions of Quality." *Harvard Business Review,* 1987, *65* (6), 101–109.

Garvin, D. *Managing Quality.* New York: Free Press, 1988.

Gayle, M. "Toward the Twenty-First Century." *Adult Learning,* 1990, *1* (4), 10–14.

Geber, B. "How to Manage Wild Ducks." *Training,* 1990, *27* (5), 29–36.

Gerlach, M. "Business Alliances and the Strategy of the Japanese Firm." *California Management Review,* 1987, *30* (1), 126–142.

Gibbs, G. *The Saco-Lowell Shops.* New York: Russell and Russell, 1950.

Goldhar, J., and Jelinek, M. "Plan for Economies of Scope." *Harvard Business Review,* 1983, *61* (6), 141–148.

Goldstein, H., and Fraser, B. S. *Training for Work in the Computer Age: How Workers Who Use Computers Get Their Training.* Washington, D.C.: National Commission for Employment Policy, U.S. Department of Labor, 1985.

Gomory, R., and Schmitt, R. "Science and Product." *Science,* 1988, *240* (4856), 1131–1132, 1203–1204.

Grayson, C., and O'Dell, C. *American Business: A Two-Minute Warning.* New York: Free Press, 1988.

Groocock, J. M. *The Chain of Quality.* New York: Wiley, 1986.

Guest, R. H. "Team Management Under Stress." *Across the Board,* 1989, *26* (5), 30–35.

Guile, B., and Brooks, H. (eds.). *Technology and Global Industry: Companies and Nations in the World Economy.* Washington, D.C.: National Academy Press, 1987.

Hall, R., Johnson, T., and Turney, P. *Measuring Up: Charting Pathways to Manufacturing Excellence.* Homewood, Ill.: Business One Irwin, 1990.

Hampton, W., and Schiller, Z. "Why Image Counts: A Tale of Two Industries." *Business Week*, June 8, 1987, pp. 138–140.

Hayes, R., and Garvin, D. "Managing as If Tomorrow." *Harvard Business Review*, 1982, *60* (3), 70–80.

Herman, S. M. "Participative Management is a Double-Edged Sword." *Training*, 1989, *26* (1), 52–57.

Hirsch, E. *Cultural Literacy: What Every American Needs to Know.* Boston: Houghton Mifflin, 1987.

Hirschhorn, L. "The Post-Industrial Economy: Labor, Skills and the New Mode of Production." *Service Industries Journal*, 1988, *8* (1), 19–38.

Hochschild, A., and Machung, A. *The Second Shift: Inside the Two-Job Marriage.* New York: Viking-Penguin, 1989.

Hodder, J., and Riggs, H. "Pitfalls in Evaluating Risky Projects." *Harvard Business Review*, 1985, *63* (1), 128–135.

Hodgson, A. "Deming's Never-Ending Road to Quality." *Personnel Management*, 1987, *19* (7), 40–44.

Hoerr, J. "Work Teams Can Rev Up Paper-Pushers, Too." *Business Week*, Nov. 28, 1988, pp. 64–72.

Hout, T. M., and Stalk, G., Jr. *Competing Against Time: How Time Based Competition Is Reshaping Global Markets.* New York: Free Press, 1990.

Hummel, R. "Behind Quality Management: What Workers and a Few Philosophers Have Always Known and How It Adds Up to Excellence in Production." *Organizational Dynamics*, 1987, *16* (1), 71–78.

Hutchins, D. "Having a Hard Time with Just-in-Time." *Fortune*, 1986, *113* (12), 64–66.

Inglehart, R. *Culture Shift in Advanced Industrial Societies.* Princeton, N.J.: Princeton University Press, 1990.

Ingrassia, P., and Patterson, G. "Is Buying a Car a Choice or a Chore?" *Wall Street Journal*, Oct. 24, 1989, sec. 2, p. 1.

Jaccaci, A. T. "The Social Architecture of a Learning Culture." *Training and Development Journal*, 1989, *43* (11), 49–51.

Johnston, R., and Lawrence, P. "Beyond Vertical Integration—The Rise of the Value-Adding Partnership." *Harvard Business Review*, 1988, *66* (4), 94–101.

Johnston, W., and Packer, A. *Workforce 2000: Work and Workers for the 21st Century.* Indianapolis, Ind.: Hudson Institute, 1987.

Juhn, C., Murphy, K., and Pierce, B. *Accounting for the Slowdown in Black-White Wage Convergence.* Conference Paper. Washington, D.C.: American Enterprise Institute for Public Policy Research, 1989.

Juran, J. M. "China's Ancient History of Managing for Quality, Part I." *Quality Progress,* 1990a, *23* (7), 31–35.

Juran, J. M. "China's Ancient History of Managing for Quality, Part II." *Quality Progress,* 1990b, *23* (8), 25–30.

Kahn, A. E. *The Economics of Regulation: Principles and Institutions.* Cambridge, Mass.: MIT Press, 1988.

Kanter, R. M. *The Change Masters: Innovation and Entrepreneurship in the American Corporation.* New York: Simon & Schuster, 1984.

Karabatsos, N. "Quality in Transition: Part 1. Account of the 80's." *Quality Progress,* 1989, *22* (12), 22–26.

Kendrick, J. "Managing Quality in Steel: Building Customer-Responsive Manufacturing." *Quality Digest,* 1988, *27* (2), 16–18.

Kerr, C. *The Future of Industrial Societies: Convergence on Continuing Diversity.* Cambridge, Mass.: Harvard University Press, 1983.

Kirrane, D. (ed.). *Training for Quality.* ASTD Info-Line, Issue 805. Alexandria, Va.: American Society for Training and Development, 1988.

Kochan, T., Mitchell, D., and Dyer, L. (eds.). *Industrial Relations Research in the 1970s: Review and Appraisal.* Industrial Relations Research Association Series. Bloomington, Ill.: Pantagraph Printing, 1982.

Konsynski, B. R., and McFarlan, E. W. "Information Partnerships—Shared Data, Shared Scale." *Harvard Business Review,* 1990, *68* (5), 114–120.

Kosters, M. *Wages and Demographics.* Conference Paper. Washington, D.C.: American Enterprise Institute for Public Policy Research, 1989.

Kraar, L. "Your Rivals Can Be Your Allies." *Fortune,* 1989, *119* (7), 66–76.

Krismann, C. *Quality Control: An Annotated Bibliography*. White Plains, N.Y.: Quality Resources, 1990.

Krugman, P. *The Age of Diminished Expectations: U.S. Economic Policy in the 1990's*. Cambridge, Mass.: MIT Press, 1990.

Kuhn, T. *The Structure of Scientific Revolutions*. Chicago: University of Chicago Press, 1970.

Kuran, T. "The Tenacious Past: Theories of Personal and Collective Conservatism." *Journal of Economic Behavior and Organization*, 1988, *10*, 143–171.

Kutscher, R. E. "Projections Summary and Emerging Issues." *Monthly Labor Review*, 1989, *112* (11), 66–74.

Kuttner, R. "Atlas Unburdened: America's Economic Interests in a New World Era." *American Prospect*, Spring 1990, pp. 90–103.

LeBoeuf, M. *How to Win Customers and Keep Them for Life*. New York: Putnam, 1987.

Lehnerd, A. "Revitalizing the Manufacture and Design of Mature Global Products." In B. Guile and H. Brooks (eds.), *Technology and Global Industry: Companies and Nations in the World Economy*. Washington, D.C.: National Academy Press, 1987.

Levy, F. *Dollars and Dreams: The Changing American Income Distribution*. New York: Russell Sage Foundation, 1987.

Lewis, J. *Partnerships for Profit: Structuring and Managing Strategic Alliances*. New York: Free Press, 1990.

Liebergott, S. *The Americans: An Economic Record*. New York: Norton, 1984.

Litan, R., Lawrence, R., and Schultze, C. (eds.). *American Living Standards*. Washington, D.C.: Brookings Institution, 1988.

Lodge, G. *Perestroika for America: Restructuring Business—Government Relations for World Competitiveness*. New York: McGraw-Hill, 1990.

McCraw, T. K. *Prophets of Regulation: Charles Francis Adams, Louis D. Brandeis, James Landis, Alfred Kahn*. Cambridge, Mass.: Belknap Press, 1984.

McDermott, B. "Training Key to Developing Autonomous Work Teams." *Training Directors' Forum Newsletter*, 1990, *6* (8), 1–3.

March, A. "The U.S. Commercial Aircraft Industry and Its Foreign Competitors." In *The Working Papers of the MIT Commission on Industrial Productivity*. Vol. 1. Cambridge, Mass.: MIT Press, 1989.

March, A. "A Note on Quality: The Views of Deming, Juran, and Crosby." *Harvard Business Review*, 1990, *68* (1), 1–3.

Milgram, P., and Roberts, J. "The Economics of Modern Manufacturing: Technology, Strategy, and Organization." *American Economic Review*, *80* (3), 1990, 511–528.

Mohanty, R. P., and Dahanayka, N. "Process Improvement: Evolution of Methods." *Quality Progress*, 1989, *22* (9), 45–48.

Mokyr, J. *The Lever of Riches: Technological Creativity and Economic Progress*. New York: Oxford University Press, 1990.

Molina, A. "1992: European Integration, Opportunities and Difficulties in High Technology Collaboration." *Futures*, 1990, *22* (5), 496–514.

Moran, L., Musselwhite, E., Orsburn, J., and Zenger, J. *Self-Directed Workteams, The New American Challenge*. Homewood, Ill.: Business One Irwin, 1990.

Morris, C. "The Coming Global Boom." *Atlantic Monthly*, 1989, *264* (4), 51–64.

Mowery, D., and Rosenberg, N. "New Developments in U.S. Technology Policy: Implications for Competitiveness and International Trade Policy." *California Management Review*, 1989, *32* (1), 107–124.

Murphy, K., and Welch, F. *Wage Differentials in the 1980s: The Role of International Trade*. Conference Paper. Washington, D.C.: American Enterprise Institute for Public Policy Research, 1989.

Nasar, S. "Do We Live as Well as We Used To?" *Fortune*, 1987, *116* (6), 32–34, 36–46.

National Advisory Committee on Semiconductors. *A Report to the President and the Congress*. Washington, D.C.: U.S. Government Printing Office, 1989.

National Institute of Standards and Technology, 1990 and 1991 Application Guidelines for Malcolm Baldrige National Quality Award.

National Research Council, Manufacturing Studies Board. *The Internationalization of U.S. Manufacturing: Causes and Consequences*. Washington, D.C.: National Academy Press, 1991.

Noyelle, T. *Services and the New Economy: Toward a New Labor Market Segmentation*. New York: National Center on Education and Employment, Teachers College, Columbia University, 1988a.

Noyelle, T. *Skills, Skill Formation, Productivity and Competitiveness: A Cross-National Comparison of Banks and Insurance Carriers in Five Advanced Economies.* Washington, D.C.: Conference on Employer-Provided Training, 1988b.

Noyelle, T. "Skill Needs in the Service Sector: The Role of Firm-Based Training." Testimony before the Joint Economic Committee, Congress of the United States, Hearings on Crisis in the Workplace: Mismatch of Jobs and Skills. Oct. 31, 1989.

Ohmee, K. "The Global Logic of Strategic Alliances." *Harvard Business Review*, 1989, *67* (2), 143–154.

Ohmee, K. *The Borderless World: Power and Strategy in the Interlinked Economy.* New York: Harper Business, 1990.

Ozeki, K., and Asaka, T. *Handbook of Quality Tools: The Japanese Approach.* Cambridge, Mass.: Productivity Press, 1988.

Paton, S. "The Malcolm Baldridge National Quality Award: A Year of Firsts." *Quality Digest*, 1991, *11* (1), 32–46.

Pennar, K. "America's Quest Can't Be Half-Hearted." *Business Week*, June 8, 1987, p. 136.

Perrault, M. "Workplace Freedom: American Workers Aren't Getting Enough." *Management World*, 1989, *18* (2), 1–6.

Personick, V. A. "Industry Output and Employment: A Slower Trend for the Nineties." *Monthly Labor Review*, 1989, *112* (11), 25–41.

Peters, T. "Time Obsessed Competition." *Management Review*, 1990, *79* (9), 16–20.

Piore, M., and Sabel, C. *The Second Industrial Divide.* New York: Basic Books, 1984.

Port, O. "The Push for Quality." *Business Week*, June 8, 1987, pp. 130–135.

The Power Report. 1989, *11* (8) (entire issue).

Priestman, S. "Bringing Quality Home." *Silicon Valley Magazine*, Oct.–Nov. 1984a.

Priestman, S. "Professional Careers: Information Specialists Replacing Librarians." *San Jose Mercury News*, Nov. 25, 1984b.

Priestman, S. "Rolm President Tries to Reassure Wary Workers." *San Francisco Examiner*, Sept. 27, 1984c.

Priestman, S. "Area Firms Re-Examine Quality-Control Process." *San Jose Mercury News*, March 31, 1985a.

Priestman, S. "SQC and JIT: Partnership in Quality." *Quality Progress*, 1985b, *18* (5), 31–34.

Razzano, R. "Retailing in the Year 2000: Future Demands Whet Retailers' Appetites." *Chain Store Age Executive*, 1987, *63* (5), 213–216.

Reich, R. B. "Education in Teamwork." *Across the Board*, 1989, *26* (5), 11.

Reichheld, F. F., and Sasser, W. E., Jr. "Zero Defections: Quality Comes to Services." *Harvard Business Review*, 1990, *68* (5), 105–111.

Reid, P. *Well Made in America*. New York: McGraw-Hill, 1990.

Roach, S. "Pitfalls on the 'New' Assembly Line: Can Services Learn from Manufacturing?" Special Economic Study for Morgan Stanley presented at Organization for Economic Cooperation and Development. International Seminar on Science, Technology and Economic Growth, Paris, June 1989.

Robinson, J. "Time's Up." *American Demographics*, 1989, *11* (7), 32–35.

Robinson, J. P. *Trends in Americans' Use of Time: Some Preliminary 1975–1985 Comparisons*. College Park, Md.: Survey Research Center, University of Maryland, 1986.

Romano, C. "Identifying Factors Which Influence Product Innovation: A Case Study Approach." *Journal of Management Studies*, 1990, *27* (1), 75–95.

Rosenberg, N. *Inside the Black Box: Technology and Economics*. New York: Press Syndicate of the University of Cambridge, 1982.

Rosenberg, N., and Birdsell, L. *How the West Grew Rich: The Economic Transformation of the Industrial World*. New York: Basic Books, 1986.

Roth, B. "A New Role for Unions." *Journal for Quality and Participation*, Sept. 1990, pp. 46–51.

Rubinstein, S. "Quality and Democracy in the Work Place." *Quality Progress*, 1988, *21* (4), 25–28.

Rummler, G. A., and Brache, A. P. *Improving Performance: How to Manage the White Space on the Organizational Chart*. San Francisco: Jossey-Bass, 1990.

Sadler, G. "Comparative Output and Productivity Patterns: U.S. and Japan, 1970–83." Unpublished data, American Productivity Center, Houston, Tex., 1977.

Sanders, E. "The Regulatory Surge of the 1970s in Historical Perspective." In E. E. Bailey (ed.), *Public Regulation: New Perspectives on Institutions and Policies.* Cambridge, Mass.: MIT Press, 1987.

Schiller, Z. "Appliance Repairmen Are Getting Lonelier." *Business Week,* June 8, 1987, p. 139.

Schrage, M. *Shared Kinds: The New Technologies of Collaboration.* New York: Random House, 1990.

Schumpeter, J. *Capitalism, Socialism and Democracy.* New York: Harper & Row, 1989.

Segalla, E. "All for Quality, and Quality for All." *Training and Development Journal,* 1989, *43* (9), 36–45.

Senge, P. M. "The Leader's New Work: Building Learning Organizations." *Sloan Management Review,* 1990, *32* (1), 7–22.

Shingo, S. *A Study of the Toyota Production System from an International Engineering Viewpoint.* Cambridge, Mass.: Productivity Press, 1989.

Shores, D. "TQC: Science, Not Witchcraft." *Quality Progress,* 1989, *22* (4), 42–45.

Silvestri, G., and Lukasiewicz, J. "Projections of Occupational Employment, 1988–2000." *Monthly Labor Review,* 1989, *112* (11), 42–65.

Sirgy, J. "A Quality-of-Life Theory Derived from Maslow's Development Perspective." *American Journal of Economics and Sociology,* 1986, *45* (3), 329–342.

Skrabec, Q. R. "Ancient Process Control and Its Modern Implications." *Quality Progress,* 1990, *23* (11), 49–52.

Smith, L. "The Wealth of Nations: The World Is Getting Richer." *Fortune,* 1987, *116* (6), 35.

Smith, S. "Personal Investing: Hogs with Wheels." *Fortune,* 1989, *119* (8), 38–40.

Spenner, K. "The Upgrading and Downgrading of Occupations: Issues, Evidence, and Implications for Education." *Review of Educational Research,* 1985, *55* (2), 125–154.

Stalk, G. "Time—The Next Source of Competitive Advantage." *Harvard Business Review,* 1988, *66* (4), 41–51.

Stalk, G. "Time—The Next Source of Competitive Advantage." *Quality Progress,* 1989, *22* (6), 61–68.

Stokes, B. "Coping with Glut." *National Journal*, 1986, *18* (44), 2608–2614.

Stromberg, R. *An Intellectual History of Modern Europe*. Englewood Cliffs, N.J.: Prentice-Hall, 1975.

Taguchi, G., and Clausing, D. "Robust Quality." *Harvard Business Review*, 1990, *68* (1), 65–75.

Technical Assistance Research Programs Institute. *Consumer Complaint Handling in America: An Update Study—Part II*. Washington, D.C.: U.S. Office of Consumer Affairs, 1986.

Teece, D. "Capturing Value from Technological Innovation: Integration, Strategic Partnership, and Licensing Decisions." In B. Guile and H. Brooks (eds.), *Technology and Global Industry: Companies and Nations in the World Economy*. Washington, D.C.: National Academy Press, 1987.

Thomas, P. *Competitiveness Through Total Cycle Time*. New York: McGraw-Hill, 1990.

Tyson, L. D. "Managed Trade: Making the Best of the Second Best." In R. Z. Lawrence and C. L. Schultze (eds.), *An American Trade Strategy, Options for the 1990's*. Washington, D.C.: Brookings Institution, 1990.

United Kingdom, Treasury. *Economic Progress Report*. No. 201. London: Colibri Press, 1989.

U.S. Congress, Office of Technology Assessment. *Technology and the American Economic Transition: Choices for the Future*. OTA-TET-238. Washington, D.C.: U.S. Government Printing Office, 1988.

U.S. Congress, Office of Technology Assessment. *Making Things Better: Competing in Manufacturing*. OTA-ITE-443. Washington, D.C.: U.S. Government Printing Office, 1990.

U.S. Department of Commerce, Bureau of the Census. *News CB89-190*. Washington, D.C.: U.S. Government Printing Office, 1989a.

U.S. Department of Commerce, Bureau of the Census. *Statistical Abstract of the United States 1989*. Washington, D.C.: U.S. Government Printing Office, 1989b.

U.S. Department of Commerce, Bureau of the Census. *U.S. Industrial Outlook*. Washington, D.C.: U.S. Government Printing Office, 1989c.

U.S. Department of Commerce, Bureau of the Census. *U.S. Industrial Outlook*. Washington, D.C.: U.S. Government Printing Office, 1990.

U.S. Department of Commerce, Bureau of Economic Analysis, "National Income and Product Accounts," historical diskettes, Tables 7.10 and 6.88, July 1989.

U.S. Department of Labor, Bureau of Labor Statistics. Bulletin No. 89-322. Washington, D.C.: U.S. Government Printing Office, 1989, updated 1990.

U.S. Department of Labor, Bureau of Labor Statistics. Unpublished data on the productivity of other nations as a percentage of American productivity, Apr. 1990a.

U.S. Department of Labor, Bureau of Labor Statistics. Unpublished data on the value of output per person in the United States and other nations, Apr. 1990b.

Utterback, J. "Innovation and Industrial Evolution in Manufacturing Industries." In B. Guile and H. Brooks (eds.), *Technology and Global Industry: Companies and Nations in the World Economy*. Washington, D.C.: National Academy Press, 1987.

Verity, J. "Another Crunch for Computer Makers." *Business Week*, Jan. 8, 1990, p. 97.

Vernon, R. "Coping with Technological Change: U.S. Problems and Prospects." In B. Guile and H. Brooks (eds.), *Technology and Global Industry: Companies and Nations in the World Economy*. Washington, D.C.: National Academy Press, 1987.

"The Visible Hand." *New Republic*, Nov. 28, 1990, pp.7–12.

von Braun, C-F. "The Acceleration Trap." *Sloan Management Review*, 1990, *49*, 49–58.

Walton, R. "From Control to Commitment in the Workplace." *Harvard Business Review*, 1985, *63* (2), 76–84.

Waylett, W. "Winning the Deming: Florida Power and Light." *Technical and Skills Training*, 1990, *1* (1), 37–43.

Waylett, W., and Beaver, P. "Winning the Deming Prize: The Role of Technical Training." Paper presented at American Society for Training and Development National Conference on Technical and Skills Training, Baltimore, Md., Oct. 1990.

Weber, J. "Getting Cozy with Their Customers." *Business Week*, Jan. 8, 1990, p. 86.

Wei, J. "The Transformation of the U.S. Chemicals Industry." In *The Working Papers of the MIT Commission on Industrial Productivity*. Vol. 1. Cambridge, Mass.: MIT Press, 1989.

Wheelwright, S., and Hayes, R. "Competing Through Manufacturing." *Harvard Business Review*, 1985, *63* (1), 99–109.

Willis, R. "Harley-Davidson Comes Roaring Back." *Management Review*, 1986, *75* (3), 20–27.

Womack, J. "The U.S. Automobile Industry in an Era of International Competition: Performance and Prospects." In *The Working Papers of the MIT Commission on Industrial Productivity*. Vol. 1. Cambridge, Mass.: MIT Press, 1989.

Wood, R. C. "The Prophets of Quality." *Quality Review*, 1988, *2* (4), 18–25.

Yamada, T., Yamada, T., and Liu, G. "Productivity of Japanese Manufacturing Industries and Their Market Competition." *Japan's Economic Challenge*. Presented to Joint Economic Committee, Congress of the United States, Oct. 1990.

Zeithaml, V. A., Rarasurakian, A., and Berry, L. L. *Delivery Quality Service*. New York: Free Press, 1990.

Zemke, R., and Schaaf, D. *The Service Edge*. New York: NAL Penguin, 1989.

Zinam, O. "Quality of Life, Quality of the Individual, Technology and Economic Development." *American Journal of Economics and Sociology*, 1989, *48* (1), 55–68.

Zuboff, S. *In the Age of the Smart Machine: The Future of Work and Power*. New York: Basic Books, 1988.

INDEX

T

U